The Civil War Trust's

OFFICIAL GUIDE
TO THE CIVIL WAR
DISCOVERY TRAIL

EDITED BY THE CIVIL WAR TRUST

Susan Collier Braselton, Senior Editor

CONTRIBUTING EDITORS:

Edgar M. Andrews III

Paul J. Birkhead

Julie K. Fix

Elliot H. Gruber

Danielle V. McMahon

Bonnie Repasi

MACMILLAN • USA

Acknowledgments

$\mathcal{T}$HE CIVIL WAR TRUST ACKNOWLEDGES with deep gratitude the assistance and support provided by its partners in the Civil War Discovery Trail: The U.S. Department of Interior, in particular the American Battlefield Protection Program staff and the staff of the National Park; The National Trust for Historic Preservation; State Partners and State Coordinators in all participating Civil War Discovery Trail states; staff at all Civil War Discovery Trail sites; and all others who provided material for this guide. Special thanks to two of the first states to join the Civil War Discovery Trail for their enthusiasm and guidance: Kentucky (David L. Morgan, State Historic Preservation Officer and Director of the Kentucky Heritage Council; Joseph E. Brent, Kentucky Heritage Council; Daniel Kidd, Kentucky Department of Travel Development) and Mississippi (Elbert Hilliard, State Historic Preservation Officer; Kenneth H. P'Pool, Deputy State Historic Preservation Officer, Mississippi Department of Archives and History; Michael Beard, Mississippi Department of Archives and History).

The Civil War Trust is not responsible for changes that occur after publication and regrets any errors and omissions in this book. We encourage your comments and suggestions by mail to: The Civil War Trust, 1225 Eye St. NW, Suite 401, Washington, D.C. 20005.

Macmillan Travel
A Simon & Schuster Macmillan Company
1633 Broadway
New York, NY 10019

Copyright © 1996 by The Civil War Trust.

ISBN 0-02-861209-4

Library of Congress Catalog Card Number: 96-76745.

Manufactured in the United States of America

Book design by George J. McKeon

Contents

THE CIVIL WAR TRUST™

Enriching Our Future By Preserving Our Past.

*T*HE MISSION OF THE CIVIL WAR TRUST is to promote appreciation and stewardship of our nation's historical, cultural, and environmental heritage through preservation of significant Civil War sites and through supporting preservation and education programs. The Civil War Trust is a private, nonprofit organization with more than 20,000 members across the country that works to preserve our nation's most important Civil War sites. Since its formation in 1991, The Civil War Trust has

- secured Congressional passage of the Civil War battlefield Commemorative Coin Act to generate private funds for battlefield preservation

- protected land at Antietam and South Mountain, Md.; Byram's Ford, Mo.; Mill Springs, Ky.; Harpers Ferry, W. Va.; Cross Keys, Va.; and Port Hudson, La.

- launched the Civil War Discovery Trail

- created the Civil War Explorer, an educational introduction to the Civil War that uses interactive multimedia technology that is available now for visitors to use at Gettysburg National Military Park, Antietam National Battlefield, and Prairie Grove State Park and soon to be expanded and more widely available

- created a Commemorative Coin Grant Program and made grants to assist in the purchase and preservation of significant battlefield land at Third Winchester, Va.; Cedar Creek, Va.; Perryville, Ky.; Mill Springs, Ky.; Corinth, Miss.; Brices Crossroads, Miss.; Spring Hill, Tenn.; Malvern Hill, Va.; Resaca, Ga.; Rich Mountain, W. Va.; and Prairie Grove, Ark.

Battlefields memorialize the ideals, courage, character, and sacrifice of the men and women who struggled for freedom to make "these United States" into the United States. These living landscapes add to the quality of our lives with their beauty and invite our visits to rest and reflect. Fewer than 15 percent of our nation's Civil War battlefields are now protected.

The Trust's national campaign unites concerned citizens, businesses, landowners, historians, public officials, and others to foster strong, community-based preservation activities.

The Civil War Trust encourages partnerships and welcomes your membership, support, and participation in its efforts. Your membership in The Civil War Trust will help to preserve the tangible reminders of our nation's history for the understanding and appreciation of future generations. For more information about membership or programs, call 1-800-CWTRUST (202-326-8420).

Foreword

*T*he Civil War defined America as a nation and left deep impressions on the character of the many communities it touched. There still remain lessons to be learned from the experiences of this turbulent era. How better to learn these lessons than by walking the streets and fields where the events unfolded?

The historic sites selected for the Civil War Discovery Trail must meet high standards to ensure historical authenticity, informative interpretive programs, and relevance to events today.

This expanded second edition of *The Civil War Trust's Official Guide to the Civil War Discovery Trail* provides an itinerary for visiting many of the places that influenced the course of the struggle. It is a tool equally valuable to the recreational traveler and to the serious student of history.

Proceeds from the sale of the *Official Guide* support the work of The Civil War Trust, a nonprofit, national membership organization that works to preserve and protect endangered Civil War battlefields.

The Trust is grateful to its national, state, and Trail site partners for their enthusiastic support for the development of the Civil War Discovery Trail.

Edgar M. Andrews III
President
The Civil War Trust

Preserving Civil War Battlefields

$\mathcal{T}$HE NATION'S CIVIL WAR HERITAGE is in grave danger! It is disappearing under buildings, parking lots, and highways. Of the 384 principal Civil War battlefields, 71 (19 percent) have already been lost. Half of the rest are now threatened by development. If we do not act swiftly to protect the remaining battlefields, within 10 years we may lose fully two-thirds of the nation's principal battlefields.

Some have asked: Why do anything more to protect the battlefields? Are not the principal battlefields already preserved in national and state parks? Can we not understand the important political and social changes that resulted from the war without studying the battles? Does not this preoccupation with "hallowed ground" romanticize violence and glorify war? These questions deserve answers.

First, an understanding of military campaigns and battles is crucial to comprehending all other aspects of the Civil War. Individual battles swayed elections, shaped political decisions, determined economic mobilization, brought women into the war effort, and influenced decisions to abolish slavery as well as to recruit former slaves as soldiers.

The Seven Days battles produced an early Union victory and changed the conflict from a limited to a total war; Antietam forestalled European recognition of the Confederacy and prompted the Emancipation Proclamation; Vicksburg, Gettysburg, and Chattanooga reversed a tide of Confederate victories that had threatened the Northern will to keep fighting; Sherman's capture of Atlanta and Sheridan's victories in the Shenandoah secured Abraham Lincoln's reelection, confirmed emancipation as a Northern war aim, and ensured continuation of the war to unconditional victory. Any different outcome might have changed the course of the war—and perhaps the world's history.

The battles were important, but why do we need to preserve the battlefields to learn from them? In part, understanding is simply a matter of being able to visualize how geography and topography shaped a battle—the pattern of fields and woods, roads and rock outcroppings, and rivers and streams. Learning cannot take place if the historical landscape has been paved over, cluttered with buildings, or carved into a different shape.

Being present on a battlefield we can experience an emotional tie to those who fought there. With a little imagination we can hear the first Rebel yell at Manassas, imagine the horror as brushfires overtook the wounded at Wilderness, experience the terror of raw recruits at Perryville, or hear the hoarse shouts of exhausted survivors of the Twentieth Maine as they launched a bayonet charge at Gettysburg's Little Round Top.

These experiences help us understand what the Civil War was all about. Understanding is not a matter of glorifying or romanticizing war. Quite the contrary, it is a matter of comprehending the grim reality of war. The battlefields are monuments to the gritty courage of the men and women who fought and died there. None condemned the war more than those who suffered the horror and trauma of battle. In 1862, a Confederate veteran of Shiloh wrote home: "O it was too shocking too horrible. God grant that I may never be the partaker in such scenes again. . . . When released from this I shall ever be an advocate of peace." Civil War veterans took the lead in creating the first national battlefield parks—not to glorify the war, but to commemorate the sacrifice of friends they had lost.

(Adapted from *Civil War Sites Advisory Commission Report on the Nation's Civil War Battlefields* [National Park Service, 1993].)

Explore The Civil War Discovery Trail

The Civil War Discovery Trail links more than 400 sites in 24 states to inspire and to teach the story of the Civil War and its haunting impact on America.

Along the Trail visitors may explore destinations such as Ford's Theater where President Lincoln was shot; Antietam National Battlefield, the site of the bloodiest one-day battle in American history; antebellum plantations in Mississippi and Tennessee; and Port Hudson, Louisiana, where hundreds of African American soldiers fought and died. The Trail includes battlefields, historic homes, railroad stations, cemeteries, and parks.

Civil War Discovery Trail sites are especially selected for their historic significance and educational opportunities. Each year new sites and states will be added to the Trail. The Civil War Discovery Trail is an initiative of The Civil War Trust, in partnership with the National Trust for Historic Preservation, the National Park Service, state agencies, and local communities.

Using This Book

For ease of use, this guide is organized first, alphabetically by state; then city; then site. Each state chapter begins with a brief overview of the role of each state in the Civil War and with an orientation map giving the general location of sites in that state. Directions in each listing lead visitors from the closest major interstate highway to the site. We suggest also using a state highway map with the maps and directions in this guide. Sites are listed under the closest town. The address listed under the site name may only be the mailing address. Whenever possible, each site listing includes a phone number to call for further information. The availability of handicapped access refers to access for persons with wheelchairs, walkers, and so forth, without having to climb stairs.

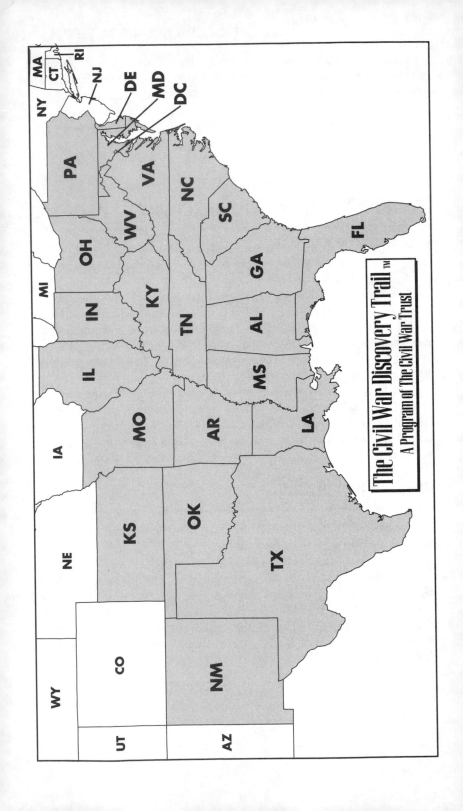

The Civil War Discovery Trail ™
A Program of The Civil War Trust

The American Civil War

by Dr. James M. McPherson

*T*he Civil War is the central event in America's historical consciousness. While the Revolution of 1776–83 created the United States, the Civil War of 1861–65 determined what kind of nation it would be. The war resolved two fundamental questions left unresolved by the revolution: whether the United States was to be a dissolvable confederation of sovereign states or an indivisible nation with a sovereign national government; and whether this nation, born of a declaration that all men were created with an equal right to liberty, would continue to exist as the largest slave-holding country in the world.

Northern victory in the war preserved the United States as one nation and ended the institution of slavery that had divided the country from its beginning. But these achievements came at the cost of 625,000 lives—nearly as many American soldiers as died in all the other wars in which this country has fought *combined*. The American Civil War was the largest and most destructive conflict in the Western world between the end of the Napoleonic Wars in 1815 and the onset of World War I in 1914.

The Civil War started because of uncompromising differences between the free and slave states over the power of the national government to prohibit slavery in the territories that had not yet become states. When Abraham Lincoln won election in 1860 as the first Republican president on a platform pledging to keep slavery out of the territories, seven slave states in the deep South seceded and formed a new nation, the Confederate States of America. The incoming Lincoln administration and most of the Northern people refused to recognize the legitimacy of secession. They feared that it would discredit democracy and create a fatal precedent that would eventually fragment the no-longer *United* States into several small, squabbling countries.

The event that triggered war came at Fort Sumter in Charleston Bay on April 12, 1861. Claiming this United States fort as its own, the Confederate army on that day opened fire on the Federal garrison and forced it to lower the American flag in surrender. Lincoln called out the militia to suppress this "insurrection." Four more slave states seceded and joined the Confederacy. By the end of 1861 nearly a million armed men confronted one another along a line stretching 1,200 miles from Virginia to Missouri. Several battles had already taken place—near Manassas Junction in Virginia, in the mountains of western Virginia where Union victories paved the way for creation of the new state of West Virginia, at Wilson's Creek in Missouri, at Cape Hatteras in North Carolina, and at Port Royal in South Carolina where the Union navy established a base for a blockade to shut off the Confederacy's access to the outside world.

But the real fighting began in 1862. Huge battles like Shiloh in Tennessee, Gaines Mill, Second Manassas, and Fredericksburg in Virginia and Antietam in Maryland foreshadowed even bigger campaigns and battles in later years, from Gettysburg in Pennsylvania to Vicksburg on the Mississippi to Chickamauga and Atlanta in Georgia. By 1864 the original Northern goal of a limited war to *restore* the Union had given way to a new strategy of "total war" to destroy the Old South and its basic institution of slavery and to give the restored Union a "new birth of freedom," as President Lincoln put it in his address at Gettysburg to dedicate a cemetery for Union soldiers killed in the battle there.

For three long years, from 1862 to 1865, Robert E. Lee's Army of Northern Virginia staved off invasions and attacks by the Union Army of the Potomac commanded by a series of ineffective generals until Ulysses S. Grant came to Virginia from the Western Theater to become general in chief of all Union armies in 1864. After bloody battles at places with names like The Wilderness, Spotsylvania, Cold Harbor, and Petersburg, Grant finally brought Lee to bay at Appomattox in April 1865. In the meantime Union armies and river fleets in the theater of war comprising the slave states west of the Appalachians won a long series of victories over confederate armies commanded by hapless, unlucky Confederate generals. In 1864–65 General William Tecumseh Sherman led his army deep into the Confederate heartland of Georgia and South Carolina, destroying their economic infrastructure while General George Thomas virtually destroyed the Confederacy's Army of Tennessee at the battle of Nashville.

By the spring of 1865 all the principal Confederate armies surrendered, and when Union cavalry captured the fleeing Confederate president Jefferson Davis in Georgia on May 10, 1865, resistance collapsed and the war ended. The long, painful process of rebuilding a united nation free of slavery began.

ALABAMA

*J*anuary 11, 1861, Alabama became the fourth state to secede from the Union. Within a short time, state troops seized the Federal arsenal at Mt. Vernon and the forts in Mobile. On February 4, 1861, delegates from six of the seven seceded states convened in Montgomery and on February 8, officially adopted the constitution of the Confederate States of America. Montgomery served as the provisional capital. On February 18, 1861, Jefferson Davis was inaugurated as president of the provisional government. The first national flag of the Confederacy was raised above the capitol on March 4, 1861. On April 12, 1861, acting on instructions that had been telegraphed from Montgomery, General P. G. T. Beauregard ordered the bombardment of Fort Sumter in Charleston, South Carolina.

During the war, 194 military land events and 8 naval engagements occurred within the boundaries of the state. Significant among these were Streight's Raid (April 26–May 3, 1863), Wilson Raid (March 22–April 16, 1865), and the Battle of Mobile Bay (August 5, 1864). The campaign for Mobile culminated in the autumn of Spanish Fort (April 8, 1865), Blakeley (April 9, 1865), and the final capitulation of the city on April 12, 1865. On May 4, 1865, at Citronelle, Alabama, General Richard Taylor finally surrendered the Confederate forces in the Department of Alabama, Mississippi, and East Louisiana.

by Robert Bradley, Alabama Department of Archives and History

Dauphin Island

1   **Site:** FORT GAINES, P.O. Box 97, Dauphin Island, AL 36528, 334-861-6992

Description: Fort Gaines is a pre–Civil War brick fort set within a few feet of the gulf. The fort was a key element in the "Battle of Mobile Bay" and after its capture was used in planning and staging the attack on Mobile. Many of the Civil War structures and courtyard buildings remain.

Admission Fees: Adults: $2; Children (7–12): $1; Groups: two for one (call in advance).

Open to Public: *Winter:* Daily: 9 A.M.–5 P.M.; *Summer:* Daily: 9 A.M.–6 P.M.

Visitor Services: Museum; gift shop; information; rest rooms; handicapped access.

Regularly Scheduled Events: *June:* Confederate encampments; Annual Battle of Mobile Bay; *Aug.:* Annual Damn the Torpedoes; *Nov.:* Women's encampment; *Second week in Dec.:* Christmas at the Fort.

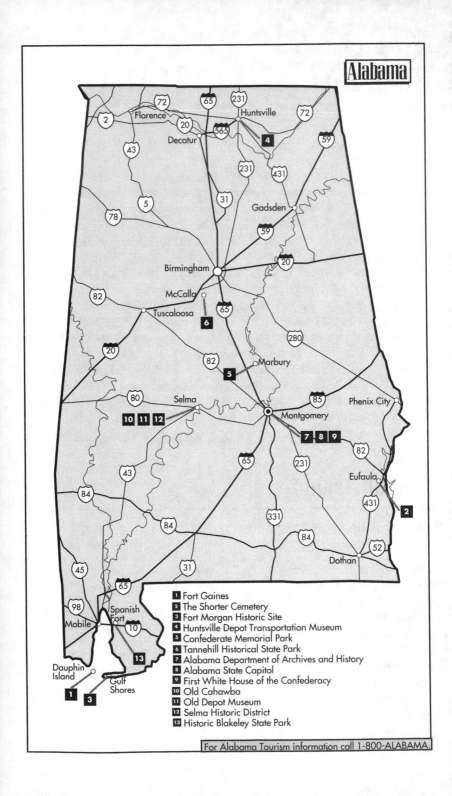

Alabama

1 Fort Gaines
2 The Shorter Cemetery
3 Fort Morgan Historic Site
4 Huntsville Depot Transportation Museum
5 Confederate Memorial Park
6 Tannehill Historical State Park
7 Alabama Department of Archives and History
8 Alabama State Capitol
9 First White House of the Confederacy
10 Old Cahawba
11 Old Depot Museum
12 Selma Historic District
13 Historic Blakeley State Park

For Alabama Tourism information call 1-800-ALABAMA.

Directions: Exit I-10 to Hwy. 193 south to Dauphin Island. Once on the island, turn left at the water tower and proceed 3 miles to Fort Gaines.

Eufaula

2 **Site:** THE SHORTER CEMETERY, 510 St. Francis Rd., Eufaula, AL 36027, 334-687-3793

Description: Cemetery belonging to the Shorter family. The graves include that of John Gill Shorter, a Civil War governor. The cemetery also houses slave plots.

Admission Fees: Free.

Open to Public: Daily: Dawn to dusk.

Visitor Services: Information.

Directions: Go to the east end of Hwy. 82 and turn south in front of the Holiday Inn. Go approximately four blocks and follow signs to cemetery.

Gulf Shores

3 **Site:** FORT MORGAN HISTORIC SITE, 51 Hwy. 180 West, Gulf Shores, AL 36542, 334-540-7125

Description: The primary defensive work at the entrance to Mobile Bay. Alabama militia seized the fort in January 1861. The fort underwent a two-week siege resulting in surrender on August 23, 1864.

Admission Fees: Adults: $2; Children (6–12): $1; Seniors: $1; Groups: half price.

Open to Public: Mon.–Fri.: 8 A.M.–5 P.M.; Sat.–Sun.: 9 A.M.–5 P.M.

Visitor Services: Museum; gift shop; information; rest rooms; handicapped access.

Regularly Scheduled Events: *First weekend in Aug.:* Living History Encampment commemorating the Battle of Mobile Bay and Siege of Fort Morgan in 1864.

Directions: South from I-10: take Hwy. 59 to Gulf Shores, AL. At Gulf Shores take AL Hwy. 180 west for 22 miles to Fort Morgan.

Fort Morgan, Gulf Shores, AL. (Photograph courtesy of Fort Morgan.)

Huntsville

4 | **Site:** HUNTSVILLE DEPOT TRANSPORTATION MUSEUM, 320 Church St., Huntsville, AL 35801, 205-539-1860; 800-239-8955

Description: The Huntsville Depot was built in 1860 as the eastern division headquarters of the Memphis & Charleston Railroad. As a vital east-west Confederate rail line, the yards, shops, depot, and trains were captured by the Federals in 1862 and used as a prison. There is legible graffiti on the third floor left by Civil War soldiers.

Admission Fees: Adults: $4; Children: $3; Seniors: $3; Groups: $.50 off.

Open to Public: Mon.–Sat.: 9 A.M.–5 P.M.

Visitor Services: Museum; gift shop; information; rest rooms; handicapped access.

Regularly Scheduled Events: *Last weekend in Apr.:* Civil War Jubilee.

Directions: From I-565: take exit 19C (Washington St.); you will see the Roundhouse on the right as you exit I-565. Proceed right and enter the free parking lot.

Marbury

5 | **Site:** CONFEDERATE MEMORIAL PARK, 437 County Rd. 63, Marbury, AL 36051, 205-755-1990

Description: Confederate Memorial Park is dedicated to preserving the memory of Alabama's heroic struggle during the War Between the States and to interpreting the site of Alabama's only Old Soldiers Home for Confederate Veterans (1902–39). The museum houses documents, uniforms, weapons, and war equipment emphasizing Alabama's participation. It also displays relics from the Soldiers Home, including photographs, books, veterans' medals, and so forth.

Admission Fees: Free.

Open to Public: *Park:* Daily: 6 A.M.–sunset; *Museum:* Daily: 9 A.M.–5 P.M.

Visitor Services: Trail; museum; gift shop; information; rest rooms; handicapped access.

Regularly Scheduled Events: *Mar.:* Confederate Flag Day ceremony; *Apr.:* Confederate Memorial Day ceremony; *Dec.:* Christmas in the South.

Directions: From I-65 south: take exit 205; go south onto U.S. 31 for 9 miles; follow signs. From I-65 north: take exit 186; go north on U.S. 31 for 13 miles; follow signs.

McCalla

6 | **Site:** TANNEHILL HISTORICAL STATE PARK, 12632 Confederate Pkwy., McCalla, AL 35111, 205-477-5711

Description: This 1,500-acre park was created around the Civil War–era iron-making furnaces. Furnaces were a major producer of iron for the Selma arsenal and were destroyed by Union cavalry raiders in 1865. The park includes a museum, more than 40 restored log cabins, and other period buildings, including a working gristmill, church, and school.

Admission Fees: Adults: $2; Children: $1; Seniors: $1.

Open to Public: *Museum:* Mon.–Fri.: 9 A.M.–5 P.M.; Sat.: 10 A.M.–5 P.M.; *Park:* Daily: 7 A.M.–dusk.

Visitor Services: Lodging; camping; trails; food; museum; gift shop; information; rest rooms; handicapped access.

Regularly Scheduled Events: *Mar.–Nov.*: Tannehill Trade Days.

Directions: From I-59: take exit 100 and follow signs (2 miles). From I-459: take exit 1 and follow signs (7 miles).

Montgomery

7 **Site:** ALABAMA DEPARTMENT OF ARCHIVES AND HISTORY, 624 Washington Ave., Montgomery, AL 36130-0100, 334-242-4363 (ext. 1)

Description: Located across the street from the State Capitol, which served as the provisional capital of the Confederate States of America, the museum and archives contain the largest collection of Civil War materials in the state. Significant among these is the department's collection of Civil War flags that are displayed on a rotational basis.

Admission Fees: Free.

Open to Public: Mon.–Fri.: 8 A.M.–5 P.M.; Sat.: 9 A.M.–5 P.M.

Visitor Services: Museum; information; rest rooms; handicapped access.

Regularly Scheduled Events: *Every third Thurs.*: Architreats, a lunchtime lecture series.

Directions: From I-85 south: exit right on Union St. Turn left at third traffic light (Washington Ave.). From Birmingham or Mobile on I-65: take interstate to I-85 north; exit right onto Court St. Stay on service road. At the seventh traffic light, turn left (Union St.). Turn left at the fourth traffic light (Washington Ave.).

8 **Site:** ALABAMA STATE CAPITOL, 468 South Perry St., Montgomery, AL 36130, 334-242-3900

Description: In 1861, Southern delegates met to discuss secession from the Union. The House Chamber voted and the decision was secession. Jefferson Davis was sworn in as the first and only president of the Confederate States of America.

Admission Fees: Free.

Open to Public: Mon.–Sat.: 9 A.M.–4 P.M.

Visitor Services: Museum; information; rest rooms; handicapped access.

Directions: From I-85: take Union St. exit; travel four blocks to Washington Ave. On-street parking is available.

---

9 Site: FIRST WHITE HOUSE OF THE CONFEDERACY, 644 Washington Ave., Montgomery, AL 36130, 334-242-1861

Description: This house was used by the provisional government of Confederate president Jefferson Davis and his family from Feb. until May 1861. In June, the government was moved to Virginia. The First White House of the Confederacy was built in 1835.

Admission Fees: Free.

Open to Public: Mon.–Fri.: 8 A.M.–4:30 P.M.

Visitor Services: Museum; information; handicapped access; rest rooms.

Regularly Scheduled Events: *Jan.:* Robert E. Lee's Birthday; *Apr.:* Confederate Memorial Day; *June:* Jefferson Davis's Birthday.

Directions: From I-85: take Union St. exit; go four blocks to Washington St. and turn left. Look for first house on the left.

Selma

10 Site: OLD CAHAWBA, 719 Tremont St., Selma, AL 36701, 334-872-8058

Description: Alabama's first State Capital and Civil War boomtown is now an archaeological park. Home to the Cahawba Rifles, 5th Alabama Regiment, this ghost town was the center of activity during the antebellum and Civil War years. It is also the site of Castle Morgan, a prison for captured Union soldiers.

Admission Fees: Free.

Open to Public: Daily: 9 A.M.–5 P.M.

Visitor Services: Trails; museum; gift shop; information; rest rooms; handicapped access; picnic area.

Regularly Scheduled Events: *Second Sat. in May:* Cahawba Festival includes reenactments, arts and crafts, music, and so forth.

Directions: Take Hwy. 80 from Montgomery to Selma. From Selma, take Hwy. 22 south for 8 miles; turn left at sign for park; follow 5 miles.

---

11 Site: OLD DEPOT MUSEUM, Selma/Dallas County Museum of History and Archives, Confederate Navy Ordnance Works, Water Ave. & Martin Luther King St., Selma, AL 36702, 334-874-2197

Description: Artifacts from the Civil War era are found in abundance at this museum. Other artifacts date from 7000 B.C. through the Gulf War.

Admission Fees: Adults: $4; Seniors: $3; Children: $1.

Open to Public: Mon.–Sat.: 10 A.M.–4 P.M.; Sun.: 2 P.M.–5 P.M.

Visitor Services: Museum; information; handicapped access.

Regularly Scheduled Events: *Mar.:* Pilgrimage; *Apr.:* Battle of Selma; *Second Sat. in Oct.:* Open House Riverfront Market.

Directions: From I-65: take Selma exit; take Hwy. 80; go over Alabama River, over Pettus Bridge; turn right on Water Ave. Street dead-ends at museum. Located at the corner of Water Ave. & Martin Luther King St.

---

12 **Site:** SELMA HISTORIC DISTRICT, Chamber of Commerce, Visitor Information Center, 2207 Broad St., Selma, AL 36701, 334-875-7485

Description: The war was almost over when Union troops under the leadership of Gen. James H. Wilson and 13,500 cavalry and mounted infantry (the Raiders) invaded Alabama. Anticipating the invasion, Selma prepared as best it could. But Lt. Gen. Nathan Bedford Forrest's highly outnumbered 2,000 men, mostly old men and boys, could not hold Wilson's Raiders. The people of Selma were doomed even before the battle on April 2, 1865. Today, Selma is a delightful, enchanting city with Civil War landmarks everywhere you turn. With historic homes, monuments, cemeteries, and battlefields, it's a one-stop shop for Civil War buffs.

Open to Public: Daily: 8 A.M.–8 P.M.

Points of Interest:

Battle of Selma
212 Pine Needle Dr.
Selma, AL 36701
334-874-4651

Grace Hall
506 Lauderdale St.

Selma, AL 36701
334-875-5744

Joseph T. Smitherman Historic Building
109 Union St.
Selma, AL 36701
334-874-2174

Old Live Oak Cemetery
110 Dallas Ave.
Selma, AL 36701
334-874-2161

Sturdivant Hall
713 Mabry St.
Selma, AL 36701
334-872-5626

White Force Cottage
811 Mabry St.
Selma, AL 36701
334-875-1714

Directions: From Montgomery: take Hwy. 80 west to Selma. From I-65 in Birmingham: exit at Clanton; take Hwy. 22 to Selma.

Spanish Fort

13 Site: HISTORIC BLAKELEY STATE PARK, 33707 State Hwy. 225, Spanish Fort, AL
36527, 334-626-0798

Description: The last major battle of the Civil War was fought at Blakeley; it ended on the same day, but after the surrender of Gen. Robert E. Lee miles away in Virginia. The Battle of Blakeley was a major news event in the coverage of the Civil War.

Admission Fees: Adults: $2; Children: $1; *Groups (25 or more):* Adults: $1.50; Children: $.75.

Open to Public: Daily: 9 A.M. to dusk.

Visitor Services: Lodging; 5 miles of nature trails; camping; information; rest rooms.

Regularly Scheduled Events: *1997 and 2000:* Major Civil War reenactments occurring; *Every year:* Civil War Demonstrations and Living History Demonstrations; *Sept.:* Blakeley Country Music Blast.

Directions: Located 5 miles north of I-10 on Hwy. 225.; 16 miles south of I-65; north of Spanish Fort, AL, in Baldwin County; 20 minutes east of Mobile; and 45 minutes west of Pensacola, FL.

ARKANSAS

$\mathcal{A}$RKANSAS played a major strategic role during the Civil War, serving as an avenue and staging area for many of the important operations involving bordering states.

In 1862, the northwest corner of the state was the major battleground. Fighting at Pea Ridge and Prairie Grove kept Missouri in the Union and helped close that section of the state as a Confederate invasion route into Missouri. Fighting in 1863 at Helena reflected that city's importance to the Vicksburg campaign. Rebel troops sought to seize the strategic river town and vital supply post, to relieve pressure on the besieged Mississippi fortress. Ironically for the southern troops, the battle was fought and lost on the day Vicksburg fell. The defeat at Helena led to the fall of Little Rock and restricted Confederate control to a small area of southwest Arkansas. In 1864, Union troops were on the move in a two-pronged operation with Louisiana-based Yankees. They sought to conquer the cotton-rich Red River area. This time, however, it was the Northern forces who tasted defeat, barely escaping to Little Rock at the conclusion of the abortive Camden Expedition.

The state witnessed the Civil War at its worst. Partisans, jayhawkers, and gangs of armed thieves terrorized rural areas of Arkansas, leaving both Union and Confederate troops with the challenge of containing the lawlessness. The war left economic devastation and a psychological bitterness in Arkansas that persisted for decades.

by Mark K. Christ, Arkansas Historic Preservation Program

Bluff City

 Site: POISON SPRING STATE PARK, Hwy. 76, Bluff City, AR 71722, 501-685-2748

Description: The Battle of Poison Spring took place on April 18, 1864, during the Camden Expedition of the Red River campaign. The Union column was bringing supplies to the Federal occupiers of Camden when attacked by Confederate troops.

Admission Fees: Free.

Open to Public: Daily: 6 A.M.–10 P.M.

Visitor Services: Trails; information.

Regularly Scheduled Events: *Mar.:* Reenactment of the Battle of Poison Spring.

Directions: From I-30: take exit 44 for Prescott. Proceed east on State Hwy. 24 through Prescott for the next 33 miles. After passing through Bragg City, look for Arkansas State Park sign for Poison Spring State Park. Turn right on State Hwy. 76 for about 5 miles. The park is located on the right.

Arkansas

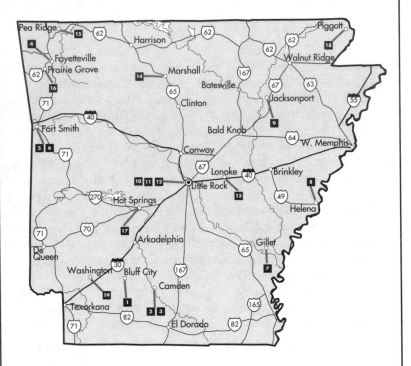

1 Poison Spring State Park
2 Fort Southerland Park
3 McCollum-Chidester House Museum
4 Headquarters House
5 Fort Smith National Cemetery
6 Fort Smith National Historic Site
7 Arkansas Post National Memorial
8 Helena, Arkansas Civil War Sites Driving Tour
9 Jacksonport State Park
10 Little Rock National Cemetery
11 Little Rock Arsenal (Museum of Natural Science and History)
12 Old State House
13 Camp Nelson Confederate Cemetery
14 Buffalo National River Civil War Heritage Trail
15 Pea Ridge National Military Park
16 Prairie Grove Battlefield State Park
17 Jenkins' Ferry State Park
18 Chalk Bluff Park
19 Confederate State Capitol at Old Washington Historic State Park

Camden

2 **Site:** FORT SOUTHERLAND PARK, 206 Van Buren St., Camden, AR 71701, 501-836-6436

Description: Fort Southerland represents an excellently preserved example of urban Civil War defensive earthworks erected along the periphery of Camden. They were erected in 1864 in anticipation of a Federal attack from Little Rock.

Admission Fees: Free.

Open to Public: Daily: Sunrise to sunset.

Visitor Services: None.

Directions: From I-30 at Prescott: take State Hwy. 24 east to Camden; turn from Hwy. 24 onto State Hwy. 4 Spur and follow 4 Spur and U.S. Hwy. 79 to Bradley Ferry Rd. Site is located two blocks down on left.

3 **Site:** McCOLLUM-CHIDESTER HOUSE MUSEUM, 926 Washington St., Camden, AR 71701, 501-836-9243

Description: This house, built in 1847, retains its furnishings brought here by steamboat in 1863 by the Chidester family. The city of Camden was occupied by Northern General Frederick Steele in 1864, during the Battle of Poison Spring.

Admission Fees: Adults: $3; Children: $1.

Open to Public: Wed.–Sat.: 9 A.M.–4 P.M.

Visitor Services: Tours; rest rooms.

Directions: From I-30 at Prescott: take State Hwy. 24 east to Camden, turn from Hwy. 24 on to State Hwy. 4 Spur and follow Washington St. to museum at 926 Washington St.

Fayetteville

4 **Site:** HEADQUARTERS HOUSE, 118 East Dickson St., Fayetteville, AR 72701, 501-521-2970

Description: Headquarters House was built in 1853 by Judge Jonas Tebbetts, a Northern sympathizer, jailed by General Ben McCulloch, and then finally released to go to St. Louis for the duration. The house was used at various times as headquarters for both the Federal and Confederate armies. The Battle of Fayetteville was fought on the house grounds and across the street on April 18, 1863. One of the doors still carries the hole made by a minié ball.

Admission Fees: Free.

Open to Public: Mon.–Fri.: 1 P.M.–4 P.M.

Visitor Services: Information.

Regularly Scheduled Events: *Apr.:* Battle of Fayetteville reenactment; *Third Sat. in Aug.:* Ice Cream Social; *Dec.:* Christmas tour.

Directions: From I-40: travel north on Rte. 71 to Fayetteville. Rte. 71 turns into College Ave. House is at corner of College Ave. & Dickson.

Fort Smith

Site: FORT SMITH NATIONAL CEMETERY, 522 Garland Ave., Fort Smith, AR 72901, 501-783-5345

Description: Burial place for Union and Confederate soldiers, including three generals and 1,500 unknown soldiers. Site offers brochure, mini-museum of local military history, and tours if arranged ahead.

Admission Fees: Free.

Open to Public: Gates open daily: 24 hours. *Office:* Mon.–Fri.: 8 A.M.–4:30 P.M.

Visitor Services: Information; rest rooms; handicapped access.

Regularly Scheduled Events: *Sun. closest to Memorial Day:* Memorial Day ceremony; *Nov.:* Veterans Day ceremony; *Dec. 7:* Pearl Harbor Day of Remembrance.

Directions: From I-540: take exit 8A (Rogers) and proceed toward downtown area. At the "Y" go to the right and take Garrison Rd. to Sixth St. Turn left on Sixth St. Cemetery is at the end of Sixth St. where it intersects Garland.

Site: FORT SMITH NATIONAL HISTORIC SITE, P.O. Box 1406, Corner of Third & Rogers, Fort Smith, AR 72902, 501-783-3961

Description: Fort Smith National Historic Site preserves the site of two military posts and the historic Federal Court for the Western District of Arkansas. The second Fort Smith (1838–71) served as a military supply and command center for both the Confederate and Union forces on the western frontier.

Admission Fees: Adults, Seniors, & Groups: $2; Children under 16: Free.

Open to Public: Daily: 9 A.M.–5 P.M.

Visitor Services: Museum; gift shop; information; rest rooms; handicapped access.

Regularly Scheduled Events: Tours and demonstrations throughout the summer.

Directions: From I-40 west: take Rogers Ave. Go west on Rogers Ave. to the end of the road downtown. From I-40 east: take exit 64B; go 6 miles east; make the first right after crossing the bridge over the Arkansas River.

Gillett

Site: ARKANSAS POST NATIONAL MEMORIAL, Rte. 1, P.O. Box 16, Gillett, AR 72055, 501-548-2207

Description: By mid-1862, Union gunboats commanded most of the Mississippi River. When the gunboats went up the White River into the heart of Arkansas, the Confederates began to prepare defenses on the Arkansas River, an important water route to the capital at Little Rock. Before the end of 1862, Confederate General

Thomas J. Churchill completed an earthen fortification at Arkansas Post called Fort Hindman or Post of Arkansas. The battle took place on January 10, 1863, when Union forces captured the fort.

Admission Fees: Free.

Open to Public: *Park:* Daily: Dawn to dusk; *Visitor Center:* Daily: 8 A.M.–5 P.M.

Visitor Services: Trails; museum; gift shop; information; rest rooms; handicapped access.

Directions: From Little Rock: take 65 south to Gould and take 212 east at Gould to Hwy. 165; take 165 north to 169 and follow to park. From Brinkley: take 49 south to Marvell and take Hwy. 1 to 165 to 169. From Forrest City: take Hwy. 1 to Dewitt and take 165 to 169.

Helena

8 **Site:** HELENA, ARKANSAS CIVIL WAR SITES DRIVING TOUR, 226 Perry St., Helena, AR 72342, 501-338-9831

Description: See Batteries A, B, C, and D and the Helena Confederate Cemetery.

Admission Fees: Free.

Open to Public: Daily: Daylight hours. *Tourist Information Center:* Daily: 8:30 A.M.–5 P.M.

Visitor Services: None.

Regularly Scheduled Events: *Columbus Day weekend in Oct.:* King Biscuit Blues Festival.

Directions: From 1-40 east: take U.S. 49 southeast to Helena. From I-40 at Memphis: take U.S. 61 south to U.S. 49. Take U.S. 49 west to Helena. Pick up driving tour brochure at the Tourist Information Center on Hwy. 49.

Jacksonport

9 **Site:** JACKSONPORT STATE PARK, P.O. Box 8, Jacksonport, AR 72075, 501-523-2143

Description: During the Civil War, Jacksonport was occupied by both Confederate and Union armies due to its strategic position accessible to the Mississippi and Arkansas rivers. Five generals used the town as their headquarters. On June 5, 1865, Confederate General Jeff Thompson, "Swampfox of the Confederacy," surrendered 6,000 troops to Lt. Colonel C. W. Davis at the Jacksonport Landing. Tour the Jacksonport Courthouse and its War Memorial Room, and the Mary Woods No. 2 steamboat, restored to the 1890s period.

Admission Fees: *Park:* Free. *Museum:* Adults: $2; Children: $1. *Riverboat:* Adults: $2; Children: $1. *Combination ticket to museum and riverboat:* Adults: $3.50; Children: $1.50.

Open to Public: *Park:* Open daily all year. *Museum:* Open all year: Wed.–Sat.: 9 A.M.– 5 P.M.; Sun.: 1 P.M.–5 P.M; closed Mon. and Tues. *Riverboat:* Open Apr. 30–Sept. 2: Sun: 1 P.M.–5 P.M.; Tues.–Thurs.: 10 A.M.– 8 P.M.; Fri.–Sat.: 9 A.M.–5 P.M.; closed Mon.

Visitor Services: Camping; trails; museum; gift shop; information; rest rooms; handicapped access.

Regularly Scheduled Events: *Sat. before Easter:* Easter egg hunt; *Autumn:* Radio-Control Fun Fly (exhibition of model airplanes); *Dec.:* Christmas open house.

Directions: From Hwy. 67 at Newport: take exit 83 and follow the Jacksonport State Park signs.

Little Rock

10 Site: LITTLE ROCK NATIONAL CEMETERY, 2523 Confederate Blvd., Little Rock, AR 72206, 501-324-6401

Description: Grounds were used as a Union campground by U.S. troops. When the troops left, the Confederates buried their dead on the west side. It was then bought by the U.S. government for a military burial ground of occupation troops. A wall was erected between Union and Confederate sections but was taken down in 1913.

Admission Fees: Free.

Open to Public: *Cemetery:* Mon.–Fri.: Dawn to dusk; *Office:* Mon.–Fri.: 7:30 A.M.–4:30 P.M.

Visitor Services: Information; rest rooms.

Regularly Scheduled Events: *Apr.:* Confederate Memorial Day; *May:* Memorial Day; *Nov.:* Veterans Day.

Directions: From I-30: take the Roosevelt Rd. exit; go east three blocks to Confederate Blvd. From I-430: take the Confederate Blvd. exit; go north about 1 mile.

11 Site: LITTLE ROCK ARSENAL (MUSEUM OF NATURAL SCIENCE AND HISTORY), MacArthur Park, Little Rock, AR 72202, 501-396-7050

Description: In February 1861, Arkansas citizens marched on Little Rock and took the arsenal, even though Arkansas had not yet seceded from the Union. For the next two years, the arsenal was under the control of the Confederacy. It was reclaimed when Federal troops took Little Rock in 1863.

Admission Fees: Adults: $2; Children & Seniors: $1.50; Groups (1–49): $10; Groups (50–100): $20.

Open to Public: Mon.–Sat.: 9 A.M.–4:30 P.M.; Sun.: 1 P.M.–4:30 P.M.

Visitor Services: Museum; gift shop; information; rest rooms; handicapped access.

Directions: From I-30: take the East Ninth St. exit. MacArthur Park lies west of the interstate, only one block from the exit.

12 **Site:** OLD STATE HOUSE, 300 West Markham St., Little Rock, AR 72201,
501-324-9685

Description: The Old State House, now an Arkansas history museum, was the state's original capitol (1836–1911). It was the site of many significant historic events, including the 1861 secession convention. In 1863, the Confederate government fled the area, and the town fell to Union troops. General Frederick Steele quartered his army in the State House during his occupation.

Admission Fees: Free.

Open to Public: Mon.–Sat.: 9 A.M.–5 P.M.; Sun.: 1 P.M.–5 P.M.

Visitor Services: Museum; gift shop; information; rest rooms; partial handicapped access.

Directions: From I-30: take the Markham St./Cantrell Rd. exit and follow the signs.

Lonoke

13 **Site:** CAMP NELSON CONFEDERATE CEMETERY, P.O. Box 431, Lonoke, AR 72086,
501-676-6403

Description: While camped near Old Austin, Arkansas, a large group of Texas Confederate soldiers were overcome by a measles epidemic, causing the deaths of several hundred. The soldiers were buried near the encampment. In 1907, the General Assembly appropriated funds to remove the remains into the area that became the cemetery. The remains were not identified on the stone markers; a monument at the cemetery tells this story.

Admission Fees: Free.

Open to Public: Daily: Dawn to dusk.

Visitor Services: Handicapped access.

Regularly Scheduled Events: *June:* Flag Day Celebration.

Directions: From I-40: take Remington exit (7 miles west of Lonoke). Take Hwy. 15 north for 2.5 miles to where it crosses and becomes Hwy. 89. Continue on Hwy. 89 to the junction of Hwy. 321. Turn right on Hwy. 321 and continue approximately 2 miles to Cherry Rd. Turn left on Cherry Rd. Site is approximately .5 mile on the right.

Marshall

14 **Site:** BUFFALO NATIONAL RIVER CIVIL WAR HERITAGE TRAIL, P.O. Box 1173,
Harrison, AR 72602, 501-741-5443, ext. 104

Description: Buffalo National River is a 95,000-acre National Park unit that preserves unique natural and cultural features of the Arkansas Ozarks. During the Civil War, the rugged terrain became a battleground between aggressive independent

Confederate units and the Union forces holding northwest Arkansas. The residents caught in the middle of the constant skirmishing lost farms, possessions, and lives. Skirmish sites, saltpeter caves, and Civil War–era farms are interpreted. For Civil War orientation, the Park staff recommends visiting the Tyler Bend Visitor Center, near Marshall, Arkansas.

Admission Fees: Free.

Open to Public: Daily: Daylight hours. *Tyler Bend Visitor Center:* Daily: 8 A.M.– 4:30 P.M.

Visitor Services: Lodging; camping; trails (some trails are rugged); museum; gift shop; information; rest rooms.

Regularly Scheduled Events: Summer tours and interpretive talks. Call for a schedule.

Directions: From I-40 at Conway: exit onto Hwy. 65 and proceed north. The Tyler Bend Visitor Center is about 10 miles north of Marshall; follow the signs. Tyler Bend Visitor Center is about 100 miles from Little Rock and about 100 miles from Springfield, MO.

Pea Ridge

15 **Site:** PEA RIDGE NATIONAL MILITARY PARK, P.O. Box 700, Pea Ridge, AR 72751-0700, 501-451-8122

Description: On March 7 and 8, 1862, the 10,500 man Union Army of the Southwest and the 16,200 man Confederate Army of the West met in combat at two separate battlefields, Leetown and Elkhorn Tavern, on the gently rolling plain called Pea Ridge. The battle at Leetown ended after the death of two Confederate generals on March 7, while the battle at Elkhorn Tavern continued until the Confederates ran out of ammunition on March 8. The decisive Union victory ensured that Missouri would remain in Federal control and paved the way for Grant's Vicksburg campaign.

Admission Fees: Adults: $2; Children under 16: Free; Cars: $4.

Open to Public: Daily: 8 A.M.–5 P.M.

Visitor Services: Trails; museum; information; rest rooms; handicapped access; bookstore.

Regularly Scheduled Events: *Weekend nearest the anniversary of the battle:* Living history exhibit; *Memorial and Veterans Days:* Commemorative ceremonies; *Summer and early autumn:* Living history demonstrations.

Directions: From I-40: exit to Hwy. 71 north; drive 60 miles to Hwy. 72 east; take 72 to Hwy. 62 east. Located on Hwy. 62, approximately 10 miles north of Rogers, AR.

Prairie Grove

16 **Site:** PRAIRIE GROVE BATTLEFIELD STATE PARK, P.O. Box 306, Prairie Grove, AR 72753, 501-846-2990

Description: The Battle of Prairie Grove was fought on December 7, 1862, between the Confederate Army of the Trans-Mississippi and the Federal Army of the Frontier. It was the last major Civil War battle in northwest Arkansas and paved the way for control of the region by the Federal army.

Admission Fees: *Park:* Free; *Museum:* Adults: $2; Children (6–12): $1.

Open to Public: *Park:* Daily: 8 A.M.–10 P.M. *Museum:* Daily: 8 A.M.–5 P.M.

Visitor Services: Civil War Explorer; trails; museum; gift shop; information; rest rooms; handicapped access.

Prairie Grove Battlefield State Park, Prairie Grove, AR. (Photograph courtesy of Prairie Grove Battlefield State Park.)

Regularly Scheduled Events: *May:* Memorial Day Tribute; *Labor Day weekend:* Clothesline Fair. *First weekend in Dec. in even-numbered years:* Battle reenactment;

Directions: From I-40 at Alma, AR: turn north on U.S. 71 for 40 miles to Fayetteville; then turn west on U.S. 62 for 10 miles to Prairie Grove Battlefield.

Prattsville

17 | **Site:** JENKINS' FERRY STATE PARK, 1200 Catherine Park Rd., Hot Springs, AR 71913, 501-844-4176

Description: This site is connected with the Battle of Jenkins' Ferry, the last major Arkansas battle in the Camden Expedition of the Red River Campaign. The April 30, 1864 battle was fought in flooded, foggy conditions as General Frederick Steele's Union army desperately and successfully withheld Confederate attacks and crossed the Saline River to escape to Little Rock.

Admission Fees: Free.

Open to Public: Daily: Dawn–10 P.M.

Visitor Services: Rest rooms; picnic area.

Regularly Scheduled Events: Small reenactment on Armed Forces Day.

Directions: From I-30: take exit 98, Hwy. 270 to Prattsville; turn right on 291; turn right on 46 to the ferryboat site.

St. Francis

18 | Site: CHALK BLUFF PARK, P.O. Box 385, Piggott, AR 72454, 501-598-2667

Description: Chalk Bluff was a strategic crossing into Missouri used by both sides during the Civil War. General Marmaduke's 1863 Raid into Mississippi ended here as he fought off pursuing Union troops.

Admission Fees: Free.

Open to Public: Daily: 8 A.M.–5 P.M.

Visitor Services: Camping; trails; rest rooms; handicapped access.

Regularly Scheduled Events: *June:* Civil War encampment.

Directions: Take U.S. 62 to St. Francis; turn west from town for 1.5 miles; then turn north for 1.25 miles to Chalk Bluff site. There are signs from St. Francis.

Washington

19 | Site: CONFEDERATE STATE CAPITOL AT OLD WASHINGTON HISTORIC STATE PARK, P.O. Box 98, Washington, AR 71862, 501-983-2684

Description: Old Washington Historic State Park offers insight into a 19th century community and builds understanding of the people, times, and events of the Territorial, Antebellum, Civil War, and Reconstruction eras in Arkansas history. This was the state capital from 1863–65 and a cultural, economic, and political center, especially after Little Rock was taken by the Union army in 1863. Site is on the Southwest Trail. Two home tours are available, the Old Town tour and the Living in Town tour, as well as the Old Washington Museum Experience, which includes the gun, blacksmith, and print museums.

Admission Fees: *Old Town Tour or Living in Town Tour:* Adults: $6.50; Children: $3.25. *Old Washington Museum Experience:* Adults: $4.25; Children: $2.25. *Day pass for both tours and all museums:* Adults: $12; Children: $6. *Family pass for both tours and all museums:* Parents and dependent children ages 6–16: $27.50.

All prices are plus tax. *Groups of 20 or more with advance reservations:* $1 off prices listed.

Open to Public: Daily: 8 A.M.–5 P.M.

Regularly Scheduled Events: *Feb.:* Valentine's Day dinner in tavern; *Mar.:* Jonquil Festival with tours, special events, arts and crafts; *Apr.:* Southwest National Rendezvous (primitive camp, seminars, arts and crafts, and exhibits); *July:* Aegis; *Sept.:* Civil War Reenactments Weekend (Old Territorial Days, primitive camp, and demonstrations); *Oct.:* Frontier Days (19th-century crafts) and Moonlight Concert; *Nov.:* Christmas Decorations and Thanksgiving Feast; *Dec.:* Christmas and Candlelight.

Directions: From I-30: take exit 30. Go north on Rte. 4 for 9 miles. Old Washington State Park is located east and west of Hwy. 4; information desk is located in 1874 Courthouse on Southwest Trail, which intersects Hwy. 4.

DELAWARE

$\mathcal{D}$ELAWARE was a slave-holding state with sympathies for the south. These sympathies caused loud discussion in the Delaware legislature, but the mood of the general populace was "go in peace." If Maryland had joined the secessionist movement, Delaware probably would have joined as well. The war did not visit Delaware except at tiny Pea Patch Island where 33,000 Confederate prisoners were kept at Fort Delaware during the war. It was a frightening, disease-ridden place where 2,740 died. The fort was known as the "Andersonville of the North."

Delaware contributed many of its sons, black and white, as soldiers to the Union and Confederate armies. Among them were members of the DuPont family—the leading family of the state. Admiral Samuel DuPont was a naval hero; Lamar DuPont, an officer of the 5th Delaware infantry, served some of his time at Fort Delaware. The state of Delaware also contributed the products of its heavy industrial base, including locomotive engines and iron clad ships, built in Wilmington's shipyards. The DuPont company turned out tons of high-quality gun powder from its mills on the Brandywine. In spite of sympathies for secession, Delaware contributed greatly to the victory for the Union and the rebirth of the nation.

by Lee Jennings, Nature Center Manager for Fort Delaware,
Fort DuPont, and Fort Penn

Delaware City

 Site: FORT DELAWARE STATE PARK, 45 Clinton St., P.O. Box 170, Delaware City, DE 19706, 302-834-7941

Description: Fort Delaware was originally constructed as a mid-19th century coastal defense site. In 1861 the War Department determined that it would be an ideal site for Confederate prisoners. During the course of the war 30,000 Confederates were imprisoned at the fort. Twenty-seven hundred died while in prison. It was reputed to be the "Andersonville of the North."

The fort is located on Pea Patch Island in the Delaware River; visitors travel to the island aboard the *Delafort*, a 90-passenger ferryboat.

Admission Fees: Adults: $4.50; Children: $3; Children 3 and under: Free; Seniors: $4.50.

Delaware

Wilmington

95

Delaware City

1

■ Fort Delaware State Park

13

Dover

1

13

For Delaware Tourism information call 1-800-441-8846.

Fort Delaware on Pea Patch Island near Delaware City, DE. (Photograph courtesy of the Fort Delaware Society.)

Open to Public: Last weekend in Apr.–last weekend in Sept.: Sat.–Sun.: 11 A.M.–4 P.M.; Mid-June–Labor Day: also open Wed.–Thurs.: 11 A.M.–4 P.M.; closed Tues.; closed Mon. except Memorial Day and Labor Day: 11 A.M.–6 P.M.

Visitor Services: Nature preserve; educational programs for groups (call in advance); trails; food; museum; gift shop; information; restrooms; handicapped access.

Regularly Scheduled Events: *First Sat. in June:* Polish Day; *First weekend in Aug.:* Garrison Weekend; Living history and Reenactments: call for schedule.

Directions: From I-95: take State Rte. 1 exit near Christiana Mall; travel south on Rte. 1 to Rte. 72 exit. Turn left onto Rte. 72 east; proceed past Star Refinery and follow signs on Rte. 9 to Delaware City. Turn left at traffic light on Clinton St.; travel about six blocks; look for State Park office and boat dock on the right.

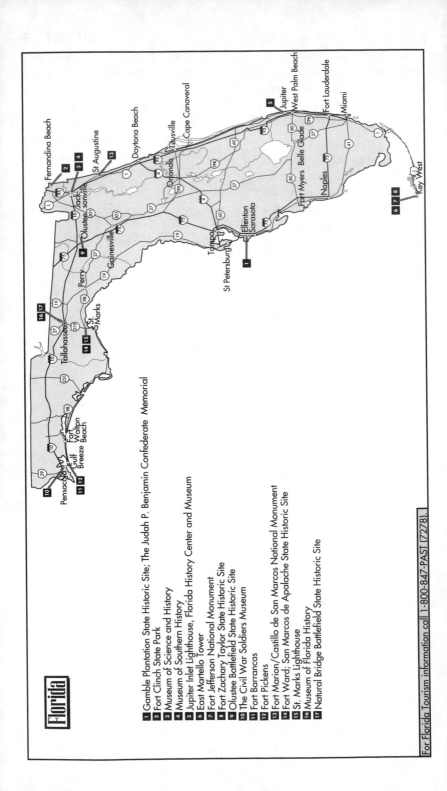

Florida

1 Gamble Plantation State Historic Site; The Judah P. Benjamin Confederate Memorial
2 Fort Clinch State Park
3 Museum of Science and History
4 Museum of Southern History
5 Jupiter Inlet Lighthouse, Florida History Center and Museum
6 East Martello Tower
7 Fort Jefferson National Monument
8 Fort Zachary Taylor State Historic Site
9 Olustee Battlefield State Historic Site
10 The Civil War Soldiers Museum
11 Fort Barrancas
12 Fort Pickens
13 Fort Marion/Castillo de San Marcos National Monument
14 Fort Ward; San Marcos de Apalache State Historic Site
15 St. Marks Lighthouse
16 Museum of Florida History
17 Natural Bridge Battlefield State Historic Site

For Florida Tourism information call 1-800-847-PAST (7278).

FLORIDA

*I*N JANUARY, 1861, Florida became the third state to secede from the Union. Governor Madison Perry and his successor, John Milton, were ardent secessionists, although the state had a sizable unionist minority. From an 1860 population of about 140,000, nearly half of whom were slaves, Florida provided 15,000 soldiers for Confederate service. Several thousand white and black Floridians joined the Federal military. The state proved most important, however, for the cattle, salt, and other supplies that it provided to the Confederacy.

Florida was the scene of one major battle and numerous small engagements. Additionally, the Union navy maintained a blockade around the peninsula throughout the war. From the outbreak of the war, Federal forces controlled Fort Jefferson in the Dry Tortugas, Fort Zachary Taylor at Key West, and Fort Pickens near Pensacola. The first fighting of the conflict nearly occurred in early 1861 at Pensacola, as Confederate troops gathered there in an attempt to force the Federals from nearby Fort Pickens. In early 1862 Confederate officials ordered the evacuation of northeast Florida and Pensacola and sent the defending troops to more active theaters of the war. Subsequently, Fernandina and St. Augustine were occupied by Federal forces, and Jacksonville suffered the first of four separate occupations.

The major battle in Florida took place on February 20, 1864 at Olustee. Political concerns played a major role in the background to the battle, as did the desire to cut off Florida supplies to the rest of the Confederacy. The fight ended in a stinging defeat for the Federals, who retreated back to their Jacksonville stronghold. Military activity in the state increased during 1864–65, with engagements at Gainesville, Marianna, Station Number 4, Fort Myers, and Natural Bridge. This last battle occurred south of Tallahassee in March 1865 and ensured that the capital would remain in Confederate hands until the war's end. Confederate forces in the state capitulated in May and early June 1865, ending the fighting in Florida. During the southern collapse a number of government officials escaped southward through Florida in an attempt to reach Cuba or the Bahamas.

by David Coles, Bureau of Archives and Records Management,
Florida Department of State

Ellenton

 Site: GAMBLE PLANTATION STATE HISTORIC SITE; THE JUDAH P. BENJAMIN
CONFEDERATE MEMORIAL, 3708 Patten Ave., Ellenton, FL 34222,
813-723-4536

Description: The mansion was the home of Major Robert Gamble and served as the center of a large sugar plantation in the antebellum period. Confederate Secretary of State Judah P. Benjamin took refuge in the house as he fled the country during the fall of the Confederacy.

Admission Fees: Adults: $3; Children (6–12): $1.50.

Open to Public: *By tour only:* Thurs.–Mon.: 9:30 A.M.; 10:30 A.M.; 1 P.M.; 2 P.M.; 3 P.M.; 4 P.M.; *Park:* 8 A.M.–dusk.

Visitor Services: Visitors center; tours.

Directions: From I-75: take exit 43; go 1 mile west on Hwy. 301.

Fernandina Beach

2 **Site:** FORT CLINCH STATE PARK, 2601 Atlantic Ave., Fernandina Beach, FL 32034, 904-277-7274

Description: The construction of Fort Clinch was begun in 1847 but was never fully completed. It was occupied by Confederate troops from early 1861 until it was evacuated under threat of a large Union naval expedition in March 1862. Union troops occupied the fort for the remainder of the war.

Admission Fees: Cars: $3.25; Adults (park & fort): $1; Children under 6: Free.

Open to Public: *Fort:* Daily: 9 A.M.–5 P.M.; *Park:* Daily: 8 A.M.–dusk.

Visitor Services: Visitors center; guided tours.

Regularly Scheduled Events: *First weekend of each month:* Reenactors join park rangers in performing sentry duty and drills; *Fri. and Sat., Apr.–Oct.:* Candlelight tours; *First weekend in May:* Special Union garrison reenactment; *Last week in Oct.:* Confederate garrison is reenacted.

Directions: From I-95: to A1A to Amelia Island to Fernandina; turn right onto Atlantic; go 2 miles.

Jacksonville

3 **Site:** MUSEUM OF SCIENCE AND HISTORY, 1025 Museum Circle, Jacksonville, FL 32201, 904-396-7061

Description: This general museum includes an exhibit on the Union transport ship Maple Leaf, which struck a Confederate mine in St. Johns River and sank in 1864. Recently discovered and partially excavated, the shipwreck has yielded well-preserved examples of military and civilian equipment.

Admission Fees: Adults: $5; Seniors & active military: $4; Children (3–12): $3.

Open to Public: Mon.–Fri.: 10 A.M.–5 P.M.; Sat.: 10 A.M.–6 P.M.; Sun. & Holidays: 1 P.M.–6 P.M.

Visitor Services: Museum.

Directions: From I-95 north: take San Marco Blvd. exit; go left onto Gary St. At stoplight take a left onto Prudential Dr.; take left into museum circle. From I-95 south: take Prudential Dr. exit to Main St; go three lights and take River Place to museum circle.

---

4 **Site:** MUSEUM OF SOUTHERN HISTORY, 4304 Herschel St., Jacksonville, FL 32210, 904-388-3574

Description: This museum displays artifacts and memorabilia from the antebellum and Civil War periods. Topics presented include camp life, military equipment, and civilian personal items. The museum has an adjoining historical research library, with genealogical research assistance available.

Admission Fees: Adults: $1; Children under 16: Free with an adult.

Open to Public: Tues.–Sat.: 10 A.M.–5 P.M.

Visitor Services: Museum; information.

Directions: From I-95: go west on I-10; then take U.S. 17 south to San Juan Ave.; turn left; go to first light (Herschel St.) and turn left; one block.

Jupiter

---

5 **Site:** JUPITER INLET LIGHTHOUSE, FLORIDA HISTORY CENTER AND MUSEUM, 805 North U.S. Hwy. 1, Jupiter, FL 33477, 407-747-6639

Description: The lighthouse was designed by then Lieutenant George G. Meade, later Federal commander at Gettysburg. Construction was completed in 1860. Early in the Civil War, Confederate sympathizers removed the illuminating apparatus and buried it in Jupiter Creek. At the end of the war, the newly appointed lighthouse keeper recovered the lighting mechanism and it was relighted in 1866.

Admission Fees: $5.

Open to Public: Sun.–Wed.: 10 A.M.–5 P.M.

Visitor Services: Museum; visitors center; information; guided tours.

Directions: From I-95: take Jupiter exit. Travel east on Indiantown Rd. to U.S. Hwy. 1. Take U.S. Hwy. 1 north approximately 2 miles to the intersection of State Rd. 707.

Key West

---

6 **Site:** EAST MARTELLO TOWER, 3501 South Roosevelt Blvd., Key West, FL 33040, 305-296-3913

Description: Built in 1862 to defend Fort Taylor from possible threat from land attack during the Civil War. No attack ever occurred, and neither the East nor West Martello Towers were finished. Today, the East Martello Tower houses a general art gallery and Key West museum.

Admission Fees: Adults: $5; Children (7–12): $1.

Open to Public: Daily: 9:30 A.M.–5 P.M.

Visitor Services: Museum; art gallery.

Directions: From A1A: turn left on South Roosevelt Blvd.

---

7 **Site:** FORT JEFFERSON NATIONAL MONUMENT, Dry Tortugas National Park, P.O. Box 279, Homestead, FL 33030, 305-247-6211

Description: This is the largest all-masonry fort in the Western Hemisphere; called the "Key to the Gulf of Mexico." It was garrisoned by Union troops throughout the Civil War and also served as a military prison. Located in the Gulf off Key West.

Admission Fees: Free.

Open to Public: Daily: 8 A.M.–4:30 P.M.

Visitor Services: Exhibits; self-guided tours.

Directions: Garden Key, Dry Tortugas, 70 miles west of Key West. Accessible only by boat or seaplane.

---

8 **Site:** FORT ZACHARY TAYLOR STATE HISTORIC SITE, P.O. Box 289, Southard St., Key West, FL 33041, 305-292-6713

Description: When Florida seceded from the Union, Federal troops in Key West quickly moved to secure Fort Taylor and prevented it from falling into Confederate hands. The cannons that have been found buried inside the fort constitute one of the largest groups of Civil War heavy artillery in existence.

Admission Fees: Cars: $3.25 plus $.50 per person; Adults: $1.50.

Open to Public: Daily: 8 A.M.–sunset.

Visitor Services: Tours (Daily, Noon & 2 P.M.)

Fort Zachary Taylor in the Florida Keys. (Photograph courtesy of Phillip M. Pollock, the Museum of Florida History.)

Regularly Scheduled Events: *Feb.:* Civil War Days reenactment and living history weekend.

Directions: Located at the southwest end of Key West, Florida, at Southard St. on Truman Annex.

Olustee

 Site: OLUSTEE BATTLEFIELD STATE HISTORIC SITE, P.O. Box 2, Olustee, FL 32072, 904-758-0400

Description: The Olustee Battlefield is the site of the only major Civil War battle fought in Florida. On February 20, 1864, a Union force of approximately 5,000 troops clashed with a Confederate force of similar size. After bloody fighting, the Union force was defeated and forced to retreat to Jacksonville.

Admission Fees: Free.

Open to Public: *State Park:* Daily: 8 A.M.– 5 P.M.; *Interpretive Center:* Thurs.–Mon.: 9 A.M.–5 P.M.

Visitor Services: Interpretive center; trails; information.

Regularly Scheduled Events: *Feb.:* Reenactment of the Battle of Olustee.

Directions: About 15 miles east of Lake City; 2 miles east of Olustee on U.S. 90.

Pensacola

 Site: THE CIVIL WAR SOLDIERS MUSEUM, 108 South Palafox Place, Pensacola, FL 32501, 904-469-1900

Description: The museum exhibits display the arms, equipment, and personal effects of Civil War soldiers, both Northern and Southern. Special areas of interest include artifacts dealing with Civil War medicine and documents related to Pensacola during the Civil War.

Admission Fees: Adults: $4; Children (6–12): $2; Children under 6: Free.

Open to Public: Mon.–Sat.: 10 A.M.–4:30 P.M.

Visitor Services: Bookstore; gift shop; museum.

Directions: From I-110: take Servantes exit; go west; then turn left onto Palafox Place.

Site: FORT BARRANCAS, 40 Gulf Island National Seashore, 1801 Gulf Breeze Pkwy., Gulf Breeze, FL 32561, 904-934-2600

Description: Confederate forces occupied this fort from early 1861 until they withdrew in May 1862. Artillery fire was exchanged in late 1861 and early 1862 with Union-held Fort Pickens in the harbor.

Admission Fees: Free.

Open to Public: *Apr.–Oct.:* Daily: 9:30 A.M.–5 P.M.; *Nov.–Mar.:* Daily: 10:30 A.M.–4 P.M.

Visitor Services: Self-guided tours.

Directions: Take Rte. 292 to U.S. Naval Air Station. Located on the base of Pensacola U.S. Naval Air Station at the south end of Navy Blvd.

Site: FORT PICKENS, 40 Gulf Island National Seashore, 1801 Gulf Breeze Pkwy., Gulf Breeze, FL 32561, 904-934-2600

Description: Originally built in 1829–34, Fort Pickens was held by Union troops throughout the Civil War. The Fort's commander refused demands that the fort surrender to state forces at the beginning of the war.

Admission Fees: Cars: $4; Persons over age 62: Free.

Open to Public: *Apr.–Oct.:* Daily: 9 A.M.–5 P.M.; *Nov.–Mar.:* Daily: 8 A.M.–4 P.M.

Visitor Services: Visitors center; guided tours.

Directions: Take U.S. 98 east across Pensacola Bay to Gulf Breeze. Take Tallahassee Hwy. 399 to Pensacola Beach; then travel 9 miles west on Fort Pickens Rd.

St. Augustine

Site: FORT MARION/CASTILLO DE SAN MARCOS NATIONAL MONUMENT, 1 Castillo Dr., St. Augustine, FL 32084, 904-829-6506

Description: Built in 1672–95 as a colonial Spanish fortress, it was later renamed Fort Marion. Confederate forces occupied this fort from early 1861 until they withdrew the next year, on arrival of a Union naval force.

Admission Fees: Adults: $2; Over 65 and under 17: Free.

Open to Public: Daily: 8:45 A.M.–4:45 P.M.

Visitor Services: Guided tours; information; exhibits.

Directions: From I-95: exit at Rte. 16 east into St. Augustine; turn right for 2 miles on San Marcos St.

St. Marks

Site: FORT WARD, SAN MARCOS DE APALACHE STATE HISTORIC SITE, P.O. Box 27, St. Marks, FL 32355, 904-925-6216

Description: These ruins are located at the confluence of the St. Marks and Wakulla rivers. The site has been occupied by Spanish, British, American, and Confederate troops. During the Civil War, Confederate soldiers built earthworks and placed artillery at the fort, which was threatened but not attacked in March 1865.

Admission Fees: Adults: $1; Children under 7: Free.

Open to Public: Thurs.–Mon.: 9 A.M.–5 P.M.

Visitor Services: Museum; visitors center; information.

Directions: Off State Rd. 363: turn right to Old Fort Rd., turn left to site. (Located south of Tallahassee).

---

15 Site: ST. MARKS LIGHTHOUSE, St. Marks National Wildlife Refuge, P.O. Box 68, St. Marks, FL 32355, 904-925-6121

Description: The lighthouse was the site of several military operations during the Civil War. In June 1862, the Union navy shelled the area, destroying a small Confederate fortification nearby. A year later, the navy returned and burned the lighthouse's interior steps, trying to prevent its use as a Confederate lookout tower.

Admission Fees: Cars: $4; Adults: $1.

Open to Public: *Refuge:* Daily: Dawn to dusk; *Lighthouse:* Armed Forces Day: 9 A.M.–10 P.M.

Visitor Services: Trails.

Directions: Located in the St. Marks National Wildlife Refuge, south of Tallahassee off County Rd. 59, south of Newport.

Tallahassee

16 Site: MUSEUM OF FLORIDA HISTORY, 500 South Bronough St., Tallahassee, FL 32399-0250, 904-488-1484

Description: The state history museum includes a Civil War exhibit that displays selected military arms, soldiers' personal effects, and battle flags carried by Florida's Confederate units. The museum also administers the state's Old Capitol that houses exhibits on the antebellum, Civil War, and Reconstruction periods in Florida's history.

Admission Fees: Free.

Open to Public: Mon.–Fri.: 9 A.M.–4:30 P.M.; Sat.:10 A.M.–4:30 P.M.; Sun. and holidays: Noon–4:30 P.M.

Visitor Services: Museum; gift shop.

Directions: From I-10: take Havana/Tallahassee exit; proceed on Monroe St. for 7 miles; turn left on Jefferson St.; travel past three stoplights to museum. Located on the ground floor of the R.A. Gray Building, 500 South Bronough St., one block west of the Capitol Building.

17 **Site:** NATURAL BRIDGE BATTLEFIELD STATE HISTORIC SITE, 1022 Desoto Park Dr., Tallahassee, FL 32301, 904-922-6007

Description: On March 6, 1865, a small battle was fought south of Tallahassee at Natural Bridge, where the St. Marks River goes underground. Confederate troops, supported by cadets and home guards, defeated a Union attempt to cross the river and forced the Union troops to retreat to the coast.

Admission Fees: Free.

Open to Public: Daily: 8 A.M.–sunset.

Visitor Services: Picnic area; information.

Regularly Scheduled Events: *Early Mar.:* Reenactment of the Battle of Natural Bridge.

Directions: Travel south from Tallahassee on State Rd. 363 to Woodville; then proceed 6 miles east of Woodville on Natural Bridge Rd.

GEORGIA

*G*EORGIA'S GEOGRAPHIC POSITION in the heart of the Confederacy made the state almost immune from invasion during the first two years of the Civil War. Its coastline was an exception. But Georgians fought in almost every battle and supplied approximately 112,000 soldiers to the Confederate cause. Former slaves, many native Georgians, served in the Forty-fourth United States Colored Infantry.

From the early months of the war, the coast of Georgia saw much activity, with the Union navy blockading the coastline in an attempt to cut off supplies to the Confederacy. Union forces invaded Georgia in September 1863 and fought the Battle of Chickamauga. Two days of hard fighting between the Confederate forces of General Braxton Bragg and the Federal army of General William S. Rosecrans ended with Rosecrans retreating to Chattanooga. Chickamauga was among the 10 bloodiest battles of the war. The cost to the Confederacy for the victory was one from which they never recovered.

The next spring, General William T. Sherman invaded Georgia, and his 100,000 men repeatedly outmaneuvered General Joseph E. Johnston's 70,000 troops. The war came to the heart of Georgia with engagements at Rocky Face Ridge, Resaca, New Hope Church, Pickett's Mill, Cassville, and Kennesaw Mountain. After being outflanked at numerous positions, including his Chattahoochee River Line, Johnston was replaced by General John B. Hood.

Atlanta was a strategic supply and communications center for the Confederacy. With no troop reinforcements available, Atlanta's fortifications were hurriedly strengthened by thousands of impressed slaves. Twelve miles of heavy fortifications surrounded the city from which General Hood launched attacks on the Union forces during three major battles in July 1864. At the conclusion of these battles and after a 40-day siege, General Hood was forced to retreat from Atlanta to avoid entrapment by Union flanking movements. On September 2, the mayor of Atlanta formally surrendered the city to the Union army. In early October, Hood turned north, hoping to cut Sherman's supply lines and lure him away from the city. Sherman then detached part of his army to follow Hood northward, and by the middle of November, Hood was well on his way to Tennessee. After Hood's departure, Sherman ordered the evacuation of the city and set much of what was left on fire. Atlanta was in flames as Sherman departed southward November 15, 1864, on his March to the Sea. After many skirmishes with Confederate cavalry and poorly organized bands of militia during his March to the Sea, he arrived in Savannah on December 22.

The end of the war came with a series of surrenders. President Jefferson Davis hoped to continue the war from the Trans-Mississippi region. He was pursued across Georgia and was captured near Irwinville in southern Georgia on May 10, 1865.

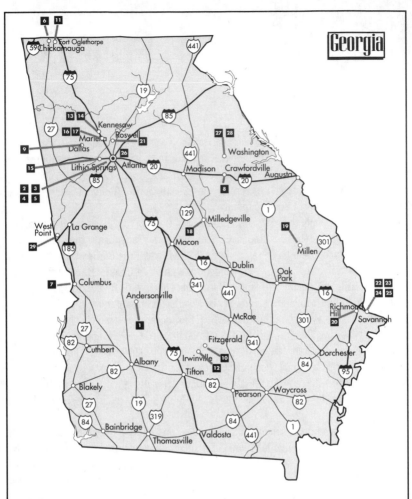

1 Andersonville National Historic Site	**16** Marietta National Cemetery
2 The Atlanta Cyclorama	**17** Western and Atlantic Passenger Depot
3 Atlanta History Center	**18** The Old Governor's Mansion
4 Georgia State Capitol	**19** Magnolia Springs State Park
5 Historic Oakland Cemetery	**20** Fort McAllister Historic State Park
6 Gordon-Lee Mansion	**21** Bulloch Hall
7 Confederate Naval Museum	**22** Fort James Jackson
8 Alexander H. Stephens State Historic Park	**23** Fort Pulaski National Monument
9 Pickett's Mill State Historic Site	**24** Green-Meldrim House
10 Blue & Gray Museum	**25** The Historic Railroad Shops and the Savannah History Museum
11 Chickamauga and Chattanooga National Military Park	**26** Georgia's Stone Mountain Park
12 The Jefferson Davis Memorial Museum and Park	**27** Robert Toombs State Historic Site
13 Kennesaw Mountain National Battlefield Park	**28** Washington Historical Museum
14 Big Shanty Museum	**29** Fort Tyler
15 Sweetwater Creek State Conservation Park	

For Georgia Tourism information call 1-800-VISIT GA

For More Information

Look for "THE PRESENCE OF THE PAST—TRACKING GEORGIA'S CIVIL WAR HERITAGE." This brochure identifies 41 selected sites, including museums, buildings, and battlefields, that represent Georgia's Civil War history. "The Presence of the Past" is available at Georgia's Welcome Centers or by calling 404-657-7294.

Andersonville

1 **Site:** ANDERSONVILLE NATIONAL HISTORIC SITE, Rte. 1, Box 800, Andersonville, GA 31711, 912-924-0343

Description: Andersonville, Georgia, was the location of Camp Sumter, a Confederate prisoner of war camp. During its 14 months of operation, 45,000 Union prisoners were held here, and 12,920 of them died and are buried in the National Cemetery. Andersonville is also the memorial to all prisoners of war in American history.

Admission Fees: Free.

Open to Public: Mon.–Sun.: 8 A.M.–5 P.M.

Visitor Services: Museum; gift shop; rest rooms; handicapped access.

Regularly Scheduled Events: *Last weekend in Feb.:* Living history commemorating the opening of the prison; *First weekend in Oct.:* Living history commemorating the dedication of the National Cemetery.

Directions: From I-75: take exit 42 (Perry); travel on GA 224 to Montezuma. Turn right on GA 26; go through the outskirts of Montezuma and Oglethorpe until the intersection with GA 49. Turn left and go approximately 11 miles. Andersonville is on the left on GA 49. Also accessible from exit 46 (Hwy. 49 south) off I-75 (Byron).

Andersonville National Historic Site, National Cemetery at Andersonville, GA. (Photograph courtesy of Eastern National.)

ANDERSONVILLE

During the Civil War, both Union and Confederate armies had to deal with thousands of prisoners and to find ways to care for them. Neither side expected a long conflict or the eventual need that arose to care for large numbers of prisoners. As the numbers of prisoners increased, special prison camps were built, many similar to the one at Andersonville, in Georgia.

Of the more than 211,400 Union soldiers captured by Confederate forces, 30,208 died in prison camps. Union forces captured 462,000 Confederates, including those surrendered at the war's close. Of these, 25,976 died in prison camps.

The most common problems confronting prisoners in both the North and South were overcrowding, poor sanitation, and an improper diet. The confined soldiers suffered terribly. Mismanagement by prison officials as well as by the prisoners themselves brought on additional hardships.

Andersonville, or Camp Sumter as it was known officially, was the largest of many Confederate military prisons established during the Civil War. It was built in early 1864 after Confederate officials decided to move the large number of Federal prisoners in and around Richmond to a place of greater security and more abundant food. During the 14 months it existed, more than 45,000 Union soldiers were confined here. Of these, almost 13,000 died of disease, poor sanitation, malnutrition, overcrowding, or exposure to the elements.

Andersonville prison ceased to exist in April and May 1865. During July and August 1865, Clara Barton, together with a detachment of laborers and soldiers and a former prisoner named Dorence Atwater, went to Andersonville to identify and mark the graves of the Union dead. Atwater, a member of the second New York Cavalry, was 19 years old when he was sent to Andersonville and became keeper of the books in which prisoners' deaths were recorded. His lists proved invaluable to Clara Barton.

Clara Barton's efforts to get medical supplies, aid, and care for the troops led President Lincoln to ask her to try to ascertain the whereabouts of missing soldiers, so relatives could be informed. This mission was what brought her to Andersonville.

Today, Andersonville National Historic Site is unique in the National Park System as the only park to serve as a memorial to all Americans ever held as prisoners of any war.

Atlanta

2 **Site:** THE ATLANTA CYCLORAMA, 800-C Cherokee Ave., SE, Atlanta, GA 30315, 404-658-7625 or 404-658-7626

Description: A painting in the round that depicts "The Battle of Atlanta." The painting is 42 feet in height, 358 feet in circumference, weighs more than 9,000 pounds, and covers a canvas area more than 16,000 square feet. A three-dimensional panorama with music and narration awaits the visitor. There is also a film narrated by James Earl Jones on the Atlanta Campaign.

Admission Fees: Adults: $5; Seniors: $4; Children (6–12): $3; Groups of adults: $4; Groups of children: $2.

Open to Public: *Fall/Winter:* Daily: 9:20 A.M.–4:30 P.M.; *Spring/Summer:* Daily: 9:20 A.M.–5:30 P.M.

Visitor Services: Museum; gift shop; information; handicapped access; rest rooms.

Directions: From I-20 east: take exit 26. Follow the signs.

3 **Site:** ATLANTA HISTORY CENTER, 130 West Paces Ferry Rd., NW, Atlanta, GA 30305, 404-814-4000

Description: The Atlanta History Center's museum interprets the key turning points in the Civil War, including the Atlanta Campaign of 1864. The museum has the largest collection of Civil War artifacts in Georgia and one of the five largest Civil War collections in the country, housing approximately 7,500 objects of all types: guns, uniforms, military equipment, and memorabilia.

Admission Fees: Adults: $7; Seniors 65+ & students 18+ with ID: $5; Youths (6–17): $4; Children 5 and under: Free. Group rates available with a reservation. Olympic rates in effect during the summer of 1996.

Open to Public: Mon.–Sat.:10 A.M.–5:30 P.M.; Sun.:12 P.M.–5:30 P.M.

Visitor Services: Wooded trails; museum; library/archives; historic houses; cafe; gift shop; information; rest rooms; handicapped access.

Regularly Scheduled Events: *Apr.:* Sheep to Shawl; *July:* Civil War encampment; *Sept.:* Folklife festival; *Nov. or Dec.:* Candlelight tours. NOTE: The Civil War Encampment *not held in 1996 due to the Olympics.*

Directions: From I-75: take the West Paces Ferry Rd. exit. Go 2.6 miles east on West Paces Ferry Rd. and the Atlanta History Center is on the right.

4 Site: GEORGIA STATE CAPITOL, 431 State Capitol, Atlanta, GA 30334, 404-651-6996

Description: In 1864, Federal troops encamped on the grounds of Atlanta City Hall. Today, Georgia's capitol stands on this site. Statues of Civil War governors and other historic figures as well as UDC historic markers are located on the grounds. Capitol museum collections include Confederate-era flags, portraits, and statuary.

Admission Fees: Free.

Open to Public: Mon.–Fri.: 8 A.M.–5:30 P.M.; Sat.: 10 A.M.–4 P.M.; Sun.: 12 P.M.–4 P.M.

Visitor Services: Museum; information; rest rooms; handicapped access.

Directions: From the south: take I-75/I-85 north; take exit 90 (Capitol Ave.). Continue through stop sign. At first light, turn left onto Capitol Ave. Capitol is 1 mile down on the left. From the north: take I-75/I-85 south; take exit 93 (Martin Luther King, Jr. Dr.). Bear right off exit onto Martin Luther King, Jr. Dr. Capitol is on the left.

---

5 Site: HISTORIC OAKLAND CEMETERY, 248 Oakland Ave., SE, Atlanta, GA 30312, 404-688-2107

Description: Oakland Cemetery is a repository for approximately 2,500 soldiers both known and unknown. It has been the site of Memorial Day services since 1866 and boasts two beautiful monuments to the Confederate dead. It is also the final resting place for five generals.

Admission Fees: Free; *Guided tours:* Adults: $3; Seniors: $2; Children: $1.

Open to Public: Daily: 8 A.M.–6 P.M.; *Business office:* Mon.–Fri.: 9 A.M.–5 P.M.

Visitor Services: Rest rooms; handicapped access; museum; gift shop.

Regularly Scheduled Events: *Oct.:* Sunday in the Park (Victorian afternoon at the cemetery).

Directions: From I-75 south: take Memorial Dr. exit 1 mile east. From I-75 north: take exit 93 onto Butler St.; make first right onto Decatur St. Go three lights to Grant St. and turn right; at stop sign turn left. The gate will be in front of you.

Chickamauga (see also Fort Oglethorpe, GA)

6 Site: GORDON-LEE MANSION, 217 Cove Rd., Chickamauga, GA 30707, 706-375-4728

Description: This antebellum mansion was completed in 1847 and is now a bed and breakfast. Located in the Chickamauga Battlefield area, the home served the Union army first as Gen. Rosecrans's headquarters and then as its main hospital during the bloodiest two days in American history, when 37,000 Civil War soldiers became casualties. The Gordon-Lee mansion is open for tours by appointment only.

Admission Fees: Group tours by appointment only: $4/person.

Open to Public: Call for appointment.

Visitor Services: Tours; museum; information; rest rooms; lodging; catering for parties and receptions.

Directions: From I-75: take exit 141. Turn left on Hwy. 2 toward the Chickamauga Battlefield. Follow Hwy. 2 for 6 miles. Turn left on Hwy. 27 south. Go through the battlefield and turn right at the first traffic signal after leaving the park. Go to the next traffic signal and turn left. Travel to the traffic signal in downtown Chickamauga and turn left. The mansion is the fourth building on the right.

Columbus

7 **Site:** CONFEDERATE NAVAL MUSEUM, P.O. Box 1022, Columbus, GA 31902, 706-327-9798

Description: The Confederate Naval Museum displays the recovered remains of the ironclad ram Jackson and sail/steam gunboat Chattahoochee. Museum exhibits interpret the Confederate Navy's innovative efforts to counter the established U.S. Navy and display artifacts recovered from the ships.

Admission Fees: Free.

Open to Public: Tues.–Fri.:10 A.M.–5 P.M.; Sat.–Sun.: 1 P.M.–5 P.M.

Visitor Services: Museum; gift shop; information; rest rooms.

Directions: Stop at the Georgia Welcome Center on the north side of Columbus and ask for directions. From I-185 south: take Victory Dr. exit; follow Victory Dr. across the river into Phenix City, AL; take first exit to right; turn left at first intersection; take first left; cross bridge back into Columbus, GA; take first right to parking lot.

Crawfordville

8 **Site:** ALEXANDER H. STEPHENS STATE HISTORIC PARK, P.O. Box 283, Crawfordville, GA 30631, 706-456-2602

Description: This historic park consists of the 1875 house and outbuildings of Alexander Stephens, vice president of the Confederacy. Located beside Stephens's home is a Confederate museum that houses one of Georgia's finest collections of Civil War artifacts.

Admission Fees: Adults: $2; Children (5–18): $1. Call for group rates.

Open to Public: Tues.–Sat.: 9 A.M.–5 P.M.; Sun.: 2 P.M.–5 P.M.; last tour at 4 P.M.

Visitor Services: Camping; trails; museum; gift shop; information; rest rooms.

Directions: From I-20: take exit 55 and follow signs to the park (approximately 2 miles).

Dallas

9 **Site:** PICKETT'S MILL STATE HISTORIC SITE, 2640 Mt. Tabor Rd., Dallas, GA 30132, 770-443-7850

Description: The Battle of Pickett's Mill involved 24,000 troops and resulted in a Confederate victory. The Union forces under General Oliver O. Howard suffered 1,600 casualties while the Confederates, under General Patrick R. Cleburne, suffered only 500. The battlefield is in an excellent state of preservation.

Admission Fees: Adults: $2; Children: $1; Groups of adults: $1.50; Groups of children: $.75; Groups of 15 or more: call for rates.

Open to Public: Tues.–Sat.: 9 A.M.–5 P.M.; Sun.: Noon–5 P.M.; closed Mon. (except federal holidays).

Visitor Services: Trails; museum; gift shop; information; rest rooms.

Regularly Scheduled Events: *First weekend in June:* Annual living history encampment; *Autumn:* Reenactment of the Confederate night attack; *All year:* Candlelight tours and weekend interpretive programs.

Directions: From I-75: take exit 120 and follow Hwy. 92 south until Hwy. 381. Take Hwy. 381 to Mt. Tabor Rd. and turn left; after 1 mile you will see the entrance on the left.

Fitzgerald

10 **Site:** BLUE & GRAY MUSEUM, Municipal Building (Old Depot), P.O. Box 1285, Fitzgerald, GA 31750, 912-423-5375

Description: Fitzgerald's Blue & Gray Museum tells a story unique in the nation: how a colony of Union veterans cleared a forest and built this town in Georgia among former enemies, replaced hatred and division with understanding and brotherhood, and organized Battalion 1, Blue and Gray. A true reuniting of America here!

Admission Fees: Adults: $1; Children: $.50.

Open to Public: *Mar.–Oct.:* Mon.–Fri.: 2 P.M.–5 P.M.

Visitor Services: Museum; rest rooms.

Regularly Scheduled Events: *Daily:* Museum conducts a Roll Call of the States for each visitor. Visitors have their picture taken with the flag of their state.

Directions: From I-75: take exit 28 in Ashburn. Go east under overpass for 5 miles. Turn right on 107; travel 20 miles straight until dead end on Merrimac Dr.; turn right on Merrimac. Go to traffic light and take a left onto Central Ave. Watch for museum signs.

Fort Oglethorpe

11 **Site:** CHICKAMAUGA AND CHATTANOOGA NATIONAL MILITARY PARK, P.O. Box 2128, Fort Oglethorpe, GA 30742, 706-866-9241

Description: This National Military Park commemorates the Battle of Chickamauga and the Battle for Chattanooga. The objective was the Chattanooga, Tennessee region, the gateway to the Deep South. Without a fight, the Union army maneuvered the Confederates out of Chattanooga and despite being defeated at Chickamauga on Sept. 19–20, 1863, they were able to hold onto the city. The Confederates, failing to properly exploit their Chickamauga victory, only lay siege to the town and two months later were defeated in the battles for Chattanooga on Nov. 23–25, 1865. Fighting on Lookout Mountain and Missionary Ridge was most decisive.

Admission Fees: Free.

Open to Public: *Visitors Center:* Daily: 8 A.M.–4:45 P.M.; Summer: 8 A.M.–5:45 P.M.; *Battlefield grounds:* 8 A.M.–dusk.

Visitor Services: Trails; museum; bookstore; information; rest rooms; handicapped access; tours.

Regularly Scheduled Events: *Sept. and Nov. on weekend closest to battle dates:* Anniversary commemorations.

Directions: From I-75 in GA: take exit 141; go west on GA 2, 6 miles to U.S. 27; turn left onto U.S. 27 to battlefield. From I-24 in TN: take exit 180B; go south on U.S. 27 to battlefield.

Irwinville

12 **Site:** THE JEFFERSON DAVIS MEMORIAL MUSEUM AND PARK, P.O. Box 422, Irwinville, GA 31760, 912-831-2335

Description: This site is where Confederate President Jefferson Davis was captured by Union forces on May 10, 1865.

Admission Fees: Adults: $1; Children: $.50; Parking: $1.

Open to Public: Tues.–Sat.: 9 A.M.–5 P.M.; Sun.: 1 P.M.–5 P.M.; closed Mon.

Visitor Services: Museum; gift shop; information; rest rooms; handicapped access.

Regularly Scheduled Events: *First Sat. in June:* Commemoration Day (Jefferson Davis's Birthday).

Directions: From I-75: take exit 26; go east 16 miles to Irwinville on GA 32; follow the signs once you are in town. The park is 1 mile north of Irwinville.

Kennesaw

13 **Site:** KENNESAW MOUNTAIN NATIONAL BATTLEFIELD PARK, 900 Kennesaw
Mountain Dr., Kennesaw, GA 30144, 770-427-4686

Description: In June of 1864, General William T. Sherman's advance toward Atlanta was delayed for two weeks at Kennesaw Mountain by Confederate General Joseph E. Johnston. The 2,884-acre National Park preserves the battleground where Johnston's army temporarily stopped the Union advance southward.

Admission Fees: Free.

Open to Public: *Visitors Center:* 8:30 A.M.– 5 P.M.; *Park:* 8 A.M.–8 P.M.

Visitor Services: Trails; museum; gift shop; information; rest rooms; handicapped access.

Regularly Scheduled Events: *June:* Anniversary commemoration.

Directions: From I-75: take exit 116 and follow signs. The park is approximately 4 miles from the interstate.

14 **Site:** BIG SHANTY MUSEUM, 2829 Cherokee St., Kennesaw, GA 30144,
770-427-2117

Description: This museum houses "The General," the train that was stolen by a group of Union soldiers known as Andrews' Raiders. The Andrews' Railroad Raid is an interesting chapter in Civil War history and has been the subject of numerous books and even a Walt Disney movie. Besides housing "The General," the museum also contains an extensive collection of Civil War artifacts.

Admission Fees: Adults: $3; Children (7–15): $1.50; Groups of 12 or more are half price.

Open to Public: Mon.–Sat.: 9:30 A.M.–5:30 P.M.; Sun.: Noon–5:30 P.M.

Visitor Services: Museum; gift shop; handicapped access.

Regularly Scheduled Events: *Apr:* Big Shanty Day; *Summer:* First and third Tues. at 10 A.M.: Storytelling on the Caboose.

Directions: From I-75: take exit 118 (Wade Green Rd.). Turn left, and it is 2.5 miles to Kennesaw site. The museum is approximately 30 miles north of Atlanta.

Lithia Springs

15 **Site:** SWEETWATER CREEK STATE CONSERVATION PARK, P.O. Box 816,
Lithia Springs, GA 30057, 770-732-5871

Description: The park features a variety of natural and cultural resources, including the ruins of the New Manchester Manufacturing Company, a Civil

War–era textile mill. General William T. Sherman's forces burned the mill and the surrounding town during their campaign for Atlanta in 1864, and the factory's female factory workers were deported to the North.

Admission Fees: Parking: $2; Free guided tours are available to groups with a reservation.

Open to Public: *Park:* Daily: 7 A.M.–9:45 P.M.; *Trails:* close at dusk.

Visitor Services: Trails; snacks; gift shop; information; rest rooms; handicapped access; boat rentals.

Regularly Scheduled Events: *Last weekend in Sept.:* New Manchester Day—a living history demonstration; *June:* Native American Day.

Directions: From I-20 west: take exit 12 (Thornton Rd. exit) and turn left onto Camp Creek Pkwy.; go .25 mile and across bridge to Blairs Bridge Rd.; go about 2 miles to a four-way stop. Turn left on Mt. Vernon Rd., which leads into the park. The park office is the first left after you cross the bridge.

Marietta

16   **Site:** MARIETTA NATIONAL CEMETERY, 500 Washington Ave., Marietta, GA 30060, 770-428-5631

Description: The National Cemetery is the burial site of more than 13,000 Union soldiers who were casualties from battles in the area such as New Hope Church, Pickett's Mill, and Kennesaw Mountain.

Admission Fees: Free.

Open to Public: *Cemetery:* Daily: Dawn to dusk; *Office:* Mon.–Fri.: 8 A.M.–4:30 P.M.

Visitor Services: Rest rooms.

Regularly Scheduled Events: Services held on Memorial Day and Veterans Day; *First week in Feb.:* Four Chaplains Day; *Second week in Sept.:* Special POW/MIA Day; *Anniversary week of Dec. 7:* Pearl Harbor Day.

Directions: From I-75 north: take exit 113; turn left onto N. Marietta Pkwy. (120 Loop). Turn left onto Cole St. The cemetery is straight ahead. There is access to the cemetery from Cole St. or Washington St.

17   **Site:** WESTERN AND ATLANTIC PASSENGER DEPOT, Marietta Welcome Center & Visitors Bureau, No. 4 Depot St., Marietta, GA 30060, 770-429-1115

Description: This Victorian brick structure was built in 1898. It was built on the site of the original passenger depot (1840s) that was burned by General William T. Sherman's troops in 1864. The depot in Marietta is where, in 1862, Andrews' Raiders boarded "The General" and began their fateful journey toward "the great locomotive chase" (Andrews' Raid). The depot is also the site from which women workers from the Roswell mills were deported to the North as prisoners of war.

Admission Fees: Free.

Open to Public: Mon.–Fri.: 9 A.M.–5 P.M.; Sat.: 11 A.M.–4 P.M.; Sun.: 1 P.M.–4 P.M.

Visitor Services: Gift shop; information; rest rooms; handicapped access.

Regularly Scheduled Events: *Last Sun. in Apr.:* Taste of Marietta—a food festival; *First & third Wed. in May, June, Sept., and*

Oct.: Past & Repast, history lecture luncheons; *First weekend in Dec.:* Marietta pilgrimage Christmas home tour.

Directions: From I-75: take exit 113. Heading west toward Marietta, proceed 2.5 miles to Mill St.; turn left onto Mill St. A parking lot is immediately on the right. The Welcome Center is across railroad tracks from parking lot.

Milledgeville

18 Site: THE OLD GOVERNORS' MANSION, 120 South Clarke St., Milledgeville, GA 31061, 912-453-4545

Description: This was the executive residence of Georgia's governors from its completion in 1838 until 1868. Governor Joseph E. Brown and his family lived in the mansion during the Civil War. General William T. Sherman spent a night at the mansion during his March to the Sea.

Admission Fees: Adults: $3; Children: $1; Groups of adults: $2, children: $.50.

Open to Public: Tues.–Sat.: 10 A.M.–4 P.M.; Sun.: 2 P.M.–4 P.M.; closed Christmas Eve–New Year's Day.

Visitor Services: Museum; gift shop; handicapped access; rest rooms.

Regularly Scheduled Events: *Thanksgiving–Christmas:* Victorian Christmas at the mansion.

Directions: From I-20: take 441 South to Milledgeville. From I-16: take the Spring St. exit to Hwy. 49 to Milledgeville. The mansion is on the corner of Hancock (Hwy. 49) and Clarke Streets, directly across from Georgia College.

Millen

 19 Site: MAGNOLIA SPRINGS STATE PARK, Rte. 5 Box 488, Millen, GA 30442, 912-982-1660

Description: Due to the overflow from Andersonville Prison, three sites were chosen to relieve the overcrowding. During the Civil War, this site was called Camp Lawton and was used as a prison camp because of its natural springs, plentiful timber for

building stockades, and nearness to the railroad. Fort Lawton was the largest prison in the world during its time.

Admission Fees: Parking: $2; free parking on Wed.

Open to Public: *Park:* Daily: 7 A.M.–10 P.M.; *Park office:* Daily: 8 A.M.–5 P.M.

Visitor Services: Lodging; camping; snacks; gift shop; information; rest rooms.

Regularly Scheduled Events: *Last weekend of Mar.:* Arts & Crafts Festival with Civil War living history encampment; *End of Nov.:* A square dance and clogging weekend; *Spring or autumn, depending on the river level:* Canoe the Ogeechee River.

Directions: From I-16 at Metter, GA: take Hwy. 121 to Millen; take a left onto 121/25. The park is 5 miles north of Millen on Hwy. 25. From I-20: exit onto Bobby Jones Expressway (Hwy. 520); go approximately 7 miles; exit on Peach Orchard Hwy. and Windsor Spring Rd. (Hwy. 25); go through first light to dead end. Turn right; go through Waynesboro (30 miles); go 17 miles south to park.

Richmond Hill

20 **Site:** FORT MCALLISTER HISTORIC STATE PARK, 3894 Ft. McAllister Rd., Richmond Hill, GA 31324, 912-727-2339

Description: Located on the south bank of the Great Ogeechee River, this park is the home of the best-preserved earthwork fortification of the Confederacy. The earthworks and bombproofs withstood bombardments by the heaviest naval guns and have been restored to their 1863–64 appearance. This beautiful coastal park offers a museum containing Civil War artifacts as well as camping and picnic facilities.

Admission Fees: Adults: $2; Children: $1; Group prices vary.

Open to Public: Tues.–Sat.: 9 A.M.–5 P.M.; Sun.: 2 P.M.–5:30 P.M.

Visitor Services: Camping; museum; gift shop; information; rest rooms; handicapped access.

Regularly Scheduled Events: *July 4:* Barbecue; *Second weekend in Dec.:* Civil War Muster.

Directions: From I-95: take exit 15; proceed 9 miles on Spur 144 to park.

Roswell

21 **Site:** BULLOCH HALL, 180 Bulloch Ave., P.O. Box 1309, Roswell, GA 30077, 770-992-1731

Description: This 1840 home was built by Major James Bulloch and was the site of the December 1853 marriage between Martha Bulloch and Theodore Roosevelt of New York (later becoming parents of President Theodore Roosevelt and grandparents of Eleanor Roosevelt, wife of President Franklin D. Roosevelt). The house is now a museum, featuring period rooms, a research library, and a Civil War artifact room. The surrounding historic district features many structures of the Civil War period. The Roswell Presbyterian Church was a Union hospital in 1864. The former locations of several mills that were burned by General Sherman are marked.

Admission Fees: Adults: $4; Children: $3.

Open to Public: Mon.–Sat.: 10 A.M.–3 P.M. (last tour at 2 P.M.); Sun.: 1 P.M.–4 P.M. (last tour at 3 P.M.).

Visitor Services: Tours; museum; information; gift shop; rest rooms; handicapped access to main floor and rest room.

Regularly Scheduled Events: *Mid-Mar.:* Great American Coverup quilt show; *Two days in early Dec.:* Reenactment of 1853 wedding; *Dec.:* Christmas at Bulloch Hall.

Directions: From I-85 or I-285: travel north on GA 400. Take Northridge exit and turn right. Take the next right onto Dunwoody Club. Stay on Dunwoody Club until you reach Roswell Rd. Turn right on Roswell Rd. Go to Historic Roswell Square and turn left at light onto Hwy. 120. The parking lot is 200 yards ahead on the right.

Savannah

22 **Site:** FORT JAMES JACKSON, 1 Old Fort Jackson Rd., Savannah, GA 31404, 912-236-5126

Description: The fort saw its greatest use as the headquarters for the Confederate defenses of the Savannah River during the Civil War and is the oldest standing fort in Georgia, dating to the 1740s.

Admission Fees: Adults: $2.50; Seniors: $1.50; Children: $1.50.

Open to Public: Daily: 9 A.M.–5 P.M.

Visitor Services: Museum; gift shop; information; rest rooms; handicapped access.

Directions: From I-16: take Montgomery St. exit; turn right on Bay St.; turn left at President St.; turn left on Woodcock Rd. and then right on Fort Jackson Rd.

23 **Site:** FORT PULASKI NATIONAL MONUMENT, P.O. Box 30757, Savannah, GA 31410-0757, 912-786-5787

Description: On April 11, 1862, Union forces overtook the fort in only 30 hours. The fall of Fort Pulaski secured Union control over Southern ports and kept Savannah from exporting cotton and importing vital military and civilian goods. This remarkably intact example of 19th-century military architecture is preserved for future generations.

Admission Fees: Adults: $2; Seniors: Free with Golden Age Passport; Children under 16: Free; Maximum charge of $4 per car.

Open to Public: Daily: 8:30 A.M.–5:15 P.M.; Call for extended summer hours.

Visitor Services: Trails; museum; gift shop; information; rest rooms; handicapped access.

Regularly Scheduled Events: *Apr.:* Siege and Reduction Weekend; *Memorial Day and Labor Day:* Troop encampment; *Dec.:* Confederate nog party and candle lantern tours.

Directions: From I-95: follow I-16 or U.S. 80 to Savannah, GA. Head east on U.S. 80 toward Tybee Island. Fort Pulaski is approximately 15 miles east of Savannah.

---

24 **Site:** GREEN-MELDRIM HOUSE, St. John's Church, 1 West Macon St., Savannah, GA 31401, 912-232-1251

Description: Restored and furnished mid-19th-century Gothic Revival–style home of Charles Green, which served as the headquarters for Union General Sherman during the winter of 1864–65. The house is owned and operated by St. John's Episcopal Church.

Admission Fees: Adults: $4; Children: $2; Groups: call for special rates.

Open to Public: Tues., Thurs., Fri., and Sat.: 10 A.M.–4 P.M.; closed Mon., Wed., and Sun.; closed two weeks before Easter, Dec. 15–Jan. 15, and the week of Nov. 10–11.

Visitor Services: Tours; information; gift shop; rest rooms.

Directions: At the end of I-16 east is Montgomery St. At first traffic signal turn right on Liberty St. Go five blocks and turn right on Bull St. Go one block to Madison Sq. The house fronts Madison Sq. between Charlton and Harris streets.

---

25 **Site:** THE HISTORIC RAILROAD SHOPS AND THE SAVANNAH HISTORY MUSEUM, 303 Martin Luther King, Jr. Blvd., Savannah, GA 31401, 912-238-1779

Description: Both sites are National Historic Landmarks. A restored 19th-century railroad terminal houses this museum and a theater that tells the history of Savannah. The Historic Railroad Shops are a railroad repair and manufacturing facility, the oldest surviving and best example of a mid-19th-century integrated railroad shop in the United States. The railroad complex was used in the filming of the movie, *Glory*, about the Fifty-fourth Massachusetts Colored Infantry.

Admission Fees: *Museum:* Adults: $3; Seniors: $2.50; Children (6–12): $1.75.

Open to Public: *Museum:* Daily: 9 A.M.–5 P.M.; *Railroad Shops:* Mon.–Sat.: 10 A.M.–4 P.M.; Sun.: Noon–4 P.M.

Visitor Services: Food; museum; gift shop; information; rest rooms; handicapped access.

Directions: Take I-16 east until it merges into Montgomery St.; turn left onto Liberty St.; go one block and turn right on Martin Luther King, Jr. Blvd. Go a half block and turn left under a brick archway into the parking lot.

Stone Mountain

26 **Site:** GEORGIA'S STONE MOUNTAIN PARK, P.O. Box 778, Stone Mountain, GA
30086, 770-498-5702

Description: This park surrounds and includes the world's largest granite outcropping, with a unique carving of three Confederate heroes (president of the Confederacy Jefferson Davis, General Stonewall Jackson, and General Robert E. Lee) on horseback. The carving is dedicated to the soldiers and sailors of the Confederacy. The park also contains a relocated and restored antebellum plantation complex, one of the largest Civil War exhibits in the state, a water-powered gristmill, a covered bridge, and the Georgia Heritage Museum.

Admission Fees: Cars: $6; there is a $25 annual pass available. Separate attractions (train, riverboat, skylift, miniature golf, antique auto museum, petting zoo, and antebellum plantation): Adults: $3.50; Children (3–11): $2.50; Call for group rates.

Open to Public: *Attractions:* Daily: 10 A.M.–5:30 P.M.; Memorial Day–Labor Day: Daily: 10 A.M.–8 P.M.. *Park:* Daily all year: 6 A.M. to midnight.

Visitor Services: Lodging; camping; trails; food; museum; gift shop; information; rest rooms; handicapped access.

Regularly Scheduled Events: *Late Mar.:* Spring Antebellum Jubilee; *First weekend after Labor Day:* Yellow Daisy Festival; *Oct.:* Tour of Southern Ghosts. Candlelight tours of the plantation are held nightly from the Friday after Thanksgiving through New Year's.

Directions: From I-285: take exit 30B (Hwy. 78); go 7 miles east and follow signs to the park.

Washington

27 **Site:** ROBERT TOOMBS STATE HISTORIC SITE, 216 East Robert Toombs Ave.,
Washington, GA 30673, 706-678-2226

Description: Home of General Robert Augustus Toombs, a successful planter, lawyer, and outspoken Georgia politician, who used his influence to persuade the state to secede from the Union. As Secretary of State to the Confederacy, general, and seasoned battle leader, he never took the Oath of Allegiance to the United States and died as an unreconstructed Rebel.

Admission Fees: Adults: $2; Children (6–18): $1; Groups of adults: $1.50; Groups of children: $.50.

Open to Public: Tues.–Sat.: 9 A.M.–5 P.M.; Sun.: 2 P.M.–5:30 P.M.; closed Mon. except federal holidays.

Visitor Services: Information; rest rooms; handicapped access to first floor.

Regularly Scheduled Events: *First Sat. in Apr.:* Spring home tour; *Last Sun. in June:* Toombs family reunion; *Second Sun. in Dec.:* Christmas tea at the Toombs House.

Directions: Washington is 45 miles east of Athens, GA, on Hwy. 78 or 60 miles west of Augusta, GA. From I-20: take Greensboro exit (Hwy. 44) to Washington; in downtown turn right on Robert Toombs Ave.

---

28 **Site:** WASHINGTON HISTORICAL MUSEUM, 308 East Robert Toombs Ave., Washington, GA 30673, 706-678-2105

Description: Exhibits in this Federal-style house (ca. 1835) highlight the Confederacy and Reconstruction as well as domestic art and local history. A guided tour is available to interpret memorabilia from the last Confederate cabinet meeting as Jefferson Davis fled south. The display includes Jefferson Davis's camp chest, original photos, signed documents, and General Robert Toombs's uniform.

Admission Fees: Adults: $2; Children: $1; Children under 5: Free; Call for special rates for groups of 15 or more.

Visitor Services: Tour; museum; information; gift shop; rest rooms.

Directions: From I-20: take exit 59 (U.S. 78). Follow U.S. 78 west for 20 miles to downtown Washington. The museum is located on E. Robert Toombs Ave.

West Point

29 **Site:** FORT TYLER, West 6th Ave., P.O. Box 715, West Point, GA 31833-0715, 706-645-1440

Description: Earthen fort built to defend strategic Chattahoochee River bridges and military depot in West Point. Site of one of the last engagements of the Civil War fought on April 16, 1865 between Union cavalry under command of Col. Oscar LaGrange and Confederates under Gen. Robert Tyler. The Confederates, numbering fewer than 300 men, managed to withstand advances by 3,500 Union soldiers for eight hours before the fort was finally captured.

Admission Fees: Free.

Open to Public: Daily: Daylight hours.

Visitor Services: Trails; handicapped access.

Regularly Scheduled Events: *Weekend in mid-Apr.:* Battle anniversary reenactment of Confederate Guard.

Directions: From I-85: take exit 1 to West Point. Cross over the Chattahoochee River and turn right on Third Ave. in downtown. Turn left on 10th St. Turn right at the historical marker on West Sixth Ave. Monument marks trail to fort.

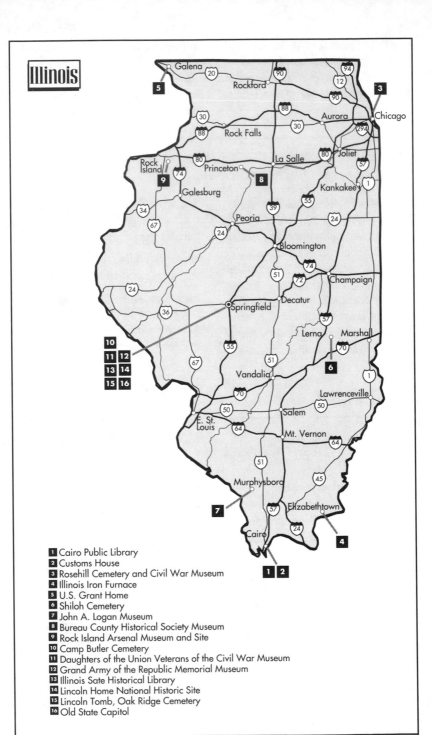

Illinois

Galena
Rockford
Aurora
Chicago
Rock Falls
La Salle
Joliet
Rock Island
Princeton
Kankakee
Galesburg
Peoria
Bloomington
Champaign
Decatur
Springfield
Lerna
Marshall
Vandalia
Lawrenceville
E. St. Louis
Salem
Mt. Vernon
Murphysboro
Elizabethtown
Cairo

1 Cairo Public Library
2 Customs House
3 Rosehill Cemetery and Civil War Museum
4 Illinois Iron Furnace
5 U.S. Grant Home
6 Shiloh Cemetery
7 John A. Logan Museum
8 Bureau County Historical Society Museum
9 Rock Island Arsenal Museum and Site
10 Camp Butler Cemetery
11 Daughters of the Union Veterans of the Civil War Museum
12 Grand Army of the Republic Memorial Museum
13 Illinois Sate Historical Library
14 Lincoln Home National Historic Site
15 Lincoln Tomb, Oak Ridge Cemetery
16 Old State Capitol

For Illinois Tourism information call 1-800-2CONNECT.

ILLINOIS

*B*y 1860, the Republican and Democratic conventions nominated as their standard bearers two political giants from Illinois: Abraham Lincoln and Stephen A. Douglas. If Lincoln's election accelerated events leading to the outbreak of war, his leadership guided a nation through war toward reconciliation in 1865.

While no major battle was fought within Illinois, it became an important supply area for much of the Western campaign. In spite of a large population with family ties to the South, Southern Illinois remained loyal to the Union cause.

More than 250,000 men from Illinois served in the Union forces. Illinois was one of a few states to exceed its quota for troops throughout the war. Through the political leadership of Abraham Lincoln and the military leadership of Ulysses S. Grant, Illinois provided extraordinary individuals to confront the nation's most serious crisis.

by Thomas Schwartz, State Historian,
Illinois Historic Preservation Agency

Cairo

1 **Site:** CAIRO PUBLIC LIBRARY, 1609 Washington Ave., P.O. Box 151, Cairo, IL 62914-0151, 618-734-1840

Description: Cairo played a critical role in the Civil War. Projecting deeply into the South, controlling major waterways and railroads, Cairo was a bastion for the Union. General Ulysses S. Grant, the Army of the Tennessee, the Siege of Vicksburg, and the Naval Battle for the Mississippi were all launched from Cairo's riverbanks. The library contains an extensive collection of primary and secondary research documents relating to the city's role in the Union army's control of the Western Theater in the Civil War. The collection also includes artifacts.

Admission Fees: Free.

Open to Public: Mon.–Fri.: 10 A.M.–5 P.M.; Sat.: 9 A.M.–Noon.

Visitor Services: Information.

Directions: From I-57: take exit 1 and proceed south on U.S. 51 to downtown Cairo. The library is located on the west side of Washington St. in the downtown business district.

2 **Site:** CUSTOMS HOUSE, 14th and Washington, Cairo, IL 62914-0724, 618-734-3637

Description: Local history museum with exhibits on Cairo's pivotal role in the Civil War, including artifacts from the U.S.S. *Cairo,* a gunboat built in the local shipyards, sunk by a Confederate torpedo in 1862 and raised in 1964.

Admission Fees: Free.

Open to Public: Mon.–Fri.: 10 A.M.–Noon and 1 P.M.–3 P.M.

Visitor Services: Museum; information.

Directions: From I-57: take exit 1 and proceed south on U.S. 51 to downtown Cairo. The Customs House is located on the east side of Washington St. in the downtown business district.

Chicago

3 **Site:** ROSEHILL CEMETERY AND CIVIL WAR MUSEUM, 5800 N. Ravenswood Ave., Chicago, IL 60660, 312-561-5940

Description: Rosehill Cemetery contains the graves of 14 Union generals, six drummer boys, and hundreds of Civil War soldiers. Members of the Eighth Illinois Cavalry, the unit that fired the first shots at Gettysburg, are buried here. Also buried here is a Chicago mayor who was charged with, and later acquitted of, assisting Confederate prisoners in escaping from Camp Douglas. A portion of the Administration building is devoted to a Civil War museum that features exhibits on the war, emphasizing the roles of those who are buried in the cemetery and the city of Chicago's part in the conflict.

Admission Fees: Free.

Open to Public: Mon.–Fri.: 9 A.M.–5 P.M.; Sat.–Sun.: 9 A.M.–4 P.M.

Visitor Services: Tours; museum; information; rest rooms; handicapped access.

Directions: From I-94 (Edens Expressway): travel east on Foster Ave. and then north on Ravenswood. From Lakeshore Dr.: travel north on Lakeshore (U.S. 41), then west on Foster to Ravenswood.

Elizabethtown

4 **Site:** ILLINOIS IRON FURNACE, U.S. Forest Service, Elizabethtown, IL 62931, 618-287-2201

Description: During the Civil War this structure was a principal furnace used for smelting iron ore. The restored structure features interpretive information; fishing, hiking, and picnicking facilities are available.

Admission Fees: Free.

Open to Public: Daily: 6 A.M.–10 P.M.

Visitor Services: Information.

Directions: Located about 5 miles from Rosiclare near the intersection of State Rtes. 146 and 34. Follow signs.

Galena

5 | **Site:** U.S. GRANT HOME, 510 Bouthillier St., Galena, IL 61036, 815-777-0248

Description: On August 18, 1865, citizens of Galena celebrated the return of its Civil War hero Gen. Ulysses S. Grant by presenting him with this handsome furnished home. The house is typical of the Italianate style and is furnished with many original items from the Grant family.

Admission Fees: Free.

Open to Public: Daily: 9 A.M.–5 P.M. NOTE: Site closes at 4 P.M., Nov.–Feb.; also closed state and federal holidays.

Visitor Services: Tours; museum; information; rest rooms.

Directions: Galena is located on U.S. 20 and State Rte. 84; follow signs to the Grant home. Galena is 160 miles from Chicago; 85 miles from Moline; and 95 miles from Madison, WI.

U.S. Grant Home, Galena, IL. (Photograph by Jim Quick.)

Lerna

6 | **Site:** SHILOH CEMETERY, Lincoln Hwy.,Lerna, IL 62440, 217-345-4088

Description: This cemetery is the final resting place for many Civil War veterans and for Thomas and Sarah Lincoln, Abraham Lincoln's father and stepmother.

Admission Fees: Free.

Open to Public: Daily: Dawn to dusk.

Visitor Services: None.

Directions: From I-47: exit at State Rte. 16 east and proceed toward Charleston; at the first traffic light turn south; follow markers to Lincoln Log Cabin State Historic Site, approximately 11 miles.

Murphysboro

7 | **Site:** JOHN A. LOGAN MUSEUM, 1613 Edith St., Murphysboro, IL 62966, 618-684-3455

Description: The John A. Logan Museum and Interpretive Center chronicles the life of this Civil War general from the time his parents arrived in Illinois until the death of his widow. The site includes a log cabin and the Dalton home, a structure purchased in 1895 by an African American Civil War veteran. The site includes an extensive collection of African American Civil War history.

Admission Fees: Adults: $1; Children: $.50.

Open to Public: *Apr.–May and Sept.–Oct.*: Sat.–Sun.: 1 P.M.–4 P.M. *June–Aug.*: Mon., Wed., Fri., Sat., and Sun.: 1 P.M.–4 P.M.

Visitor Services: Tours; museum; information; gift shop; rest rooms; handicapped access.

Directions: From I-57: take State Rte. 13 west to Murphysboro; the museum is located two blocks off Rtes. 13 and 149 (Walnut St.).

Princeton

8 | **Site:** BUREAU COUNTY HISTORICAL SOCIETY MUSEUM, 109 Park Ave. West, Princeton, IL 61356-1927, 815-875-2184

Description: The 93d Illinois Infantry was mustered from Bureau County for service in the Union army. The County Historical Museum contains an outstanding and extensive collection of artifacts and documents associated with the regiment. The collection is well researched and documented.

Admission Fees: Adults: $2; Children: $.50.

Open to Public: Mon. and Wed.–Sun.: 1 P.M.–5 P.M.; Closed Tues.

Visitor Services: Tours; museum; information; gift shop.

Directions: From I-80: take Princeton exit; proceed into Princeton (this road becomes Main St.). Continue on Main through two business districts to the four-way stop, just before the courthouse. Turn right onto Park. Park curves around, and the museum is located at the end of the curve, across from the courthouse.

Rock Island

9 | **Site:** ROCK ISLAND ARSENAL MUSEUM AND SITE, Attn.: SIORI-CFM, Rock Island Arsenal, Rock Island, IL 61299-5000, 309-782-5021

Description: This was the site of a Union prison. A cemetery here contains graves of

nearly 2,000 Confederate prisoners. The adjoining national cemetery is the burial place of Union prison personnel and veterans. The museum contains military collections from all wars and features an extensive small-arms collection.

Admission Fees: Free.

Open to Public: Daily: 10 A.M.–4 P.M.

Visitor Services: Museum; information; gift shop; rest rooms; handicapped access; food available Mon.–Fri.

Directions: From I-74 or I-280: follow signs.

Springfield

10 **Site:** CAMP BUTLER CEMETERY, 5063 Camp Butler Rd., Springfield, IL 62702, 217-522-5764

Description: This was once the site of a Union Civil War training camp and Confederate prison. It is now a cemetery for veterans and their dependents.

Admission Fees: Free.

Open to Public: Mon.–Fri.: 8 A.M.–4:30 P.M.

Visitor Services: Information; rest rooms.

Directions: From I-72: exit at Camp Butler Rd.; continue north on Camp Butler Rd. to the cemetery entrance.

11 **Site:** DAUGHTERS OF THE UNION VETERANS OF THE CIVIL WAR MUSEUM, 503 South Walnut, Springfield, IL 62707, 217-544-0616

Description: Collections of this museum include Civil War medals, photographs, currency, drums, uniforms, and a complete set of the official records.

Admission Fees: Free.

Open to Public: Mon.–Fri.: 9 A.M.–Noon and 1 P.M.–4 P.M.

Visitor Services: Museum; gift shop.

Directions: From I-55: take the South Grand Ave. west exit to Walnut.

12 **Site:** GRAND ARMY OF THE REPUBLIC MEMORIAL MUSEUM, 629 South Seventh, Springfield, IL 62701, 217-522-4373

Description: This museum includes a large assortment of Civil War memorabilia, including tintypes by Civil War photographer Matthew Brady.

Admission Fees: Free; however, donations are welcomed.

Open to Public: Tues.–Sat.: 10 A.M.–4 P.M.

Visitor Services: Museum.

Directions: From I-55: take the South Grand Ave. west exit to Ninth St.; turn north on Ninth St. to Cook St.; turn west on Cook St. to Seventh.

13 **Site:** ILLINOIS STATE HISTORICAL LIBRARY, 1 Old State Capitol Plaza, Springfield, IL 62701, 217-524-6358

Description: The Illinois State Historical Library collects the political, social, business, and military history of the State of Illinois. The collections include many Civil War letters, manuscripts, photographs, maps, and other memorabilia. The collections also include the largest single collection devoted to the prepresidential career of Abraham Lincoln.

Admission Fees: Free.

Open to Public: Mon.–Fri.: 8:30 A.M.–5 P.M.; Closed on state and national holidays.

Visitor Services: Museum; information; rest rooms.

Directions: From I-55: take the Clear Lake exit to Ninth St.; turn south on Ninth to Adams St.; turn west on Adams St. to the Old State Capitol Plaza. The Library is located in the underground facility below the Old State Capitol.

---

14 Site: LINCOLN HOME NATIONAL HISTORIC SITE, 413 South Eighth St., Springfield, IL 62701, 217-492-4150

Description: The Lincoln Home National Historic Site preserves four city blocks surrounding the only home ever owned by Abraham Lincoln. Erected in 1839, the house was purchased by Lincoln in 1844 and served as the Lincolns' home for 17 years until their departure for Washington, D.C. in 1861.

Admission Fees: Free.

Open to Public: Daily: 9 A.M.–5 P.M.

Visitor Services: Tours; museum; gift shop; visitors center; rest rooms.

Directions: From I-55: take the South Grand Ave. west exit to Ninth St.; turn north on Ninth St. and proceed to Capitol Ave.; turn west on Capitol Ave. to Eighth St.; turn south to the Lincoln Home Visitors Center.

---

15 Site: LINCOLN TOMB, Oak Ridge Cemetery, Springfield, IL 62702, 217-782-2717

Description: The 117-foot-tall tomb is constructed of granite and is the final resting place of President Abraham Lincoln, his wife, Mary, and three of their four children. Near the entrance is a bronze bust of Lincoln. The tomb designer, Larkin Mead, created the monumental bronze military statues and the statue of Lincoln on the terrace. Mead's design has been popularly interpreted as symbolizing Lincoln's role in the preservation of the Union.

Admission Fees: Free.

Open to Public: Daily: 9 A.M.–5 P.M. NOTE: Site closes at 4 P.M. in Nov.–Feb.; Closed New Years Day, Martin Luther King Day, Presidents Day, General Election Day, Veterans Day, Thanksgiving, and Christmas.

Visitor Services: Tours; museum; information; rest rooms; and handicapped access.

Directions: From I-55: take Sangamon Ave. exit to Peoria Rd; turn south on Peoria Rd. to North Grand Ave.; go west on North Grand Ave. to Monument Ave.; go north on Monument to the cemetery.

16 **Site:** OLD STATE CAPITOL, 1 Old State Capitol Plaza, Springfield, IL 62701, 217-785-7961

Description: The Old State Capitol is a magnificently restored Greek Revival building that served as the center of the Illinois government from 1839 to 1876. U.S. Senator Stephen Douglas and a young legislator, Abraham Lincoln, were powerful figures of the time who frequented the halls of the Capitol. Abraham Lincoln delivered his famous "House Divided" speech in the Representatives Hall and lay in state there before his interment in the Oak Ridge Cemetery.

Admission Fees: Free.

Open to Public: Daily: 9 A.M.–4:30 P.M.; Closed state and national holidays.

Visitor Services: Tours; museum; gift shop; visitors center; rest rooms; handicapped access from elevator in kiosk south of the main entrance; braille guide available.

Directions: From I-55: take Clear Lake exit to Ninth St.; turn south on Ninth St. to Adams St.; turn west on Adams St. to the Old State Capitol.

Indiana

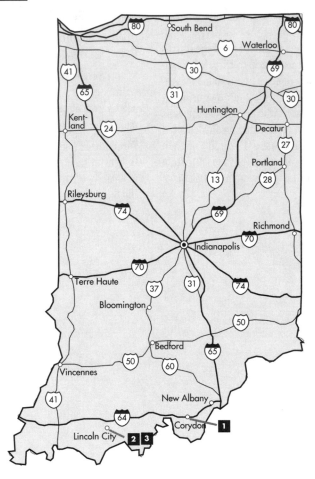

1 Corydon Battlefield
2 Lincoln Boyhood National Memorial
3 Lincoln Amphitheater and Lincoln State Park

INDIANA

*I*ndiana supplied more than men, money, and munitions in the Civil War. Led by autocratic Gov. Oliver P. Morton—the "War Governor"—Indiana anchored the resolve of the western states to help save the Union.

When men and materiel were most needed to shore up Northern armies, President Lincoln called on Morton, and his ally responded. Boldly playing his cards in politics and war, Morton defied his opponents in the Indiana legislature, over and over coming up with the troops Lincoln required to fight the war. Morton operated outside his state as well, marshaling support throughout the Midwest. When he could not raise funds from his own lawmakers, Morton borrowed from men of wealth. Railroad financier James Lanier of Madison, Indiana, first lent Morton $400,000 to finance the war effort, then later an additional $600,000—a million dollars!—much of which Morton kept in his own safe, and all of which was eventually repaid.

The Civil War raged only miles away from Indiana, below the Ohio River. The flames of fighting, in fact, lapped onto the Hoosier State in July 1863, when a large Confederate force, led by Gen. John Hunt Morgan, crossed the Ohio just downriver from Louisville, and proceeded northward, primarily in search of fresh horses for Confederate cavalry.

Just south of the little town of Corydon, the original state capital of Indiana, a hastily gathered "home guard" of about 600 threw up a line of defense in a deep woods, pitting themselves against Morgan's 4,000 regular troops. The home guard, made up mostly of men too young or too old to be off to war, laid down intense fire, but eventually "skedaddled" when Morgan wheeled up his artillery. Later that day, July 9, 1863, Morgan was informed that Lee had been defeated at Gettysburg. Confederate wounded were taken to the Presbyterian Church and were cared for by women from the town. Lest anyone try to harm the fallen Southerners, one of the women stood with a gun ready at the church door to protect the wounded enemy men.

Morgan was soon on his way, but the delay at the Battle of Corydon allowed Union pursuers to be hard on his heels, and probably diminished the success of Morgan's Raid. As the Union soldiers passed through town the next day, those same Corydon women braved the dust and heat to fetch water for the fast-marching Northern soldiers. The efforts of one of those women, Miss Abbie Slemmons, proved too exhausting, and she died of fatigue and fever some days later—another casualty of a cruel war.

In all, Indiana sent 196,363 men to the Civil War, but more than one-eighth of them never returned: 7,243 died in battle, and another 17,785 succumbed to the diseases of war. As they have in every war, Hoosiers demonstrated in the Civil War their bravery and determination—and on more than one occasion, their compassion.

by William Doolittle, Creative Projects, Louisville, Ky.;
research assistance by William B. Doolittle Sr.

Corydon

---

1   **Site:** CORYDON BATTLEFIELD, c/o 202 East Walnut St., Corydon, IN 47112, 317-232-2537

Description: The Battle of Corydon was the only Civil War battle in Indiana and the only battle site north of the Ohio River. The site commemorates the effort of Confederate Gen. John Hunt Morgan to spread the war to the north. The Corydon Battlefield is a five-acre park located on the east side of State Rte. 135, just south of Corydon. The park is a heavily wooded area covered with hardwood trees, some of which date from 1863. Although the park area looks much as it did in 1863, a gravel drive to a parking lot on the property, several historic markers, and a log cabin moved to the site in the 1930s represent changes to the historic landscape.

Admission Fees: Free.

Open to Public: Daily: 24 hours.

Visitor Services: Information.

Directions: From I-64: take State Rte. 135 south through Corydon. The battle site is approximately 1 mile south of the city.

Lincoln City

---

2   **Site:** LINCOLN BOYHOOD NATIONAL MEMORIAL, P.O. Box 1816, Lincoln City, IN 47552, 812-937-4541

Description: This was the boyhood home of Abraham Lincoln, where he lived from age 7 to 21. The park includes the Memorial Visitor Center; the gravesite of Nancy Hanks Lincoln, Abraham Lincoln's mother; and the Lincoln Living Historical Farm, a typical 19th-century farm on the Indiana frontier.

Admission Fees: Adults: $2; Maximum of $4/family.

Open to Public: Daily: 8 A.M.–5 P.M.; closed Thanksgiving, Christmas, and New Year's Day.

Visitor Services: Trails; tours; museum; visitors center; rest rooms; handicapped access to Memorial Visitor Center.

Regularly Scheduled Events: *Feb., Sun. closest to Lincoln's birthday:* Lincoln Day.

Directions: From I-64: exit at U.S. Hwy. 231 and travel south for 8 miles. Travel east on IN Hwy. 162 at Gentryville. Proceed 2 miles to site.

Memorial Building at the Lincoln Boyhood National Memorial in Indiana. (Photograph courtesy of the National Park Service.)

---

3 **Site:** LINCOLN AMPHITHEATER AND LINCOLN STATE PARK,
Box 7-21, Lincoln City, IN 47552-0126, 800-264-4ABE;
Park: 812-937-4710

Description: Within walking distance of the Lincoln homestead, the Lincoln Amphitheater, America's most beautiful outdoor covered stage presents a musical drama for all ages. *Young Abe Lincoln* recreates the pioneer upbringing of our 16th president from age 7 to 21. The Lincoln story reveals how his greatness developed from a humble origin, made rich by his mother's love and his own passion for learning. The amphitheater is located in the 1,747-acre state park.

Admission Fees: *Drama:* Adults: $10; Children: $6; Seniors 60+: $9; Groups: $8/person. *Park:* $2/in-state vehicle, $5/out-of-state vehicle. NOTE: additional charges for camping and boat rental.

Open to Public: *Drama performances:* Mid-June–Mid-Aug.: Tues.–Sun. at 8 P.M. *Box office:* Mid-June–Mid-Aug.: Mon.: 9 A.M.–5 P.M.; Tues.–Sun.: 9 A.M.—8 P.M. Off-season hours (Mid-Aug.–Mid-June): Mon.–Fri.: 9 A.M.–4:30 P.M. *Park:* Daily, all year: 7 A.M.–11 P.M.

Visitor Services: *Drama:* information; gift shop; food; rest rooms; handicapped access. *Park:* Camping; picnicking; hiking; swimming; boating; fishing.

Regularly Scheduled Events: *June (call for date):* Opening night celebration.

Directions: From I-64: take exit 57; take U.S. 162 to Lincoln State Park. Amphitheater is located in State Park.

1 Fort Scott National Historic Site
2 Mine Creek Battlefield State Historic Site

*I*n Kansas, the Civil War began in 1854 as North and South fought to impose their cultural systems on the new territory. Westerners, the great majority of settlers in the Kansas Territory, often tried to ignore the conflict as they pursued their peaceful day-to-day activities, but when forced to choose sides, most went with the antislavery cause. When the national Civil War erupted in 1861, Kansans overwhelmingly supported the Union and rushed to enlist in disproportionate numbers.

Although thousands of Kansans served in the Eastern theaters of battle, the major focus of the new state was on the Missouri-Kansas border. Old hatreds from the territorial period were pursued in the continuing border war. Time and again, Kansas Jayhawkers swept into western Missouri to rob, pillage, and burn. Guerrillas from Missouri struck back with a vengeance. Quantrell's destruction of Lawrence in 1863 is the best-known incident, but many other Kansas localities suffered the wrath of Quantrell and his kind.

Certain Native Americans saw the war as an opportunity to stop the western spread of settlement in Kansas. As Federal troops and the militia watched for invasion from the east, the natives of the Plains struck from the west. Raids throughout north-central Kansas drew away soldiers who had hoped to fight rebels, not Native Americans.

Regular battles in the state centered primarily on Price's Raid in October 1864. Gen. Sterling Price's Confederate troops had marched across Missouri in search of recruits and supplies. They were turned back at the Battle of Westport, Missouri, on October 23 and retreated southward through Kansas. Union cavalry struck them at the Marais des Cygnes River, at Mine Creek, and at the Little Osage River. The greatest havoc came at Mine Creek, where two Confederate generals were captured and Price's rear guard was overwhelmed. He escaped destruction but at the cost of thousands of men and most of his wagon train.

by Dale E. Watts, Kansas State Historical Society

Fort Scott

Site: FORT SCOTT NATIONAL HISTORIC SITE, Old Fort Blvd., Fort Scott, KS 66701, 316-223-0310

Description: Fort Scott mirrored the course of western settlement along the middle border. From 1842–53, troops helped keep peace on this Indian frontier. Between 1854 and 1861, the years of "Bleeding Kansas," the town was caught up in the violent struggle between "free-soilers" and slaveholders. During the Civil War, the fort served as the headquarters of the Army of the Frontier, a supply depot, a refugee center for displaced

Indians, and a base for one of the first black regiments raised during the war, the First Kansas Colored Infantry.

Admission Fees: Ages 17 and over: $2.

Open to Public: Daily: 8 A.M.–5 P.M.; Closed Thanksgiving, Christmas, and New Year's Day; call for extended summer hours.

Visitor Services: Tours; information; visitors center; museum; gift shop; rest rooms; limited handicapped access.

Regularly Scheduled Events: *Spring:* Civil War encampment; *Summer:* Evening programs; *Sept.:* Mexican War encampment; *Fall:* American Indian heritage weekend; *First weekend in Dec.:* Frontier Candlelight tour.

Directions: Located about 90 miles south of Kansas City and 60 miles north of Joplin, MO. U.S. 69 and U.S. 54 intersect at Fort Scott; the fort is in the center of town.

Pleasanton

2 **Site:** MINE CREEK BATTLEFIELD STATE HISTORIC SITE, c/o Kansas State Historical Society, 6425 SW Sixth, Topeka, KS 66615-1099, 913-272-8681

Description: On October 25, 1864, some 10,000 Union and Confederate troops clashed at Mine Creek. They had been fighting off and on for several days as Gen. Sterling Price's Confederates marched through Missouri and then were turned back at the Battle of Westport. The Union cavalry caught up with the rear guard of Price's wagon train at Mine Creek and crushed them in one of the greatest cavalry charges of the Civil War. A portion of the battlefield is being preserved by the state of Kansas. Interpretive trail loops on both sides of Mine Creek are now in place. A major interpretation center with attendant programs opens in the summer of 1997.

Admission Fees: Free.

Open to Public: Daily: Daylight hours.

Visitor Services: Trails. NOTE: Museum, gift shops, visitors center, and rest rooms scheduled starting in summer 1997.

Regularly Scheduled Events: *Late Oct.:* Encampment or festival.

Directions: From I-70 or I-435: take U.S. 69 south; take KA 52 west 2 miles south of Pleasanton; proceed 1 mile and turn left (south) on a county road for .5 mile to the site parking lot.

Bridge over Mine Creek at Mine Creek Battlefield in Kansas. (Photograph courtesy of the Kansas State Historical Society.)

KENTUCKY

*T*he smoke and fire of the Civil War have long since faded from Kentucky's landscape, but its legacy remains a vital part of the Commonwealth's history. Kentuckians figured prominently at the highest levels of the conflict. Both the U.S. president, Abraham Lincoln, and the Confederate president, Jefferson Davis, were born in Kentucky—less than a year and 100 miles apart.

The irony of the opposing leaders' origins highlights Kentucky's deep divisions. While the state never officially left the Union—retaining Frankfort as the state capital—a Confederate capital was established at Bowling Green. There was a star for Kentucky on the Southern flag. More than 45,000 men left their Kentucky homes to fight for the South, while twice that number fought for the Union—including 20,000 African Americans, the second-highest number among all the states.

Trying to avoid the conflict, Kentucky declared itself neutral. This neutrality quickly vanished, as both Union and Confederate forces, recognizing the strategic importance of the state, sought to gain control—leading to a number of significant battles. Resentful of Union treatment during the war, Kentucky later became so southern-sympathetic that it was said "Kentucky seceded after the war."

by Daniel Kidd, Kentucky Department of Travel Development

---

*F*or More Information

There are 25 significant places featured in "Kentucky's Civil War Heritage Tour" in the *Kentucky Heritage Tours* magazine. In numerous aspects, Kentucky's Civil War role was unique, and this tour is designed to help you understand and appreciate that position. Call 800-225-TRIP (8747) for a copy, or write: Kentucky Department of Travel Development, Ste. 2200, 500 Mero St. Frankfort, KY 40601-1968.

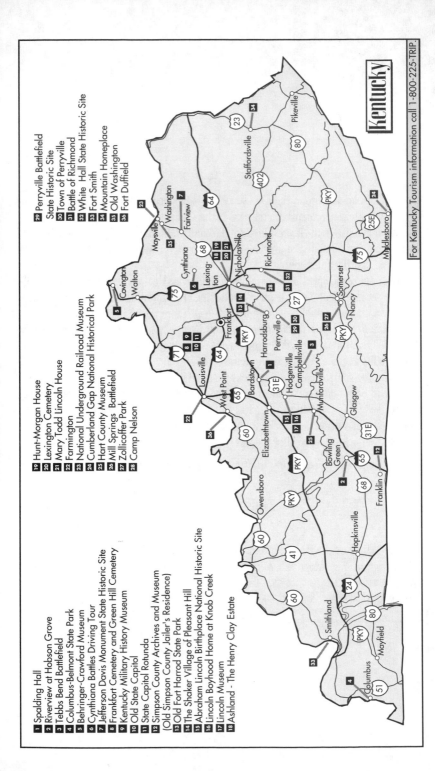

kentucky

1 Spalding Hall
2 Riverview at Hobson Grove
3 Tebbs Bend Battlefield
4 Columbus-Belmont State Park
5 Behringer-Crawford Museum
6 Cynthiana Battles Driving Tour
7 Jefferson Davis Monument State Historic Site
8 Frankfort Cemetery and Green Hill Cemetery
9 Kentucky Military History Museum
10 Old State Capitol
11 State Capitol Rotunda
12 Simpson County Archives and Museum
   (Old Simpson County Jailer's Residence)
13 Old Fort Harrod State Park
14 The Shaker Village of Pleasant Hill
15 Abraham Lincoln Birthplace National Historic Site
16 Lincoln Boyhood Home at Knob Creek
17 Lincoln Museum
18 Ashland - The Henry Clay Estate

19 Hunt-Morgan House
20 Lexington Cemetery
21 Mary Todd Lincoln House
22 Farmington
23 National Underground Railroad Museum
24 Cumberland Gap National Historical Park
25 Hart County Museum
26 Mill Springs Battlefield
27 Zollicoffer Park
28 Camp Nelson

29 Perryville Battlefield
   State Historic Site
30 Town of Perryville
31 Battle of Richmond
32 White Hall State Historic Site
33 Fort Smith
34 Mountain Homeplace
35 Old Washington
36 Fort Duffield

For Kentucky Tourism information call 1-800-225-TRIP.

Bardstown

1 **Site:** SPALDING HALL, 114 North Fifth St., Bardstown, KY 40004, 502-348-2999

Description: Spalding Hall is a large, federal-style brick building erected in 1826 as part of the former St. Joseph's College. It was used as a hospital during the Civil War. Now a museum, Spalding Hall includes a room featuring Civil War artifacts and memorabilia. The museum guide can provide information on Bardstown's role in the Civil War.

Admission Fees: Free.

Open to Public: May–Oct.: Mon.–Sat.: 9 A.M.–5 P.M.; Sun.: 1 P.M.–5 P.M. Nov.–Apr.: Mon.–Sat.: 10 A.M.– 4 P.M.; Sun.: 1 P.M.–4 P.M.

Visitor Services: Museum; rest rooms.

Directions: From Southbound Bluegrass Pkwy.: take exit 25; turn right onto U.S. 150, which becomes Stephen Foster Ave. Turn right at the fourth traffic light (circle halfway around the county courthouse in the center of town) onto North Fifth St. From Northbound Bluegrass Pkwy.: take exit 21; travel north (turn left) on U.S. 31E. Turn right on West Stephen Foster Ave.; proceed to first traffic light and turn left onto North Fifth St.

Bowling Green

2 **Site:** RIVERVIEW AT HOBSON GROVE, 1100 West Main St., Bowling Green, KY 42102, 502-843-5565

Description: The Hobson House, an Italianate mansion, was partially constructed before the Civil War. Col. William Hobson, son of builder Atwood Hobson and the youngest Union colonel on record, requested that Brig. Gen. Simon Bolivar Buckner, commanding Southern officer during the Confederate occupation of Bowling Green, spare the property. Buckner filled the basement of the unfinished mansion with Confederate ammunition. Atwood Hobson, one of the most ardent Union supporters in southern Kentucky, brought a French military professor to his home for the purpose of instructing William and his contemporaries in French military tactics ("Zouaves"). Atwood, president of a local bank, borrowed $30,000 to advance the Union cause. He also purchased 300 rifles to arm local citizens against the Confederates.

Admission Fees: Adults: $3.50; Children: $1.50; Groups: Call in advance to arrange.

Open to Public: Mon.–Sat.: 10 A.M.– 4 P.M.; Sun.: 1 P.M.–4 P.M.

Visitor Services: Tours; museum; gift shop; rest rooms; no handicapped access, but a video will be available to those unable to take the guided tour.

Directions: From southbound I-65: take exit 28 and follow signs to Bowling Green via U.S. 68/80. Turn right on Sixth Ave., which becomes Hobson Lane and leads to Hobson Grove Park; follow signs. From northbound I-65: take exit 20 onto the Green River Pkwy. Take Morgantown Rd. exit onto U.S. 231. Turn right toward Bowling Green. Turn left onto Hobson Lane and follow signs.

Campbellsville

---

3 | **Site:** TEBBS BEND BATTLEFIELD, Taylor County Tourist Commission, Courthouse, Broadway and Court, P.O. Box 4021, Campbellsville, KY 42719, 502-465-3786

Description: The 1863 Battle of Tebbs Bend/Green River Bridge took place on a bend in the Green River 8 miles from Campbellsville and was an early omen of the disaster to befall General John Hunt Morgan on his Great Indiana and Ohio Raid. There is no signage at the site; however, a self-guided driving tour brochure of the battlefield is available at the tourist commission or at Green River Lake Park Interpretive Center.

Admission Fees: Free.

Open to Public: Daily: Dawn to dusk. *Tourist Commission:* Mon.–Fri.: 8:30 A.M.–4:30 P.M.

Visitor Services: Rest rooms, picnic area, Atkinson-Griffin House/Confederate Hospital museum at Green River Lake Park, adjacent to battlefield.

Directions: From Campbellsville: obtain driving tour brochure at the Tourist Commission located on the courthouse square that is on Hwy. 55. Take Hwy. 55 south for 8 miles and turn right on Morgan-Moore Trail to begin tour. From the south: take exit 49 off Cumberland Pkwy. to Columbia and follow Hwy. 55 north for 12 miles to Green River Lake Park. Obtain brochure at the Interpretive Center. Return to park entrance; turn right on Hwy. 55 and travel 2 miles. Turn left on the Morgan-Moore Trail to begin tour.

Columbus

---

4 | **Site:** COLUMBUS-BELMONT STATE PARK, KY 58 and KY 123/80, P.O. Box 8, Columbus, KY 42032, 502-677-2327

Description: This is the site of a massive chain and anchor used to block the passage of Union gunboats during the Civil War. There is also a Confederate cannon, a network of earthen trenches, and a museum that was a Civil War hospital.

Admission Fees: *Museum:* $.50; Groups: $.35.

Open to Public: May–Sept.: Daily: 9 A.M.–5 P.M.; Open weekends only in Apr. & Oct.

Visitor Services: Camping; trails; museum; gift shop; rest rooms; snack bar; picnic area.

Regularly Scheduled Events: *Early Oct.:* Civil War Days.

Directions: From Purchase Pkwy.: take exit 1, U.S. 51 north to Clinton; go northwest on KY 58 to Columbus and the park.

Covington

5 **Site:** BEHRINGER-CRAWFORD MUSEUM, 1600 Montague Rd., P.O. Box 67,
Covington, KY 41012, 606-491-4003

Description: Covington's Behringer-Crawford Museum preserves the area's natural and cultural heritage. It is located in the 1848–80 Devou family home in the 700-acre Devou Park. The permanent collections span 450 years, including a fine display of Civil War artifacts. Also, a battery in the park offers interpretive Civil War signage.

Admission Fees: Adults: $2; Children: $1; Seniors: $1.

Open to Public: Tues.–Fri.: 10 A.M.–5 P.M.; Sat.–Sun.: 1 P.M.–5 P.M.

Visitor Services: Gift shop; museum; rest rooms; handicapped access; private library.

Regularly Scheduled Events: *June:* Periodic Civil War reenactments; Beer & Brat festival; *Nov.–Dec.:* Holiday trains & Victorian house decorations.

Directions: From I-71/75: take exit 192; go west on Fourth St.; follow signs to Devou Park.

Cynthiana

6 **Site:** CYNTHIANA BATTLES DRIVING TOUR, 117 Court St., Cynthiana, KY 41031,
606-234-5236

Description: Confederate General John Hunt Morgan fought two battles here: the first in 1862 and the second in 1864. A self-guided tour brochure of the battles is available at the Cynthiana/Harrison County Chamber of Commerce.

Admission Fees: Free.

Open to Public: *Chamber office:* Mon.–Fri.: 9 A.M.–4 P.M.

Visitor Services: None.

Directions: From I-75: take exit 126 at Georgetown; go northeast on U.S. 62 through Oxford and Leesburg to U.S. 27 and into Cynthiana; the chamber office is behind the Harrison County Courthouse on Main St.

Fairview

7 **Site:** JEFFERSON DAVIS MONUMENT STATE HISTORIC SITE, U.S. 68, P.O. Box 10,
Fairview, KY 42221-0010, 502-886-1765

Description: The monument is a 351-foot-high stone obelisk that marks the site where, on June 3, 1808, Jefferson Davis, the only president of the Confederacy was born. There is an elevator to an observation room high atop the structure for a panoramic view of the western Kentucky countryside.

Admission Fees: Adults, Children, and Seniors: $1; School groups: $.50.

Open to Public: May–Oct.: Daily: 9 A.M.– 5 P.M.; Closed Nov. 1–Apr. 31.

Visitor Services: Gift shop; rest rooms; handicapped access.

Regularly Scheduled Events: *First week-end in June:* Jefferson Davis birthday celebration; Miss Confederacy pageant; Living history camps; Artillery and infantry demonstrations.

Directions: Take Pennyrile Pkwy. south to Hopkinsville where it ends; go approximately 10 miles east on U.S. 68 to Fairview.

Frankfort

8 **Site:** FRANKFORT CEMETERY AND GREEN HILL CEMETERY, 215 East Main St. Frankfort, KY 40601, 502-227-2403

Description: Frankfort Cemetery is a highly scenic cemetery whose southern edge overlooks the Kentucky River, the State Capitol, and the town of Frankfort. The cemetery has been described as "Kentucky's Westminister" because so many famous people are buried here. A brochure gives the location of the graves of many Civil War notables, the Confederate monument and surrounding unknown graves, and the state military monument that tells about Kentucky's role in the Civil War. Green Hill Cemetery, 2 miles east on Main St., features a memorial to the 154 African American soldiers from Franklin County who fought in the Civil War, as well as graves of some of those soldiers.

Admission Fees: Free.

Open to Public: Brochures available at the Frankfort Cemetery office: Mon.–Fri.: 8 A.M.– 4 P.M. or the Frankfort Tourist Information Center (100 Capitol Ave.) on weekends. *Cemeteries:* Mon.–Sat.: 7:30 A.M.– dusk;

Sun.: 8 A.M.–dusk. NOTE: Buses and motor-coaches are not allowed in the Frankfort Cemetery.

Visitor Services: Information.

Directions: From I-64: take exit 58 (Frankfort/Versailles). Travel on U.S. 60 toward Frankfort and follow signs for downtown Frankfort and East Main St.; U.S. 60 turns left at the intersection with U.S. 460 and becomes East Main St. Turn left onto East Main St.; and then turn left into the paved way between a Chevron gas station and the sign for "859 East Side Shopping Center." This way becomes Atwood Ave.; follow it around curve and look for sign for Green Hill Cemetery on the left. Turn into cemetery's circular lane and go one-third around the circle; the monument is approximately 75 feet away to the right. To proceed to Frankfort Cemetery: Return to East Main St. and turn left. Travel 1.5 miles; turn left at traffic light onto Glenn's Creek

Rd.; immediately turn right into cemetery. To reach the Tourist Center: continue on East Main past the turn to Frankfort Cemetery. Turn left onto Capitol Ave. Tourist Center is at 100 Capitol Ave. on the right.

---

9 | **Site:** KENTUCKY MILITARY HISTORY MUSEUM, East Main St. at Capitol Ave., P.O. Box H, Frankfort, KY 40602, 502-564-3265

Description: The Kentucky Military History Museum is housed in the Old State Arsenal and has a large collection of Kentucky Confederate memorabilia, including identified uniforms, flags, guns, and other weapons. During the war, the arsenal was a cartridge factory for the Union army, as well as a regional supply center for Northern troops from Midwestern states.

Admission Fees: Free.

Open to Public: Mon.–Sat.: 9 A.M.–4 P.M.; Sun. & holidays: Noon–4 P.M.

Visitor Services: Museum; handicapped access; rest rooms.

Directions: From I-64: take exit 58; go 5 miles west on U.S. 60 (U.S. 60 turns into East Main St.); museum is located on the left before Capitol Ave. Bridge.

---

10 | **Site:** OLD STATE CAPITOL, Broadway & Lewis St., c/o Kentucky Historical Society, Box H, Frankfort, KY 40602, 502-564-3016

Description: This 1829 Greek Revival masterpiece was the only non-Confederate capitol captured by Southern troops. Here Kentucky's legislature voted to maintain official neutrality, although the state later became bitterly divided. So resentful of wrongful Union treatment, Kentucky— following the war's end—became so Southern-sympathetic that it was observed, "Kentucky seceded after the war!"

Admission Fees: Free.

Open to Public: *Museum:* Mon.–Fri.: 9 A.M.–4 P.M.; Sat.: Noon–5 P.M.; Sun.: 1 P.M.– 5 P.M. *Library:* Mon.–Fri.: 8 A.M.–4 P.M.; Sat.: 9 A.M.–4 P.M.

Visitor Services: Handicapped access; rest rooms; gift shop.

Directions: From I-64: take exit 58, go 5 miles west on U.S. 60 (U.S. 60 turns into East Main St.) to downtown; follow signs.

---

11 | **Site:** STATE CAPITOL ROTUNDA, c/o Information Desk, 700 Capitol Ave., Frankfort, KY 40601, 502-564-3449

Description: The rotunda of Kentucky's handsome 1910 State Capitol features statues of prominent Kentuckians, including Abraham Lincoln, sculpted by A. Weinman, and Jefferson Davis, sculpted by Frederick C. Hibbard. Both leaders were born in Kentucky—less than a year and 100 miles apart.

Admission Fees: Free.

Open to Public: Mon.–Fri.: 8 A.M.–4:30 P.M.; Sat.: 8:30 A.M.–4:30 P.M.; Sun.: 1 P.M.–4:30 P.M.

Visitor Services: Handicapped access; information; food.

Directions: From I-64 west: take exit 58; go 5 miles west on U.S. 60 (East Main St.) to bridge, follow U.S. 60 up Capitol Ave. to building. From I-64 east: take exit 52; go north on U.S. 127, east on U.S. 60, and follow signs.

Franklin

12 | **Site:** SIMPSON COUNTY ARCHIVES AND MUSEUM (OLD SIMPSON COUNTY JAILER'S RESIDENCE), 206 North College St., Franklin, KY, 42134, 502-586-4228

Description: Confederate prisoners, or Union officers, or maybe both, executed drawings (thought to be in charcoal) on plaster walls in a second-story room of this circa 1835 brick house. The drawings portray soldiers on both sides, one bearing a striking resemblance to the "Thunderbolt of the Confederacy," Brig. Gen. John Hunt Morgan. One of the displays tells of Franklin native Marcellus Jerome Clarke, the best known of Kentucky's Civil War guerrillas, who went by the nom de guerre, "Sue Mundy."

Admission Fees: Free.

Open to Public: Mon.–Fri.: 9 A.M.–4 P.M.; closed Sat. and Sun.

Visitor Services: Museum; rest rooms; handicapped access to first floor only.

Regularly Scheduled Events: *Apr.:* Civil War encampment and skirmish.

Directions: From I-65 southbound: take exit 6 and travel west on KY 100 to Franklin. Turn right on 31W (Main St.); turn left on Kentucky Ave. Go one block and turn right on North College to stone jail and brick house. From I-65 northbound: take exit 2; turn left onto 31W north and travel into Franklin. 31W becomes Main St. Turn left onto Kentucky Ave. Go one block to North College St. and turn right.

Harrodsburg

13 | **Site:** OLD FORT HARROD STATE PARK, Lexington and College Streets (U.S. 68 & U.S. 127), P.O. Box 156, Harrodsburg, KY 40330-0156, 606-734-3314

Description: Located on the grounds of this state park is the Lincoln Marriage Temple, a brick pavilion enshrining the cabin in which the parents of President Abraham Lincoln were wed on June 12, 1806. Also, the "Mansion Museum" features Confederate and Union rooms.

Admission Fees: Adults: $3.50; Children: $2; Groups (20 or more): Adults: $3; Children: $1.50.

Open to Public: *Museum & Fort:* Mar. 16–Oct. 31: 8:30 A.M.–5 P.M.; Nov. 1–Mar. 15: 8 A.M.–4:30 P.M.; *Fort only extended hours:* mid-June–Aug.: 8:30 A.M.–8 P.M.

Visitor Services: Museum; gift shop; rest rooms; handicapped access.

Regularly Scheduled Events: *May 1:* May Day celebration; *Mid-June:* Old Fort Harrod heritage Festival; *End of Oct:* Halloween ghost tour; *Mid-Nov.:* Holiday gala tour.

Directions: From Bluegrass Pkwy.: take exit 59, travel 15 miles south on U.S. 127 to intersection of U.S. 127 and U.S. 68.

---

14 **Site:** THE SHAKER VILLAGE OF PLEASANT HILL, 3501 Lexington Rd.
(on U.S. 68, 7 miles northeast of Harrodsburg), Harrodsburg, KY 40330,
606-734-5411

Description: The Shaker Village of Pleasant Hill is a restored indoor and outdoor living history museum that interprets the lives of the Shakers. This unique American religious community is located on a turnpike that was a strategic conduit for both Union and Confederate soldiers throughout the Civil War, but especially during the 1862 Kentucky campaign. The Shakers were both Unionists and emancipationists, but their dedication to pacifism prevented their participation in the conflict. The Shakers extended generous hospitality to both armies as they marched through the village. The only non-Shaker buried in the cemetery is a Confederate soldier who died there shortly after the nearby battle of Perryville. Also, the Shaker Landing on the Kentucky River was critical to the Union effort throughout the war.

Admission Fees: Adults: $9; Children (6–11): $4.50; Groups: Call in advance for special prices for more than 20 people.

Open to Public: Daily: 9:30 A.M.–5 P.M.

Visitor Services: Trails; tours; museum; gift shop; rest rooms; food; lodging; conference facilities; partially handicapped accessible.

Regularly Scheduled Events: *Sept.:* Civil War living history weekend.

Directions: From I-64/75 near Lexington: access New Circle Rd. (KY 4) from exit 115 (Newtown Pike), exit 113 (Paris Pike/N. Broadway), or exit 110 (Winchester Rd.) and go east or south to U.S. 68. Travel south on U.S. 68, a Kentucky Scenic Byway, for 21 miles to the Shaker Village of Pleasant Hill.

Hodgenville

15 **Site:** ABRAHAM LINCOLN BIRTHPLACE NATIONAL HISTORIC SITE,
2995 Lincoln Farm Rd., Hodgenville, KY 42748, 502-358-3137

Description: The 116-acre park features the enshrined cabin traditionally thought to be Lincoln's birthplace and the spring where the Lincoln family drew water.

Admission Fees: Free.

Open to Public: Apr., May, and Labor Day–Oct.: 8 A.M.–5:45 P.M.; June–Labor Day: 8 A.M.–6:45 P.M.; Nov.–Mar.: 8 A.M.–4:45 P.M.

Visitor Services: Rest rooms; handicapped access.

Regularly Scheduled Events: *Sun. before the Mon. holiday in Jan.:* Martin Luther King's Birthday; *Feb. 12:* Lincoln's Birthday; *Weekend closest to July 16–17:* Founder's Day; *Second week in Oct.:* Lincoln Days festival; *Second Thurs. in Dec.:* Christmas in the Park.

Directions: From I-65: take exit 81; go east on KY 84, approximately 9 miles.

Site: LINCOLN BOYHOOD HOME AT KNOB CREEK, 7120 Bardstown Rd., Hodgenville, KY 42748, 502-549-3741

Description: Lincoln's Boyhood Home is a replicated log cabin made of material from another cabin, this one erected in 1800. The Lincoln family resided on the site from 1811–16 before leaving for Indiana due to faulty land title and ensuing disputes.

Admission Fees: Adults: $1; Children: $.50; Seniors: $.75; Groups: Book in advance.

Open to Public: Memorial Day–Labor Day: 9 A.M.–7 P.M.; Apr.–Memorial Day: 9 A.M.–5 P.M.; Labor Day–Oct.: 9 A.M.–5 P.M.; Closed Nov. 1–Mar. 31.

Visitor Services: Gift shop; museum; handicapped access; rest rooms.

Directions: From I-65: take exit 81, KY 84 northeast into Hodgenville; go 6 miles northeast on U.S. 31E; property is on the left.

Site: LINCOLN MUSEUM, 66 Lincoln Square, Hodgenville, KY 42748, 502-358-3163

Description: On the square in downtown Hodgenville, birthplace of Abraham Lincoln, is the Lincoln Museum—featuring 12 scenes with realistic wax models from Lincoln's life. There is also an art collection, a film, and Civil War memorabilia.

Admission Fees: Adults: $3; Children: $1.50; Seniors and Military: $2.50; Groups (12 or more): Adults: $2; Children: $1.

Open to Public: Mon.–Sat.: 8:30 A.M.–5 P.M.; Sun.: 12:30 P.M.–5 P.M.

Visitor Services: Gift shop; rest rooms; museum.

Regularly Scheduled Events: *Feb.:* Lincoln's Birthday; *Second weekend in Oct.:* Lincoln Days festival.

Directions: From I-65: take exit 81; go east on KY 84 approximately 10 miles into Hodgenville.

Lexington

18 **Site:** ASHLAND—THE HENRY CLAY ESTATE, 120 Sycamore Rd., Lexington, KY
40502, 606-266-8581

Description: Ashland, a National Historic Landmark, was the home of "the Great Compromiser," Henry Clay, from 1811 until his death in 1852. Clay was a U.S. Senator, Speaker of the House, Secretary of State, and a presidential candidate three times. He is especially noted for his devotion to the Union, and during his time, he tried valiantly to prevent the ensuing Civil War. Ashland was rebuilt in the 1850s by Clay's son. A Civil War skirmish took place near Ashland, and the house was used as a hospital afterward. The estate includes 20 acres, several antebellum dependencies, and a large, formal garden.

Admission Fees: Adults: $5; Students (13–College): $3; Children (6–12): $2; Children under 6: Free.

Open to Public: Feb.–Dec.: Tues.–Sat.: 10 A.M.–4:30 P.M.; Sun.: 1 P.M.–4:30 P.M. NOTE: Tours on the hour; last tour at 4 P.M. Closed Mon.; closed the month of Jan.

Visitor Services: Tours; museum; gift shop; food; rest rooms.

Regularly Scheduled Events: *Summer:* Reenactments; Abraham and Mary Todd Lincoln living history: call for special events; *Dec.:* Christmas events.

Directions: From I-64/75: Take exit 115 (Newtown Pike), exit 118 (Paris Pike/North Broadway), or exit 110 (Winchester Rd.) to New Circle Rd. (KY 4). Go east on KY 4 to Richmond Rd. (U.S. 25); take Richmond Rd. north 1 mile to Sycamore Rd. Ashland is at the corner of East Main (Richmond Rd.) and Sycamore Rd.

19 **Site:** HUNT-MORGAN HOUSE, 201 North Mill St., Lexington, KY 40507,
606-253-0362

Description: Built in 1814 for the first millionaire west of the Allegheny Mountains, this Federal mansion was later the home of General John Hunt Morgan—the "Thunderbolt of the Confederacy"—and Nobel prize recipient Thomas Hunt Morgan. Period furnishings and two upstairs rooms exclusively house Civil War memorabilia.

Admission Fees: Adults: $5; Children: $2; Groups (12 or more): $3.

Open to Public: Tues.–Sat.: 10 A.M.–4 P.M.; Sun.: 2 P.M.–5 P.M.

Visitor Services: Gift shop; museum; rest rooms.

Regularly Scheduled Events: *Spring:* Restoration seminars; *Dec.:* Holiday tours.

Directions: From I-64/75: take exit 113; go south on North Broadway; go west (left) on West Second and almost immediately right on Mill St.; the house is two blocks down.

Site: LEXINGTON CEMETERY, 833 West Main St., Lexington, KY 40508, 606-255-5522

Description: Two self-guided tours are available: one for trees and the other for historical interest. The latter points out gravesites of Civil War luminaries such as Confederate Generals John Hunt Morgan and John C. Breckinridge. Also, relatives of Mary Todd Lincoln are interred here, as are both Union and Confederate soldiers, the latter being honored by two notable monuments.

Admission Fees: Free.

Open to Public: Daily: 8 A.M.–5 P.M.

Visitor Services: Information.

Directions: From I-64/I-75: take exit 115, south on Newtown Pike (Hwy. 922), to West Main St. (Hwy. 421); go right on West Main and turn into large stone cemetery gatehouse on the right. Information is available at offices in gatehouse, or at the Lexington Convention and Visitors Bureau on Vine St.

Site: MARY TODD LINCOLN HOUSE, 578 West Main St., P.O. Box 132, Lexington, KY 40501, 606-233-9999

Description: First Lady Mary Todd Lincoln resided in this fashionable brick residence between the ages of 14 and 21, and Abraham Lincoln was a guest here following their marriage. Personal articles from the Lincoln and Todd families are on display. Restored garden to the rear.

Admission Fees: Adults: $5; Children (6–12): $2; Groups (20 or more): $3.50.

Open to Public: Tues.–Sat.: 10 A.M.– 4 P.M.; last tour 3:15 P.M.

Visitor Services: Museum; handicapped access; gift shop.

Directions: From I-64/75: take exit 115; go south on Newtown Pike (Hwy. 922), cross New Circle Rd. (Hwy. 4) and go to West Main St. (Hwy. 421). Go left on West Main, and house is on the right on the corner of West Main and Tucker, just before Rupp Arena.

Louisville

22 **Site:** FARMINGTON, 3033 Bardstown Rd., Louisville, KY 40205, 502-452-9920

Description: Farmington is an 1810 house that was built based on plans designed by Thomas Jefferson. The site interprets life on the plantation from 1812 through the Civil War, including the roles of African Americans who lived at Farmington. Joshua Fry Speed, son of the original owners of Farmington, went to Springfield, Illinois, in 1835 and later shared living quarters in Springfield with future president Abraham Lincoln. Speed became Lincoln's most trusted friend and confidant, and Lincoln spent six weeks as a guest at Farmington in 1841. Joshua Fry Speed served as Lincoln's advisor on western affairs during the Civil War but declined the president's offer to appoint him secretary of state. However, his brother, James Speed, did serve as attorney general during Lincoln's second term.

Admission Fees: Adults: $4; Children (6–17): $2; Children under 6: Free; Seniors: $3; Groups: Call for rates.

Open to Public: Mon.–Sat.: 10 A.M.–4:30 P.M.; Sun.: 1:30–4:30 P.M. Closed Jan. 1, Easter, Derby (first Sat. in May), Thanksgiving, Christmas Eve, and Christmas Day.

Visitor Services: Tours; museum; information; gift shop; visitors center; rest rooms; wheelchair lift to first floor.

Regularly Scheduled Events: *Apr.:* Plant sales; *First Sat. in May:* Kentucky Derby breakfast; *June:* Craft Fair; *Dec.:* Lunchtime theater; Candlelight tours; Civil War reenactments and encampments: call for schedule; Blacksmith activities for children's groups and on weekends: call for schedule.

Directions: From I-265 (Henry Watterson Expressway): take exit 15; go north on Bardstown Rd. and follow signs to Farmington (less than .5 mile).

Maysville

23 | **Site:** NATIONAL UNDERGROUND RAILROAD MUSEUM, 115 East Third St., Maysville, KY 41056, 606-564-6986

Description: Slave census records, artwork, and agricultural implements are among the artifacts and memorabilia displayed in this tribute to an important segment of the antislavery movement, the Underground Railroad.

Admission Fees: Adults: $2; Children: $1; Seniors: $1; Groups: Call for rates for 10 or more.

Open to Public: Mon.–Sat.: 10 A.M.–4 P.M.; closed Sun. except by advance appointment.

Visitor Services: Museum; rest rooms; accessibility limited by one 4-inch step.

Directions: From the Ashland-Alexandria ("AA") Hwy. (KY 9): exit at U.S. 68; follow U.S. 68 north to the Simon Kenton Memorial Bridge. The museum is located by the bridge.

Middlesboro

24 | **Site:** CUMBERLAND GAP NATIONAL HISTORICAL PARK, U.S. 25E South, P.O. Box 1848, Middlesboro, KY 40965, 606-248-2817

Description: Cumberland Gap is the historic mountain pass on the Wilderness Road that opened the pathway for westward migration. During the Civil War, Cumberland Gap was first held by the South, then captured by Union troops. Each side held the gap twice.

Admission Fees: Free.

Open to Public: Mid-June–Labor Day: Daily: 8 A.M.–6 P.M.; Labor Day–mid-June: Daily: 8 A.M.–5 P.M.

Visitor Services: Gift shop; rest rooms; trails; museum; information; camping; handicapped access.

Directions: From I-75: take exit 29 at Corbin; follow signs on U.S. 25 E (Cumberland Gap Pkwy.) through Middlesboro. The park is .25 mile south of Middlesboro, KY.

Munfordville

25 Site: HART COUNTY MUSEUM, 109 Main St., P.O. Box 606, Munfordville, KY 42765, 502-524-0101

Description: Hart County's seat of government is Munfordville, site of a Civil War battle in 1862. The museum includes Civil War memorabilia related to the battle of Munfordville and to Munfordville natives, CSA Brig. Gen. Simon Bolivar Buckner (later governor of Kentucky) and USA Maj. Gen. Thomas Wood. Buckner and Wood were childhood friends and classmates at West Point, an association that well illustrates Kentucky's deep divisions during the Civil War. Museum staff can direct you to sites of the Battle of Munfordville.

Admission Fees: Free.

Open to Public: Mon.–Fri.: 10 A.M.–2 P.M.; call to arrange Sat. and Sun. visits.

Visitor Services: Museum; rest rooms.

Regularly Scheduled Events: *Sept.:* Battle of Munfordville reenactment.

Directions: From I-65: take exit 64 (U.S. 31W) 1 mile south into Munfordville. U.S. 31W becomes Main St. Museum is in two-story brick building next to city hall.

Nancy

26 Site: MILL SPRINGS BATTLEFIELD, Hwy. 235, P.O. Box 814, Somerset, KY 42502, 606-679-5725

Description: The Battle of Mill Springs was the first major Union victory of the Civil War. This victory turned the Confederate flank in Kentucky and opened up an invasion route to east Tennessee and even Nashville. Confederate General Felix K. Zollicoffer was killed in this battle; he was the first general killed in the west. The

Union forces were commanded by General George H. Thomas, who would later gain fame as "the Rock of Chickamauga."

Admission Fees: Free.

Open to Public: Daily: Dawn to dusk.

Visitor Services: Information; handicapped access; tours.

Regularly Scheduled Events: *Weekend closest to Jan. 19 and Memorial Day:* Battle of Mill Springs commemoration ceremony.

Directions: From I-75: take the London/U.S. 80 exit; follow U.S. 80 west to Somerset. At Somerset take the Cumberland Pkwy. west. (U.S. 80 and the Parkway are the same route briefly in Somerset.) From the Cumberland Pkwy. take the second left and then the first right. You will then be headed west on KY 80. Proceed approximately 9 miles to Nancy. At Nancy turn left (south) on KY 235. Proceed approximately one mile to Zollicoffer Park on the left.

---

27 **Site:** ZOLLICOFFER PARK, Hwy. 235, 1 mile south of Nancy, Nancy, KY 42544, 606-679-5725

Description: Zollicoffer Park marks the site of the fiercest fighting in the Battle of Mill Springs, an important early–Civil War conflict. The park is named for Confederate General Felix K. Zollicoffer, mortally wounded in the battle. There are two interpretive signs and a half mile of trails.

Admission Fees: Free.

Open to Public: Daily: Dawn to dusk.

Visitor Services: Information.

Regularly Scheduled Events: *Weekend closest to Jan. 19 and Memorial Day:* Battle of Mill Springs commemoration ceremony.

Directions: *See* Mill Springs Battlefield listing.

Nicholasville

28 **Site:** CAMP NELSON, Off U.S. 27 South, 8 miles south of Nicholasville, Chamber of Commerce, 611 North Main St., Nicholasville, KY 40356, 606-887-4351

Description: Camp Nelson was a major Union supply depot for the armies of the Ohio and Cumberland. It supplied the Union invasion of Knoxville and the Battles of Saltville in southwest Virginia. It was also the third-largest recruiting base for African American soldiers in the United States, with more than 10,000 black soldiers recruited here. On request, the visitors

center at Camp Nelson National Cemetery shows a video highlighting the history of Camp Nelson. A 10-stop driving tour highlights the county's Civil War history.

Admission Fees: Free.

Open to Public: *Site:* Daily: Dawn to dusk; *Chamber of Commerce office:* Mon.–Fri.: 9 A.M.–5 P.M.

Visitor Services: Information; driving tour.

Directions: From I-75: take exit 110 (U.S. 60) west to New Circle Rd. (KY 4) in Lexington. Follow KY 4 east to the Nicholasville Rd. exit; take Nicholasville Rd. (U.S. 27) south approximately 10 miles to Nicholasville and proceed to Chamber of Commerce office at 611 North Main. Camp Nelson is 8 miles farther south on U.S. 27.

Perryville

29 Site: PERRYVILLE BATTLEFIELD STATE HISTORIC SITE, P.O. Box 296, Hwy. 1920, Perryville, KY 40468-9999, 606-332-8631

Description: Kentucky's greatest Civil War battle took place outside Perryville on October 8, 1862. It was the South's last serious attempt to gain possession of the state, and a museum on the grounds interprets the battle and its aftermath.

Admission Fees: *Museum:* Adults: $2; Children: $1; Groups (10 or more): Adults: $1.50; Children: $.50.

Open to Public: Daily: 9 A.M.–5 P.M.; Closed Nov. 1–Mar. 31.

Visitor Services: Gift shop; rest rooms; museum; handicapped access; trails.

Regularly Scheduled Events: *Weekend closest to Oct. 8:* Battle reenactment.

Directions: From Bluegrass Pkwy.: take exit 59; go 24 miles south on U.S. 127 through Harrodsburg to Danville; take 127/150 bypass; go west (turn right) on U.S. 150; go 9 miles to Perryville; north (turn right) on KY 1920.

The Dug Road at Perryville Battlefield, Perryville, KY. (Photograph courtesy of The Civil War Trust.)

30 Site: TOWN OF PERRYVILLE, U.S. 68 and U.S. 150, P.O. Box 65, Perryville, KY 40468, 606-332-1862

Description: The entire town of Perryville, 1990 population 815, has been a National Register district since 1976. Looking much as it did during the 1862 Battle of Perryville (*see* Perryville Battlefield State Historic Site), this is one of the most intact mid-19th-century communities in the state. Remnants of the battle's aftermath remain to a large extent, and a new interpretive center is planned.

Admission Fees: Free.

Open to Public: Daily: Dawn to dusk.

Visitor Services: Food; gas; gift shop; rest rooms; lodging.

Regularly Scheduled Events: *Weekend closest to Oct. 8:* Battle of Perryville reenactment.

Directions: From Bluegrass Pkwy.: take exit 59; go 24 miles south on U.S. 127 through Harrodsburg to Danville; take 127/150 bypass; go west (turn right) on U.S. 150 for 9 miles to Perryville.

Richmond

31 Site: BATTLE OF RICHMOND, c/o Tourism Commission, City Hall, 359 Main St., P.O. Box 250, Richmond, KY 40476-0250, 606-623-1000 (ask for Tourism Commission)

Description: The Battle of Richmond was part of the important 1862 Perryville campaign. Richmond was the site of one of the Confederacy's greatest victories. A self-guided tour brochure and taped narrative are available at the Richmond Tourism Commission in city hall. The eight "stations" of the driving tour begin at the top of Big Hill southeast of Berea and end at the Madison County Courthouse in Richmond.

Admission Fees: Refundable deposit for tape: $5.

Open to Public: *Tourism office:* Mon.–Fri: 8 A.M.–5 P.M.

Visitor Services: Rest rooms; information.

Directions: From I-75: take exit 90; U.S. 25 South becomes Main St.

32 Site: WHITE HALL STATE HISTORIC SITE, 500 White Hall Shrine Rd., Richmond, KY 40475-9159, 606-623-9178

Description: Cassius Marcellus Clay, "the Lion of White Hall," was an outspoken emancipationist, newspaper publisher, and minister to Russia under his friend Abraham Lincoln. This Italianate mansion, furnished in period pieces, was built for Clay and has many noteworthy features.

Admission Fees: Adults: $4; Children: $2.50; Groups (10 or more): Adults: $3. Children: $2.

Open to Public: Apr.–Labor Day: Daily: 9 A.M.–5 P.M.; Labor Day–Oct.: Wed.–Sun.

9 A.M.–5 P.M.; Closed from end of Oct. to Apr. 1.

Visitor Services: Handicapped access; gift shop.

Regularly Scheduled Events: *Sept.:* Living history weekend; *Oct.:* Ghost Walk; *Dec.:* A Victorian Christmas.

Directions: From I-75: take exit 95; travel on Hwy. 627; cross U.S. 25; the house is located at the end of Hwy. 627.

Smithland

33 **Site:** FORT SMITH, c/o Smithland Area Chamber of Commerce, P.O. Box 196, Smithland, KY 42081, 502-928-2446

Description: The star-shaped, earthen Fort Smith was constructed by Union forces after Gen. Ulysses S. Grant seized Paducah in 1861. The fort was part of a larger complex designed to protect the mouth of the Cumberland River at the Ohio River. From this location, soldiers were sent down the Cumberland River to participate in the expedition against Forts Henry and Donelson near the Tennessee/Kentucky border. As many as 2,000 Union troops were stationed in Smithland during the Civil War. By 1864, the fort was manned by a contingent of the 13th U.S. Colored Heavy Artillery. Several of these men are buried in the cemetery adjacent to the fort.

Admission Fees: Free.

Open to Public: Daily: Daylight hours; obtain brochure at the Chamber of Commerce: Mon.–Fri.: 9 A.M.–4:30 P.M.

Visitor Services: Trails; information (at chamber office).

Regularly Scheduled Events: *Apr.:* Artillery demonstration/living history.

Directions: From I-24: take exit 31 onto Rte. 453. Travel approximately 15 miles to Smithland. To chamber office: at caution light in Smithland, turn right; proceed one block; turn right on Level St.; the chamber office is located behind the school bus garage. To Fort Smith: at the caution light in Smithland, turn left; proceed up the hill and into the cemetery; follow the road to a water tower. Travel on foot on the trail to the right (west) of the tower approximately 50 feet; the fort is on the right.

Staffordsville

34 **Site:** MOUNTAIN HOMEPLACE, Rte. 2275, P.O. Box 1850, Staffordsville, KY 41256, 606-297-1850

Description: Mountain Homeplace recreates life in Johnson County from 1850 to 1875. The historic buildings that have been assembled here include a one-room schoolhouse, a blacksmith shop, and other buildings and implements used to operate a farm. Interpreters provide oral information about the Civil War in this area of Kentucky. An award-winning video shown at the visitors center features actor Richard Thomas who spent summers with his family in Johnson County during his youth. The video includes a segment about Johnson County's tenuous situation during the Civil War. Both sides had ardent sympathizers here, and neither the Union nor the Confederate flags were allowed to fly above the county courthouse.

Admission Fees: Adults: $5; Children: $3; Seniors: $4; Groups: Call in advance for special rates.

Open to Public: Wed.–Sat.: 10 A.M.–6 P.M.; Sun.: 1 P.M.–6 P.M.

Visitor Services: Trails; tours; museum; information; gift shop; visitors center; rest rooms.

Directions: From the west on I-64: take exit 98 (several miles east of Winchester) and travel south on Mountain Pkwy. for approximately 70 miles to Salyersville. Turn left on U.S. 460 and proceed 15 miles to KY 40. Turn left onto KY 40 and proceed approximately 3.5 miles. Turn right on Paintsville Lake Rd. (Rte. 2275) past intersection with Hwy. 172 and follow signs. From the east on I-64: take exit 191 (south of Catlettsburg); proceed south on U.S. 23 for 59 miles to the intersection with U.S. 460; turn right on U.S. 460 and travel approximately 3.5 miles. Turn right on Paintsville Lake Rd. (Rte. 2275) past intersection with Hwy. 172 and follow signs.

Washington

35 | **Site:** OLD WASHINGTON, 2215 Old Main St., P.O. Box 227, Washington, KY 41096, 606-759-7411

Description: Civil War associated sites within this 1785 outpost for pioneers traveling the Buffalo Trace include the birthplace and childhood home of Confederate Gen. Albert Sidney Johnston; the Methodist Episcopal Church South, significant for African American history; Paxton Inn, a documented Underground Railroad station; and the site of the slave auction that inspired Harriet Beecher Stowe to write *Uncle Tom's Cabin*.

Admission Fees: Adults: $3; Children: $1.

Open to Public: *Apr.–Dec.:* Mon.–Sat.: 10 A.M.–4:30 P.M.; Sun.: 1 P.M.–4:30 P.M.; closed Jan.–Mar.

Visitor Services: Tours; museum; information; gift shop; visitors center; rest rooms; food.

Directions: From Ashland-Alexandria Hwy. ("AA" Hwy./KY 9): exit at U.S. 68 and travel 2 miles south. Old Washington borders old U.S. 68 to the east of new U.S. 68.

West Point

36 | **Site:** FORT DUFFIELD, 509 Elm St., West Point, KY 40177, 502-922-4260

Description: 1861 Union fortification protecting supply route from Louisville over the Old L&N Turnpike. One of the best preserved and largest forts in Kentucky, it was designed to be manned by 1,000 troops.

Admission Fees: Free.

Open to Public: Daily: Dawn to dusk.

Visitor Services: Trails; information; handicapped access.

Regularly Scheduled Events: *Memorial Day:* Reenactment.

Directions: From I-65: take exit 125 west on I-265 (Gene Snyder Freeway) to U.S. 31 W/60; cross bridge into Hardin County and watch for entrance sign on left, or turn right into town of West Point and go to visitors center in a red caboose at Fourth & Main St.

LOUISIANA

$\mathcal{L}$ ouisiana was not a major battleground, because it was essentially taken out of the war by mid-1863. But several important battles and campaigns were fought in the state, more than 500 engagements in all.

New Orleans was naturally a primary target for Union attack. The South's largest city and major port, possession of New Orleans was necessary for control of the Mississippi. Additionally, New Orleans was the site of large commercial, financial, and industrial firms. In April 1862, a Union fleet under Flag Officer David G. Farragut began operations against the Crescent City. Farragut's vessels steamed past Forts Jackson and St. Philip early on April 24 and destroyed the small Confederate fleet that supported them. Confederate troops evacuated New Orleans rather than submit to a bombardment. The city surrendered to Farragut, and Union troops began occupying New Orleans on May 1.

In the spring of 1863, General Nathaniel P. Banks's Union army moved against the Confederate stronghold at Port Hudson, acting in conjunction with General Ulysses S. Grant's attack on Vicksburg, Mississippi. The siege of Port Hudson lasted from May 23 to July 9, the longest genuine siege in American military history. Confederate General Franklin Gardner surrendered to Banks after hearing of the fall of Vicksburg. The last Confederate stronghold on the Mississippi fell into Union hands, placing the river under Federal control and splitting the Confederacy in two.

In mid-March 1864, General Banks launched the Red River campaign. His objective was to drive General Richard Taylor's Confederate army from Louisiana and to plant the Union flag in the interior of Texas. After an initial retreat, Taylor attacked the Union army near Mansfield on April 8, and the Confederates inflicted a severe defeat on the Federals. Banks retreated to Pleasant Hill during the night, and Taylor attacked again the next day. The Battle of Pleasant Hill was a draw. Taylor's success in the Red River campaign delayed Union victory in the war by several months. Only small skirmishes occurred in the state after the Red River campaign. In mid-May 1865, Confederate Gen. Edmund Kirby Smith contacted Union Gen. Edward R. S. Canby about a surrender of the Trans-Mississippi Department. Terms were worked out and signed on May 26. The war was finally over for Louisiana.

by Dr. Arthur W. Bergeron, Jr.

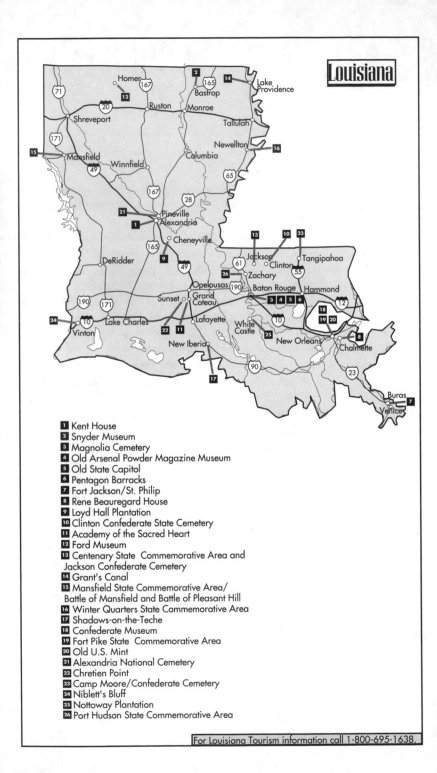

Louisiana

1 Kent House
2 Snyder Museum
3 Magnolia Cemetery
4 Old Arsenal Powder Magazine Museum
5 Old State Capitol
6 Pentagon Barracks
7 Fort Jackson/St. Philip
8 Rene Beauregard House
9 Loyd Hall Plantation
10 Clinton Confederate State Cemetery
11 Academy of the Sacred Heart
12 Ford Museum
13 Centenary State Commemorative Area and
Jackson Confederate Cemetery
14 Grant's Canal
15 Mansfield State Commemorative Area/
Battle of Mansfield and Battle of Pleasant Hill
16 Winter Quarters State Commemorative Area
17 Shadows-on-the-Teche
18 Confederate Museum
19 Fort Pike State Commemorative Area
20 Old U.S. Mint
21 Alexandria National Cemetery
22 Chretien Point
23 Camp Moore/Confederate Cemetery
24 Niblett's Bluff
25 Nottoway Plantation
26 Port Hudson State Commemorative Area

For Louisiana Tourism information call 1-800-695-1638.

For More Information

"The Louisiana Civil War Heritage Guide," available through the Louisiana Office of Tourism, outlines significant military actions in Louisiana during the Civil War (such as the role it played in the capture of the Mississippi River). The guide also highlights some of the economic and social issues in the state at the time and lists cultural attractions of the era that are of interest to visitors.

A copy of the guide can be obtained through the state's 10 Welcome Centers or by calling 800-695-1638 or 504-342-8119.

Alexandria

1 **Site:** KENT HOUSE, 3601 Bayou Rapides Rd., P.O. Box 12248, Alexandria, LA 71315-2248, 318-487-5998

Description: Kent House, a raised French-Creole cottage built in 1796, is the oldest remaining structure in Central Louisiana. The courageous owner, Robert Hynson, refused to leave his home, thus preventing Union troops retreating from the battle of Mansfield from setting it on fire. Unfortunately, Hynson could not save his stock or outbuildings from the ravaging army. Many of Kent House's destroyed structures are replicated with antebellum dependencies from other plantations. The complex includes a kitchen, slave cabins, carriage house, milk house, blacksmith shop, and sugar mill. The site features living history events throughout the year.

Admission Fees: Adults: $5; Children (6–12): $2; Children under 6: Free; Seniors: $4.

Open to Public: Mon.–Sat.: 9 A.M.–5 P.M.; Sun.: 1–5 P.M.

Visitor Services: Tours; museum; information; gift shop; rest rooms.

Directions: From I-49: exit onto MacArthur Blvd. Remain on MacArthur until it intersects Bayou Rapides Rd. Turn left on Bayou Rapides Rd. Continue .5 mile; turn left to Kent House.

Bastrop

2 **Site:** SNYDER MUSEUM, 1620 East Madison St. (U.S. 165N), Bastrop, LA 71220, 318-281-8760

Description: This museum highlights local history, including a special display dedicated to the Civil War. It also houses a genealogical section.

Admission Fees: Free.

Open to Public: Tues.–Sun.: 10 A.M.–3 P.M.

Visitor Services: Rest rooms.

Directions: From I-20: take Rte. 165 through Monroe to Bastrop. Rte. 165 becomes East Madison St. Located on U.S. 165 North.

Baton Rouge

3 **Site:** MAGNOLIA CEMETERY, located at North Dufrocq and Main Streets, c/o Foundation for Historical Louisiana, 900 N. Blvd., Baton Rouge, LA 70802, 504-387-2464

Description: Much of the heaviest fighting of the Battle of Baton Rouge took place in this cemetery on August 5, 1862. The battle pitted Union forces under the overall command of Brig. Gen. Thomas Williams against Confederate forces of Maj. Gen. John C. Breckinridge. Though Union forces were pushed back to the river, guns from the Federal fleet forced Confederate withdrawal after expected support from the Rebel ironclad gunboat *Arkansas* did not materialize. The ferocity of the attack, however, convinced the Federal command to withdraw their forces to protect New Orleans, allowing Gen. Breckinridge to fortify Port Hudson. This delayed Federal domination of the Mississippi River until July 1863. Confederate soldiers who died at Magnolia Cemetery are buried in a mass grave. A brochure is available from the address listed above and at the site.

Admission Fees: Free.

Open to Public: Daily: Daylight hours.

Visitor Services: None.

Regularly Scheduled Events: *Aug. 5:* Battle of Baton Rouge commemoration.

Directions: From I-10: exit onto Florida St. Circle around; the cemetery is bounded by Florida and Laurel Streets and 19th and 22d Streets, near downtown Baton Rouge.

Site: OLD ARSENAL POWDER MAGAZINE MUSEUM, P.O. Box 94125, Baton Rouge, LA 70804-9125, 504-342-0401

Description: When Louisiana seceded from the Union on January 26, 1861, the governor ordered the state militia to seize the arsenal. Shortly thereafter, Louisiana joined the Confederate States of America, and the weapons, ammunition, and powder that was stored in the Baton Rouge compound was rushed to the embattled Southern armies. In May 1862, Union forces recaptured Louisiana's capital city. Federal troops occupied the arsenal and the fortifications.

Admission Fees: Adults: $1; Students: $.50.

Open to Public: Mon.–Fri.: 9 A.M.–4 P.M.; Sat.: 10 A.M.–4 P.M.; Sun.: 1 P.M.–4 P.M.

Visitor Services: Self-guided tours; museum; interpretive center.

Directions: From I-10: take Capital Access/Governor's Mansion exit. Keep straight toward the State Capitol. Arsenal is located on the State Capitol grounds, between the capital building and the governor's mansion.

Site: OLD STATE CAPITOL, 100 North Blvd., Baton Rouge, LA 70804, 504-342-0500

Description: This building served as the State House of Louisiana until the state capital was moved to Opelousas to avoid capture by Federal troops. The Gothic structure was burned in 1862 when it was a federal prison. On the grounds is the grave of Henry Watkins Allen, Confederate governor of Louisiana and brigadier general.

Admission Fees: Adults: $4; Children, Seniors, and Veterans: $2.

Open to Public: Tues.–Sat.: 10 A.M.–4 P.M.; Sun.: Noon–4 P.M.

Visitor Services: Tours; museum.

Directions: From I-10: take Government St. exit; turn left at light. Keep straight on Government St. until it changes to River Rd. Keep straight until you pass the Centroplex Complex (on right); turn right at North Blvd. The Old State Capitol can be seen on the right.

---

6 **Site: PENTAGON BARRACKS, 959 North Third St., Baton Rouge, IA, 504-342-1866**

Description: The Pentagon Buildings were constructed in 1819–29 to house United States troops and were used as a garrison until 1877. From 1861–62, the barracks was held by the Confederates. It served as quarters for many famous soldiers, including Generals Wade Hampton, Robert E. Lee, and Stonewall Jackson.

Admission Fees: Free.

Open to Public: Tues.–Sat.: 10 A.M.–4 P.M.; Sun.: 1 P.M.–4 P.M.

Visitor Services: Museum; interpretive center; rest rooms; tours.

Directions: From I-10: take Capital Access/Governor's Mansion exit. Keep straight around Capitol until you see a flashing light; turn left. The Pentagon Barracks is the two story brick building on the right. Parking lot in front.

Buras

7 **Site: FORT JACKSON/ST. PHILIP, P.O. Box 7043, Buras, LA 70041, 504-657-7083**

Description: This restored fort (1822–32) was built to defend New Orleans and the mouth of the Mississippi River.

Admission Fees: Free.

Open to Public: Daily: 7 A.M.–5 P.M.; *Museum:* Daily: 9 A.M.–4:30 P.M.

Visitor Services: Museum; walking tours.

Directions: From I-10 through New Orleans: cross the New Orleans Bridge going west to Gretna. Get onto Westbank Expressway; proceed 1.5 miles to LA Hwy. 23. The fort is 6 miles south.

Chalmette

8 **Site:** RENE BEAUREGARD HOUSE, JEAN LAFITTE NATIONAL HISTORICAL PARK AND PRESERVE, 8686 West St. Bernard Hwy., Chalmette, LA 70043, 504-589-4430

Description: Located on the Battle of New Orleans (War of 1812) site, this two-story, cement-covered house was the home of Judge Rene Beauregard, son of Confederate General P. G. T. Beauregard.

Admission Fees: Free.

Open to Public: Daily: 8:30 A.M.–5 P.M.

Visitor Services: Interpretive center; information; tours; rest rooms.

Directions: From I-10 through the city of New Orleans: take I-610 east. Take Chalmette/Littlewood exit south to I-510 to State Service Rd. 47; turn right onto St. Bernard Hwy. After 2 miles the Chalmette National Park sign will be visible.

Cheneyville

9 **Site:** LOYD HALL PLANTATION, 292 Loyd Bridge Rd., Cheneyville, LA 71325, 318-776-5641

Description: This beautifully restored Greek Revival–Italianante mansion was used by the Union and Confederate troops during the Civil War. Tales of ghosts dating to that era are included in the tour.

Admission Fees: Adults: $5; Children (6–12): $3; Children under 6: Free.

Open to Public: Tues.–Sat.: 10 A.M.–4 P.M.; Sun.: 1 P.M.–4 P.M.

Visitor Services: Tours; lodging.

Directions: From I-49 north: take exit 61 on Hwy. 167 north (Turkey Creek); go 1.8 miles, turn right; go 1 mile to plantation.

Clinton

 10 **Site:** CLINTON CONFEDERATE STATE CEMETERY, East Feliciana Parish, Marston St., Clinton, LA 70722, 504-683-8753

Description: This four-acre cemetery contains remains of hundreds of Civil War troops from both sides. Because Clinton was connected to the Mississippi River by railroad, the town received many sick and wounded soldiers from nearby Port Hudson.

Admission Fees: Free.

Open to Public: Daily: Dawn to dusk.

Visitor Services: None.

Directions: Located north of Baton Rouge on LA 67 in Clinton; go straight to the caution light; turn left on St. Helen St.; turn left on Bank St.; go two blocks and turn right. Continue one and a half blocks. Cemetery is on the right.

Grand Coteau

11 **Site:** ACADEMY OF THE SACRED HEART, P.O. Box 310, Grand Coteau, LA 70541, 318-662-5275

Description: Catholic girls school established in 1821 and known for its beautiful formal gardens and oak alley. The Academy has remained in continuous operation through fire, epidemics, and the Civil War. In 1863, Gen. Banks headed Federal troops pouring into the Teche country, and he made his headquarters at Grand Coteau for a brief time. His daughter attended a Sacred Heart school in New York and the superior of the convent there requested that the general look after the nuns at Grand Coteau. The general protected the students and the nuns and even provided food and supplies to the convent, allowing the school to remain open during the war.

Admission Fees: Adults: $5; Children: $3; Seniors: $3.

Open to Public: Mon.–Fri.: 10 A.M.–3 P.M.; Sat.–Sun.: 1 P.M.–4 P.M.

Visitor Services: Tours; museum; information; gift shop; rest rooms.

Directions: Take I-10 to Opelousas; exit to I-49. Follow I-49 toward Opelousas to the Grand Coteau/Sunset exit. Exit on Hwy. 93 toward Grand Coteau. Hwy. 93 becomes Main St. Turn left at the traffic light onto Church St. Follow Church St. to the academy.

Homer

12 **Site:** FORD MUSEUM, 519 South Main St., Homer, LA 71040, 318-927-9190

Description: Homer was the departing point for Louisiana Confederate soldiers via railroad. The museum houses a fascinating collection of memorabilia and artifacts of north Louisiana hill country, including activities during the Civil War.

Admission Fees: $1.

Open to Public: Mon.–Fri.: 10 A.M.–4 P.M.; Sat.: 10 A.M.–2 P.M.; Sun.: 2 P.M.–4 P.M.

Visitor Services: Tours.

Directions: From I-20 west: take exit at Minden; follow U.S. 79 for approximately 20 miles. The museum is on the right at the first light in Homer.

Jackson

13 **Site:** CENTENARY STATE COMMEMORATIVE AREA AND JACKSON CONFEDERATE CEMETERY, Centenary address: P.O. Box 574, Jackson, LA 70748, 504-634-7925; Cemetery address: P.O. Box 546, St. Francisville, LA 70775, 504-635-3739

Description: Centenary State Commemorative Area is a former college that interprets the history of education in Louisiana. The college buildings were used as hospitals for Confederate soldiers from 1862–63. A small skirmish was fought on the grounds on August 3, 1863. The Jackson Confederate Cemetery across the street from this site contains more than 100 unmarked graves of soldiers who died during the war.

Admission Fees: *Centenary State Commemorative Area*: Adults: $2; Children under 12 and Adults 62 and over: Free; Buses: $60. *Jackson Confederate Cemetery*: Free.

Open to Public: *Centenary State Commemorative Area:* Daily: 9 A.M.–5 P.M.

Jackson Confederate Cemetery: Daily: Daylight hours.

Visitor Services: *Centenary State Commemorative Area:* Tours; museum; information; visitors center, rest rooms; handicapped access. *Jackson Confederate Cemetery:* None.

Directions: Take I-10 north through Baton Rouge. Exit at U.S. 61; turn right. Turn right at LA 10 and follow signs to Centenary State Commemorative Area, which is located at East College and Pine Streets in the town of Jackson in East Feliciana Parish. Jackson Confederate Cemetery is located adjacent to Centenary State Commemorative Area; information on the cemetery can be obtained at Centenary State Commemorative Area.

Lake Providence

14 Site: GRANT'S CANAL, 600 Lake St., Lake Providence, LA 71254, 318-559-5125

Description: This is all that remains of Grant's attempt to circumvent the fortifications at Vicksburg through the back waters of Louisiana. It is approximately 1,000 feet long.

Admission Fees: Free.

Open to Public: Daily: Dawn to dusk.

Visitor Services: None.

Directions: From Vicksburg: travel on I-20 west to Tallulah. In Tallulah, take the U.S. 65 north exit to Lake Providence. Grant's Canal is located on U.S. 65 at the northern end of Lake Providence.

Mansfield

15 Site: MANSFIELD STATE COMMEMORATIVE AREA/BATTLE OF MANSFIELD AND BATTLE OF PLEASANT HILL, 15149 Hwy. 175, Mansfield, LA 71052, 318-872-1474

Description: The Battle of Mansfield took place on April 8, 1864. Under the leadership of General Richard Taylor, an army of fewer than 9,000 Confederate soldiers defeated 13,000 Union troops of General Nathanial Banks. The day after the Battle of Mansfield, on April 9, the fierce Battle of Pleasant Hill was fought with both sides taking heavy losses and withdrawing from the field after dark. Local historians have been constructing a series of marble road markers denoting and interpreting the Battle of Pleasant Hill. The marker-trail leads the visitor on the road from Mansfield, with a chronology of events. Markers are located on U.S. Hwy. 175 between Mansfield State Commemorative Area and Pleasant Hill.

Admission Fees: Adults: $2; Seniors and children under 12: Free.

Open to Public: Daily: 9 A.M.–5 P.M.

Visitor Services: Museum; maps and interpretive programs of the battle; rest rooms.

Regularly Scheduled Events: *Apr.:* Reenactments and living history program.

Directions: From I-20: go through Shreveport to Hwy. 171 south; go approximately 35 miles to Mansfield; turn onto U.S. 84 west. From I-49: exit at U.S. 84 west.

Newellton

16 **Site:** WINTER QUARTERS STATE COMMEMORATIVE AREA, Rte. 1, P.O. Box 91, Newellton, LA 71357, 318-467-5439

Description: Winter Quarters, a home listed on the National Register of Historic Places, stands today as a rare survivor of the ravages of the Civil War and as a tribute to the courage of one woman. Julia Nutt not only saved her home, but also preserved the architectural work of her talented planter and inventor husband, Dr. Haller Nutt. The home was taken over by Grant's troops during the Civil War.

Admission Fees: Adults: $2; Children 12 and under and Adults 62 and over: Free.

Open to Public: Daily: 9 A.M. 5 P.M.

Visitor Services: Tours; museum; information; visitors center; rest rooms.

Directions: From 1-20: take the Tallulah (U.S. 65) exit south. Travel on U.S. 65 south to Newellton. Take Parish Rd. 605 to 608. Winter Quarters is located on 608, 6 miles east of Newellton, across from St. Joseph Lake.

New Iberia

17 **Site:** SHADOWS-ON-THE-TECHE, 317 East Main St., New Iberia, LA 70560, 318-369-6446

Description: This 1834 plantation home and gardens on the banks of Bayou Teche is one of the most authentically restored and interpreted pre–Civil War historic sites in America. In 1863, the home was under Federal occupation. It was built by sugar planter David Weeks and was donated by the family to the National Trust for Historic Preservation.

Admission Fees: Adults: $6; Children (6–11): $3. Groups (12 or more with reservations): $4.50.

Open to Public: Daily: 9 A.M.–4:30 P.M.

Visitor Services: Museum; information; gift shop; rest rooms; handicapped access.

Regularly Scheduled Events: *Every other year (call for more information):* Civil War encampment.

Directions: From I-10: take exit 103A. Take Evangeline Thruway (Hwy. 90); take LA 14 exit off Hwy. 90; take left off ramp on Center St.; go to end. In New Iberia, turn left at E. Main St. Located at 317 E. Main St.

New Orleans

18 Site: CONFEDERATE MUSEUM, 929 Camp St., New Orleans, LA 70130, 504-523-4522

Description: This is the oldest museum in Louisiana. Civil War memorabilia include flags, uniforms, weapons, medical instruments, currency, and personal effects of President Jefferson Davis, General Robert E. Lee, and other Southern leaders.

Admission Fees: Adults: $4; Children: $2.

Open to Public: Mon.–Sat.: 10 A.M.–4 P.M.

Visitor Services: Tours.

Directions: From Baton Rouge: take I-10 to New Orleans. Take Business District/ Tchoupitoulas St. exit; turn left at Calliope St. Continue to Camp St. and turn right. Get in left hand lane. The Confederate Museum is located on the corner of Camp and Howard Streets.

19 Site: FORT PIKE STATE COMMEMORATIVE AREA, Rte. 6, Box 194, New Orleans, LA 70129, 504-662-5703

Description: Before the actual start of the Civil War, the Louisiana militia captured Fort Pike. Confederates held it until Union forces took New Orleans in 1862, whereupon the Southerners evacuated the fort. In spite of much activity, not a single cannonball was ever fired in battle from Fort Pike.

Admission Fees: Adults: $2; Children under 12: Free; Seniors (62 & over): Free.

Open to Public: Daily: 9 A.M.–5 P.M.

Visitor Services: Museum; picnic area; rest rooms; tours.

Directions: Fort Pike is located on U.S. 90, 23 miles east of downtown New Orleans. From downtown New Orleans, get on I-12 toward Slidell. At Slidell, get on I-10 and exit left at exit 263. Keep straight until the road forks right.

20 **Site:** OLD U.S. MINT, 400 Block of Esplanade Ave., New Orleans, LA 70116, 504-568-6968

Description: Operational from 1838–1909, the Old U.S. Mint at peak produced $5 million in coins monthly. For a short time during the Civil War, it was the only mint of the Confederate states. Now part of the Louisiana State Museum, the building has been restored and houses many popular exhibits plus a collection of historical documents.

Admission Fees: Adults: $4; Children: $3.

Open to Public: Tues.–Sun.: 9 A.M.–5 P.M.

Visitor Services: Tours.

Directions: Take I-10 to Elysian Fields; go south toward the river; turn right to Esplanade Ave.

Pineville

21 **Site:** ALEXANDRIA NATIONAL CEMETERY, 209 East Shamrock St., Pineville, LA, 318-449-1793

Description: Established in 1867 as a burial site for Civil War soldiers. Contains graves of soldiers from every American war since the Spanish-American War.

Admission Fees: Free.

Open to Public: Daily: 8 A.M.–4 P.M.

Visitor Services: None.

Directions: Located on U.S Hwy. 165, north of Alexandria (across Red River Bridge).

Sunset

22 **Site:** CHRETIEN POINT, Rte. 1, P.O. Box 162, Sunset, LA 70584, 318-662-5876

Description: This plantation became the site of the "Battle of the Red River Campaign." Several skirmishes took place on Chretien land and a major battle was fought on Bayou Bourbeau, approximately a mile to the rear of the mansion. A bullet hole can be found in one of the front doors.

Admission Fees: Adults: $5.50; Children: $2.75.

Open to Public: Daily: 10 A.M.–5 P.M.; last tour at 4 P.M.

Visitor Services: Bed & Breakfast; tours.

Directions: From I-49 (from Lafayette): take exit 97 onto LA 93. Go straight through Cankton, continue for 2 miles; turn left. Go one block, turn right. From I-10: take exit 97; go north approximately 8 miles; take a left onto Hwy. 356 toward Bristol. Go one block and turn right on Chretien Point Rd.; the plantation is on the left (1 mile).

Tangipahoa

23 **Site:** CAMP MOORE/CONFEDERATE CEMETERY, U.S. Hwy. 51, Tangipahoa, LA 70465, 504-229-2438

Description: Established in the summer of 1861, Camp Moore, named after Civil War Governor Thomas Moore, served as one of the largest Confederate training bases in the Southern states. The Confederate cemetery, adjacent to Camp Moore, contains the remains of more than 400 Confederate soldiers.

Admission Fees: Adults: $2; Children: $1; Children under 6: Free.

Open to Public: Tues.–Sat.: 10 A.M.–4 P.M.

Visitor Services: Museum; trails; information.

Directions: From Hammond: follow U.S. 51 north. Camp Moore is located on U.S. 51, .5 mile north of the village of Tangipahoa.

Vinton

24 **Site:** NIBLETT'S BLUFF, Rte. 1, P.O. Box 358, Vinton, LA 70668, 318-589-7117

Description: Overlooking the Old Sabine River, Niblett's Bluff is the site of an old Civil War encampment. Confederate breastworks may still be seen.

Admission Fees: Overnight RV: $10; Tent with electricity: $10; Cabins: $20; Tent: $5.

Open to Public: Daily: 6 A.M.–10 P.M.

Visitor Services: Trails; lodging; camping; rest rooms.

Directions: From I-10: take exit at Tommey Sparks; follow 109; go north for 2.9 miles. At yellow light look for directional sign on left.

White Castle

25 **Site:** NOTTOWAY PLANTATION, P.O. Box 160, White Castle, LA 70788, 504-545-2730

Description: This is the largest plantation home in the South, an outstanding example of the opulent lifestyle enjoyed by the wealthy sugar planter before the Civil War. The three-story mansion has 64 rooms

and was considered immense even by the standards of the antebellum "Golden Age."

Admission Fees: Adults: $8; Children (5–12): $3.

Open to Public: Daily: 9 A.M.–5 P.M.

Visitor Services: Restaurant (open daily 11 A.M.–3 P.M.); overnight accommodations with reservations; tours.

Directions: From I-10: go over Mississippi River Bridge at Baton Rouge; take Plaquemine exit south to LA 1. Continue down LA 1 for 20 miles. Nottoway Plantation is on the left.

Zachary

26 **Site:** PORT HUDSON STATE COMMEMORATIVE AREA, 756 West Plains (Port Hudson Rd.), Zachary, LA 70791, 504-654-3775

Earthwork fortification and walking trail at Port Hudson State Commemorative Area, Port Hudson, LA. (Photograph courtesy of Port Hudson State Commemorative Area.)

Description: Port Hudson was the longest siege in U.S. military history. The Union force of 30,000 to 40,000 was held off by 6,800 Confederate soldiers from May 23 to July 9, 1863. This conflict is also one of the first in which free black soldiers fought on the side of the Union. The site includes a national cemetery with more than 3,000 Union soldiers, most of whom are unknown.

Admission Fees: Adults: $2; Seniors and children under 12: Free.

Open to Public: Daily: 9 A.M.–5 P.M.

Visitor Services: Trails; interpretive center; rest rooms; gift shop.

Regularly Scheduled Events: *Last weekend in Mar.:* Reenactment.

Directions: Take I-10 to U.S. 61 (to Natchez); take St. Francisville exit (I-10 intersects with U.S. 61 at this point); turn right. Port Hudson is 14–17 miles straight ahead on the left.

Maryland

For Maryland Tourism information call 1-800-MD IS FUN (634-7386).

1 Fort McHenry National Monument & Historic Site
2 Maryland Historical Society, Museum and Library of Maryland History
3 Fort Frederick State Park Civilian Conservation Corps Museum
4 Surratt House Museum & Visitor Center
5 Thomas Viaduct
6 Fort Washington Park
7 Barbara Fritchie House & Museum
8 Monocacy National Battlefield
9 Mount Olivet Cemetery
10 National Museum of Civil War Medicine
11 Clara Barton National Historic Site
12 Marietta Manor
13 Point Lookout State Park & Civil War Museum
14 Antietam National Battlefield
15 Kennedy Farmhouse
16 Dr. Samuel A. Mudd Home & Museum

Maryland

$\mathcal{A}$t the outbreak of the Civil War, Maryland could be described as both a Northern and a Southern state. Strong unionist sentiment was present, but also a great deal of sympathy for the Confederacy. Maryland relied on both free and slave labor and contained large plantations, small farms, and a great city.

On April 19, 1861, Maryland's two sides came to blows in the streets of Baltimore when Massachusetts troops, marching through the city, engaged a crowd of Southern sympathizers. To safeguard the national capital, Maryland had to be secured to the Union. Federal troops turned the guns of Fort McHenry on the city itself and imprisoned public officials with known secessionist tendencies. General Ben "Beast" Butler seized the railroads around Annapolis, while John Garrett, president of the B&O Railroad, promised his company's support to Lincoln. Meanwhile, Governor Hicks moved the General Assembly to unionist Frederick to insure the imprisoned legislators could not participate. In response, thousands of Marylanders headed south to join the Confederate army.

Larger numbers of Marylanders served in the Union forces than in the Confederate army. They confronted each other at such battles as Front Royal and Culps Hill (Gettysburg). Maryland witnessed the bloodiest day of the Civil War at the Battle of Antietam on September 17, 1862, with more than 23,000 killed or wounded that day. Lee's army invaded the state on two other occasions—on his way to Pennsylvania in 1863 and during General Early's 1864 raids on Washington, which included the Battle of Monocacy. Lee's setback at Antietam may have given Lincoln the opportunity to announce his Emancipation Proclamation; but his executive order did not apply to Maryland, which abolished slavery with a state law about a year before the 13th Amendment. Many African Americans from Maryland served in the Union forces, fighting to gain or insure their freedom. When soldiers of both sides returned home, Maryland healed its wounds more easily than the rest of the nation.

Baltimore

Site: FORT MCHENRY NATIONAL MONUMENT & HISTORIC SITE, East Fort Ave., Baltimore, MD 21230-5393, 410-962-4290 or 410-962-4291

Description: This historic site documents the history of Fort McHenry, including its construction from 1798 to 1803; its bombardment during the War of 1812; the writing of "The Star-Spangled Banner"; and its use as a Civil War prison, WWI hospital and WWII U.S. Coast Guard training center.

Admission Fees: Adults: $2; Children under 17: Free.

Open to Public: Daily: 8 A.M.–5 P.M.; call for extended summer hours.

Visitor Services: Rest rooms; handicapped access.

Regularly Scheduled Events: *June 14:* Flag Day festivities; *Second Tues. in Sept.:*

Defenders Day (commemorates the Battle of Baltimore).

Directions: From I-95: take exit 55 (Key Hwy.). Follow posted signs.

ANTIETAM

Antietam National Battlefield, Sharpsburg, MD. (Photograph by Dennis Kan, courtesy of The Civil War Trust.)

The Battle of Antietam (or Sharpsburg) on September 17, 1862, climaxed the first of Confederate General Robert E. Lee's two attempts to carry the war into the North. About 40,000 Southerners were pitted against the 87,000-man Federal Army of the Potomac under Union General George B. McClellan. And when the fighting ended, the course of the American Civil War had been greatly altered.

After his great victory at Manassas in August, Lee had marched his Army of Northern Virginia into Maryland, hoping to find vitally needed men and supplies. McClellan followed, first to Frederick (where through rare good fortune a copy of the Confederate battle plan, Lee's Special Order No. 191, fell into his hands), then, westward 12 miles to the passes of South Mountain. There on September 14, at Turner's, Fox's, and Crampton's gaps, Lee tried to block the Federals. But because he had split his army to send troops under General Thomas J. "Stonewall" Jackson to capture Harpers Ferry, Lee could only hope to delay the Northerners. McClellan forced his way through, and by the afternoon of September 15, both armies had established new battle lines west and east of Antietam Creek near the town of Sharpsburg. When Jackson's troops reached Sharpsburg on the 16th, Harpers Ferry having surrendered the day before, Lee consolidated his position along the low ridge that runs north and south of the town.

The battle opened at dawn on the 17th when Union General Joseph Hooker's artillery began a murderous fire on Jackson's men in the Miller cornfield north of town. Hooker's troops advanced, driving the Confederates before them, and Jackson reported that his men were "exposed for near an hour to a terrific storm of shell, canister, and musketry."

About 7 A.M., Jackson was reinforced and succeeded in driving the Federals back. An hour later Union troops under General Joseph Mansfield counterattacked and by 9 o'clock had regained some of the lost ground. Then, in an effort to extricate some of Mansfield's men from their isolated position near the Dunker Church, Union General John Sedgewick's division of Edwin V. Sumner's corps advanced into the West Woods. There Confederate troops struck Sedgewick's men on both flanks, inflicting appalling casualties.

Meanwhile, Union General William H. French's division of Sumner's corps moved up to support Sedgewick but veered south into Confederates under General D. H. Hill posted along an old sunken road separating the Roulette and Piper farms. For nearly four hours, from 9:30 A.M. to 1 P.M., bitter fighting raged along this road (afterward known as Bloody Lane) as French, supported by Union General Israel B. Richardson's division, also of Sumner's corps, sought to drive the Southerners back. Confusion and sheer exhaustion finally ended the battle here and in the northern part of the field generally.

Southeast of town, Union General Ambrose E. Burnside's troops had been trying to cross a bridge over Antietam Creek since 9:30 A.M. Some 400 Georgians had driven them back each time. At 1 P.M. the Federals finally crossed the bridge (now known as Burnside Bridge) and, after a two-hour delay to reform their lines, advanced up the slope beyond. By late afternoon they had driven the Georgians back almost to Sharpsburg, threatening to cut off the line of retreat for Lee's decimated Confederates. Then, about 4 P.M. Confederate General A. P. Hill's division, left behind by Jackson at Harpers Ferry to salvage the captured Federal property, arrived on the field and immediately entered the fight. Burnside's troops were driven back to the heights near the bridge they had earlier taken. The Battle of Antietam was over. The next day Lee began withdrawing his army across the Potomac River.

More men were killed or wounded at Antietam on September 17, 1862, than on any other single day of the Civil War. Federal losses were 12,410, Confederate losses 10,700. Although neither side gained a decisive victory, Lee's failure to carry the war effort effectively into the North caused Great Britain to postpone recognition of the Confederate government. The battle also gave President Abraham Lincoln the opportunity to issue the Emancipation Proclamation, which, on January 1, 1863, declared free all slaves in states still in rebellion against the United States. Now the war had a dual purpose: to preserve the Union and end slavery.

by Julie K. Fix, The Civil War Trust

Site: MARYLAND HISTORICAL SOCIETY, MUSEUM AND LIBRARY OF MARYLAND HISTORY, 201 West Monument St., Baltimore, MD 21201, 410-685-3750

Description: Home of Francis Scott Key's original handwritten version of "The Star-Spangled Banner," the nation's largest 19th-century silver collection, Peale family paintings, and a superb fine and decorative arts collection.

Admission Fees: Adults: $4.50; Seniors: $3; Children 12 and over: $3; Students with ID: $3. Families: $8; Free admission: Sat.: 9 A.M.–11 A.M.

Open to Public: *Museum:* Tues.–Fri.: 10 A.M.–5 P.M.; Sat.: 9 A.M.–5 P.M.; Sun.: 1 P.M.–5 P.M. *Library:* Tues.–Fri.: 10 A.M.–4:30 P.M.; Sat: 9 A.M.–4:30 P.M.

Visitor Services: Handicapped access.

Directions: From I-95: take exit 53 (395N); stay to the right and follow signs to Martin Luther King Blvd.; go north on Martin Luther King for 1.5 miles to Druid Hill. Turn left on Park Ave. Parking lot is on left.

Big Pool

Site: FORT FREDERICK STATE PARK CIVILIAN CONSERVATION CORPS MUSEUM, 11100 Fort Frederick Rd., Big Pool, MD 21711, 301-842-2155

Description: This historic fort (built in 1756) and museum interpret military history as well as military and civilian lifestyles.

Admission Fees: Free.

Open to Public: *Fort:* Apr.–Oct.: Daily: 8 A.M.–sunset. Call for museum hours.

Visitor Services: Camping; rest rooms; handicapped access.

Regularly Scheduled Events: *Apr.:* Market fair and rifle frolic; *Last full weekend in July:* Military field days; *Third week of Sept.:* Governor's invitational firelock match; *Oct.:* Ghost walk.

Directions: From I-70: take exit 12; follow signs.

Clinton

Site: SURRATT HOUSE MUSEUM & VISITOR CENTER, 9118 Brandywine Rd., Clinton, MD 20735, 301-868-1121

Description: Presents a variety of programs and events that recapture the history of mid-19th-century life and focuses on the fascinating web of the Lincoln conspiracy.

Admission Fees: Adults: $1.50; Children (5–18): $.50; Seniors: $1.

Open to Public: Mar.–Dec.: Thurs.–Fri.: 11 A.M.–3 P.M.; Sat.–Sun.: Noon–4 P.M.; open other days for special events.

Visitor Services: Library; gift shop; museum.

Regularly Scheduled Events: *Feb:* Antique Valentine exhibit; *Apr. & Sept.:* John Wilkes Booth escape route tour; *Nov.:* Annual open house; *Dec.:* Victorian Christmas.

Directions: From I-95: take exit 7 (Rte. 5) south; exit at Rte. 223 west; take left onto Brandywine Rd.

Elkridge

 Site: THOMAS VIADUCT, West of U.S. 1, Levering Ave., Elkridge, MD 21227, 410-313-1900

Description: Built in 1835, this bridge was part of the main railroad between Baltimore and Washington, which allowed boat and rail transport to move troops and supplies during the Civil War. It is the oldest multiarched curved bridge in the world and is still in use.

Admission Fees: Free.

Open to Public: Daily: Dawn to dusk.

Visitor Services: None.

Directions: From I-95: take exit 41 (Rte. 175); go east to Rte. 1 (1 block); go north on Rte. 1 to Elkridge (about 5 miles); go past Harbor Tunnel Hwy. sign; turn at next left; follow signs for Patapsco State Park; road goes under the viaduct.

Fort Washington

Site: FORT WASHINGTON PARK, 13551 Fort Washington Rd., Fort Washington, MD 20744, 301-763-4600

Description: Outstanding example of 19th-century seacoast fortifications and the only permanent fortification ever constructed to defend the nation's capital. During the first year of the Civil War, the fort controlled river access to Alexandria, Georgetown, and Washington, D.C., and maintained a training base for state militia troops from the North. The site was an active military post from 1808 through the end of World War II, but never fired a shot in anger. Military and civilian living history presented from Feb. to Nov.

Admission Fees: Cars: $4.

Open to Public: Daily: 9 A.M.–dark.

Visitor Services: Trails; museum; gift shop; rest rooms; handicapped access.

Regularly Scheduled Events: Torchlight tours, Civil War garrison weekends and cannon firing demonstrations. Call for special events.

Directions: From I-95: take Indian Head Hwy. (Hwy. 210 south) until you see Fort Washington Rd.; follow to the end.

Frederick

7 **Site:** BARBARA FRITCHIE HOUSE & MUSEUM, 154 West Patrick St., Frederick, MD 21701, 301-698-0630

Description: On September 10, 1862, as General "Stonewall" Jackson and his troops were leaving Frederick, Barbara Fritchie, at age 95, earned her place as a legendary American heroine by defying those she believed to be wrong. This replica of the Barbara Fritchie House preserves many of her belongings.

Admission Fees: Adults: $2; Children under 12: $1.50; Seniors: $1.50.

Open to Public: Apr.–Nov. 30: Mon., Thurs., Fri. & Sat.: 10 A.M.–4 P.M.; Sun.: 1 P.M.–4 P.M.

Visitor Services: Tours; gift shop.

Directions: From I-70: take exit 54 toward Frederick; in Frederick turn left onto Patrick St.

8 **Site:** MONOCACY NATIONAL BATTLEFIELD, 4801 Urbana Pike, Frederick, MD 21701-7307, 301-662-3515

Description: Site of July 9, 1864 battle where Confederate forces, under Lt. General Jubal Early, en route to Washington D.C., were delayed for a day by Union forces under Major General Lew Wallace. This battle allowed time for General Grant to deploy Union troops around the defenseless capital, saving it from Confederate invasion.

Admission Fees: Free.

Open to Public: *Visitors Center:* Memorial Day–Labor Day: Daily: 8 A.M.–4:30 P.M.; rest of the year: Wed.–Sun.: 8 A.M.–4 P.M.

Visitor Services: Visitors center; rest rooms; handicapped access.

Directions: From I-270: take exit 26 (Rte. 80 north); travel .2 mile and turn left on Rte. 355 north; battlefield is 3.7 miles.

9 **Site:** MOUNT OLIVET CEMETERY, 515 South Market St., Frederick, MD 21701, 301-662-1164

Description: Site of the Francis Scott Key Monument, as well as the graves of Governor Thomas Johnson, Barbara Fritchie, and more than 800 Confederate Civil War soldiers.

Admission Fees: Free.

Open to Public: Daily: Dawn to dusk.

Visitor Services: None.

Directions: From I-70: take exit 54 (Rte. 355) toward Frederick and follow the signs. Cemetery is .25 mile west of Rte. 355.

10 **Site:** NATIONAL MUSEUM OF CIVIL WAR MEDICINE, P.O. Box 470, 48 East Patrick St., Frederick, MD 21705, 301-695-1864

Description: The National Museum of Civil War Medicine is dedicated to telling the medical story of the Civil War. Unprepared for an unparalleled emergency that killed over 600,000 Americans, both North and South mobilized to meet the need, and changed the practice of medicine in the process. The museum features exhibits, a video, a museum store, and special events and is continually expanding.

Admission Fees: Free.

Open to Public: Tues.–Fri.: 9 A.M.–5 P.M.; Sat.–Sun.: Noon–5 P.M.; closed Mon.

Visitor Services: Museum.

Regularly Scheduled Events: *Aug:* National Conference on Civil War Medicine.

Directions: From I-270 and I-70: travel north on Market St. (Rte. 355 and 85). Turn right on Church St. Go one block and turn right on Maxwell Alley. Museum is on Patrick St. at the end of the alley.

Glen Echo

11 **Site:** CLARA BARTON NATIONAL HISTORIC SITE, 5801 Oxford Rd., Glen Echo, MD 20812, 301-492-6245

Description: Built in 1891, this house was the final home of Clara Barton, founder of the American Red Cross. The house also served as the headquarters and warehouse space for the American Red Cross from 1897–1904. The museum houses a collection of furnishings used by Clara Barton in her Glen Echo home.

Admission Fees: Free.

Open to Public: Daily: 10 A.M.–5 P.M.; tours hourly at the half hour.

Visitor Services: Handicapped access to first floor; tours; rest roooms.

Regularly Scheduled Events: *Apr. & Sept.:* Biannual Lamplight open house.

Directions: From I-495: take exit 40 on outer loop or exit 41 on the inner loop; follow signs for MacArthur Blvd; turn left onto MacArthur Blvd.; go east past Glen Echo Park on left; take next left onto Oxford Rd.

Glenn Dale

12 **Site:** MARIETTA MANOR, Prince George's County Historical Society, 5626 Bell Station Rd., Glenn Dale, MD 20769, 301-464-5291

Description: Marietta is a federal-style brick house (1812) built by Supreme Court Justice Gabriel Duvall (1752-1844). Its furnishings are from 1812–1900, and the home is interpreted during the years of the Duvall family.

Admission Fees: Free.

Open to Public: *Library:* Sat.: Noon–4 P.M. *Museum:* Sun.: Noon–4 P.M. and by appointment; call for expanded hours.

Visitor Services: None.

Directions: From I-95: take exit 20A (Annapolis Rd. Rte. 450 east); proceed 4 miles; turn left on Rte. 193W; turn left on Bell Station Rd.

Scotland

---

13 **Site:** POINT LOOKOUT STATE PARK & CIVIL WAR MUSEUM, Rte. 5, Scotland, MD 20687, 301-872-5688

Description: Museum documents local history during the Civil War era. The site originally functioned as a Civil War Union hospital, then became a Union prisoner-of-war camp. More than 52,000 prisoners passed through the facility.

Admission Fees: *Museum:* Free; *Fort Lincoln and picnic area:* $2.

Open to Public: *Park:* Daily: 8 A.M.–sunset; *Museum:* May–Sept.: Daily: 10 A.M.–6 P.M.

Visitor Services: Handicapped access; trails; boat rentals; camping; visitors center.

Regularly Scheduled Events: *Second weekend in June.:* Blue & Gray days; *Last weekend in Oct.:* Ghostwalk; *First weekend in Nov.:* Lighthouse tour.

Directions: From I-95: take exit 7; follow Rte. 5 south for 65 miles.

Sharpsburg

---

14 **Site:** ANTIETAM NATIONAL BATTLEFIELD, Sharpsburg Pike, Sharpsburg, MD 21782, 301-432-5124

Description: Site of the bloodiest single-day battle in American history. An 8.5-mile tour road leads through the battlefield with more than 300 markers, monuments, and Civil War cannons.

Admission Fees: Adults: $2; Family: $4.

Open to Public: Daily: 8:30 A.M.–5 P.M.; Summer: 8:30 A.M.–6 P.M.

Visitor Services: Civil War Explorer; trails; museum; rest rooms; handicapped access; visitors center.

Regularly Scheduled Events: *First weekend in Dec.:* The Illumination; *First Sat. in July:* Maryland symphony and fireworks.

Directions: From I-70: take exit 29 to Rte. 65 south for approximately 10 miles.

---

15 **Site:** KENNEDY FARMHOUSE, 2406 Chestnut Grove Rd., Sharpsburg, MD 21783, 301-432-2666

Description: Staging area where John Brown and his Provisional Army of the United States planned and prepared for their Harpers Ferry raid during the summer of 1859. This farmhouse is a National Historic Landmark.

Admission Fees: Free.

Open to Public: *Farmhouse:* May–Oct.: Sat.–Sun.: 9 A.M.–5 P.M. *Grounds:* open all year.

Visitor Services: None.

Directions: From I-70: take U.S. Rte. 340 west; follow the signs.

Waldorf

16 **Site:** DR. SAMUEL A. MUDD HOME & MUSEUM, P.O. Box 1046, LaPlata, MD 20646, 301-645-6870

Description: St. Catherine on the Zechia is the home and plantation of Dr. Samuel A. Mudd, who set the leg of John Wilkes Booth, assassin of President Lincoln. For this deed, Dr. Mudd was sent to Fort Jefferson Prison, Dry Tortugas Island, Florida, for life, but was pardoned in 1869 by President Andrew Johnson.

Admission Fees: Adults: $3; Children: $1.

Open to Public: Apr.–Nov.: Wed: 11 A.M.–3 P.M.; Sat.–Sun.: Noon–4 P.M.

Visitor Services: Handicapped access; rest rooms.

Regularly Scheduled Events: *Apr. & Sept.:* John Wilkes Booth escape route tour.

Directions: From U.S. Rte. 301 at Waldorf: take Rte. 5; then left on Rte. 205; right on Poplar Hill Rd. for approximately 4 miles. Turn right on Dr. Samuel Mudd Rd.; travel .4 mile to the house.

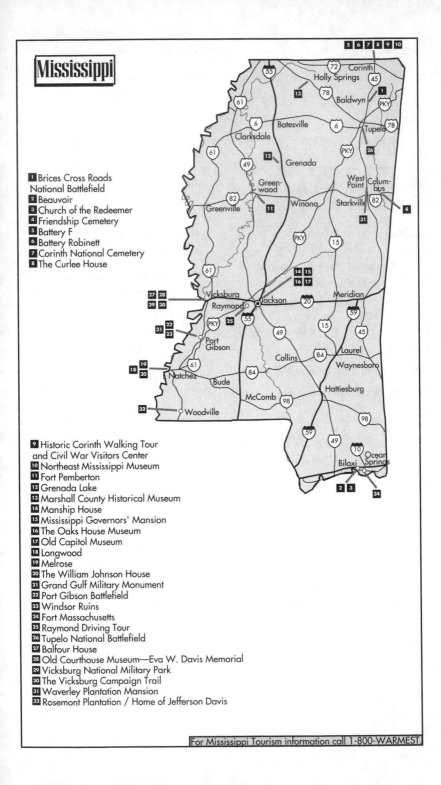

Mississippi

1 Brices Cross Roads
National Battlefield
2 Beauvoir
3 Church of the Redeemer
4 Friendship Cemetery
5 Battery F
6 Battery Robinett
7 Corinth National Cemetery
8 The Curlee House

9 Historic Corinth Walking Tour
and Civil War Visitors Center
10 Northeast Mississippi Museum
11 Fort Pemberton
12 Grenada Lake
13 Marshall County Historical Museum
14 Manship House
15 Mississippi Governors' Mansion
16 The Oaks House Museum
17 Old Capitol Museum
18 Longwood
19 Melrose
20 The William Johnson House
21 Grand Gulf Military Monument
22 Port Gibson Battlefield
23 Windsor Ruins
24 Fort Massachusetts
25 Raymond Driving Tour
26 Tupelo National Battlefield
27 Balfour House
28 Old Courthouse Museum—Eva W. Davis Memorial
29 Vicksburg National Military Park
30 The Vicksburg Campaign Trail
31 Waverley Plantation Mansion
32 Rosemont Plantation / Home of Jefferson Davis

For Mississippi Tourism information call 1-800-WARMEST

MISSISSIPPI

In late April 1862, following the Battle of Shiloh, a Union army besieged a smaller Confederate force entrenched at Corinth in defense of the vital crossroads of the Memphis & Charleston and the Mobile & Ohio railroads. The Federals built some 14 miles of offensive earthworks between Shiloh and Corinth, and during the night of May 29, the Confederates, whose defensive works had by then become untenable, secretly slipped out of Corinth, abandoning the crossroads to the North. Following the Confederate failure to recapture Corinth in October, General Ulysses S. Grant led his army into northwestern Mississippi from his camp in Tennessee. Grant's first attempt to get to Vicksburg to wrest control of the Mississippi River from the Confederacy failed due to Union defeats at Coffeeville, Holly Springs, and Chickasaw Bayou in December 1862.

After failing to approach Vicksburg from the north, through the bayous of the Mississippi's delta in the winter of 1863, Grant decided to attempt yet another invasion of Mississippi, this time from the south. At the end of April he sent two-thirds of his army down the western shore of the Mississippi, while the Union navy, which had run the batteries of Vicksburg on the evening of April 22, attacked the Rebel fortress at Grand Gulf on the 29th. This assault failed, but the persistent Grant landed his troops even farther south at Bruinsburg on April 30. During the following 200 days, Grant's soldiers marched over a triangular route more than 200 miles long and defeated Confederate forces, commanded by General John Pemberton, at Port Gibson on the 1st, Raymond on the 12th, Jackson on the 14th, and Champion Hill, the major battle of the campaign, on the 16th. Then, as Pemberton withdrew into Vicksburg's formidable works, his rear guard was routed at the Big Black River Bridge. When two bloody attempts to take the city by storm failed, Grant laid siege to Vicksburg for six weeks. Cut off from the rest of the Confederacy, the besieged had all but run out of food and medical supplies by early July, and Pemberton was forced to surrender on July 4, 1863.

During 1864 Mississippi suffered a number of Union raids, most significantly the Meridian Expedition, in which the Federals marched from Vicksburg eastward across the state to Meridian, destroying everything of military value in their path. During the remainder of 1864, as William T. Sherman marched on Atlanta, his lengthening supply lines were threatened by Confederate cavalry leader Nathan Bedford Forrest. To divert the aggressive Forrest from those lines, Sherman ordered three successive Union expeditions into North Mississippi. Battles at Brices Cross Roads and Tupelo, skirmishing at Oxford, and a celebrated raid by Forrest on Memphis ensued between June 10 and August 11, 1864. Of these, the battle at Brices Cross Roads, in which Forrest's force totally defeated their more numerous Union enemy, was the most significant.

by Michael F. Beard, Mississippi Department of Archives and History

---

ℱor More Information

Mississippi recently produced a *Civil War Guide* (32 pages), organized regionally, that gives visitor contact information for approximately 75 sites, including battlefields and fortifications, cemeteries, historic communities, homes, and sites associated with the political history of the war. The guide also contains a general essay on the war in the state, a chronology of significant events from secession to surrender, a selected reading list, and photographs. It is available free by writing Mississippi Department of Tourism Development, P.O. Box 1705, Ocean Springs, MS 39566-1705; or call: 1-800-WARMEST.

Baldwyn

1 **Site:** BRICES CROSS ROADS NATIONAL BATTLEFIELD, Natchez Trace Pkwy., Rural Rte. 1, NT-143, Tupelo, MS 38801, 601-680-4025

Description: At Brices Cross Roads in June 1864, a battle was fought that served to keep Confederate General Nathan Bedford Forrest from altering the supply line that was essential to the success of Union General William T. Sherman. While considered a Confederate victory, Sherman persevered and went on to win the Atlanta campaign.

Admission Fees: Free.

Open to Public: Daily: Dawn to dusk.

Visitor Services: Gift shop; information; rest rooms; handicapped access.

Directions: From I-45: proceed north to Baldwyn, Mississippi; go west on MS 370 about 6 miles to park.

Biloxi

2 **Site:** BEAUVOIR, 2244 Beach Blvd., Biloxi, MS 39531, 601-388-1313

Description: Seaside retirement estate of Confederate President Jefferson Davis. Estate served as the Mississippi Confederate Soldiers' Home from 1903 to 1957. See the restored home, soldiers' home and hospital (now a military museum), cemetery and tomb of the unknown

Confederate soldier. Became the location of the Jefferson Davis Presidential Library.

Admission Fees: Adults: $5; Children: $2.50; Seniors: $4.50; Groups (20 or more): $4.

Open to Public: Daily: 9 A.M.–4:30 P.M.

Visitor Services: Museum; gift shop; library; information; rest rooms; handicapped access.

Regularly Scheduled Events: *Mar.:* Spring Pilgrimage; *Apr.:* Confederate Memorial Day; *Oct.:* Fall Muster; *Dec.:* Candlelight Christmas.

Directions: From I-10 east: exit onto Lorraine-Cowan Rd. traveling south; turn left (east) on U.S. Hwy. 90 (Beach Boulevard) to Beauvoir at the intersection of U.S. Hwy. 90 and Beauvoir Ave. (Beauvoir is 8 miles from I-10.) From I-10 west: exit onto I-110; proceed toward the Gulf to U.S. Hwy. 90.; turn right (west) on U.S. 90 to Beauvoir Ave. (Beauvoir is 9 miles from I-10.)

---

3 **Site:** CHURCH OF THE REDEEMER, Corner of Hwy. 90 (Beach Blvd.) and Bellman St., 610 Water St., Biloxi, MS 39530, 601-436-3123

Description: Confederate President Jefferson Davis worshiped here and was a member of the vestry. Other Confederate generals who were church members during the time they lived in Biloxi were Lt. Gen. Alexander P. Stewart, Brig. Gen. Joseph Davis, and Brig. Gen. Samuel W. Ferguson. The church offers tours and an exhibit of Confederate and Davis memorabilia, featuring the Davis pew, Confederate flag and cross, and a letter from Davis.

Admission Fees: Free.

Open to Public: Daily: 9 A.M.–5 P.M.

Visitor Services: Information; tour.

Regularly Scheduled Events: *Mar.:* Spring Pilgrimage; *Second Sun. in Sept.:* Blessing of the Animals.

Directions: From I-10: take I-110 to Hwy. 90 east (exit 1A). Church is on Hwy. 90 at Bellman St. Distance to Church is 5.5 miles from I-10.

Columbus

4 **Site:** FRIENDSHIP CEMETERY, P.O. Box 1408, Columbus, MS 39703, 601-328-2565

Description: Burial site of four Confederate generals, more than 2,000 Confederate soldiers, veterans from every war the United States has fought, as well as distinguished authors, legislators, and people from all walks of life. Site of America's first Decoration Day (1866), inspiring the writing of the poem "The Blue and the Gray." This site relates to the theme of reconciliation after the Civil War, because the Ladies of Columbus put flowers on the graves of both Confederate and Union soldiers who had been buried there during the war.

Admission Fees: Free.

Open to Public: Daily: 7 A.M.–sunset.

Visitor Services: Locator service is available.

Regularly Scheduled Events: Spring Pilgrimage includes "Tales from the Crypt."

Directions: 69 miles from I-55 on 82 E; 68 miles from I-20 on 45 N.

Corinth

5 | **Site:** BATTERY F, P.O. Box 45, Corinth, MS 38835-0045, 601-287-1328

Description: Battery F is one of the six outer batteries built by the Union army in a position to provide support fire on Oct. 3, 1862. It was captured the evening of Oct. 3, 1862. Battery F is a well preserved earthwork about 150 feet long with a parapet between 3 feet and 6 feet high. Facing northwest, Battery F protected the Memphis & Charleston Railroad. The battery was the northernmost of the detached batteries protecting approaches along roads and railroads.

Admission Fees: Free.

Open to Public: Daily: Daylight hours.

Visitor Services: Information.

Directions: From I-40 at Jackson, TN: exit onto Hwy. 45 south to Corinth (50 miles). From Hwy. 45, take Memphis exit onto Hwy. 72 east. Turn north at the intersection of Hwy. 72 and Alcorn Dr.; turn at the first right onto Smithbridge Rd. to Pinelake subdivision. Battery F is located at the corner of Bitner and Davis Streets in the subdivision.

6 | **Site:** BATTERY ROBINETT, P.O. Box 45, Corinth, MS 38834, 601-287-1328

Description: Battery Robinett is a reconstruction of one of seven batteries constructed by the Federal army following the Siege of Corinth in the spring of 1862. It was the scene of the most famous event of the Battle of Corinth.

Admission Fees: Free.

Open to Public: Daily: Dawn to dusk.

Visitor Services: Trails; information.

Directions: From I-40 at Jackson, TN: exit onto Hwy. 45 south to Corinth (50 miles). From Hwy. 45, take Memphis exit onto Hwy. 72 east. From Hwy. 72 E turn left onto Fulton Dr. at shopping center with Kroger Store.; follow Fulton Dr. to Linden St.; turn left at this intersection. Battery Robinett will be on the left. Entrance at top of hill approximately .25 mile from Fulton Dr./ Linden St. intersection on left.

7 | **Site:** CORINTH NATIONAL CEMETERY, Horton St., Corinth, MS 38834, 901-386-8311

Description: On April 13, 1866, the Secretary of War authorized immediate action to provide a final resting place for the honored dead who died in Civil War battles for control of the railroad in and around Corinth, Miss. This beautiful 20-acre cemetery is the resting place for 1,793 known and 3,895 unknown Union soldiers.

Admission Fees: Free.

Open to Public: Mon.–Fri.: 8 A.M.–4:30 P.M.

Visitor Services: Information; rest rooms.

Regularly Scheduled Events: Veterans Day and Memorial Day events.

Directions: From I-40 at Jackson, TN.: exit onto Hwy. 45 south; drive to Corinth (50 miles) and exit onto Hwy. 72 (the Memphis exit) east. Follow signs off Rte. 72 in Corinth.

---

8 | **Site:** THE CURLEE HOUSE, 705 Jackson St., Corinth, MS 38834, 601-287-9501

Description: The Curlee House was used in the Civil War as headquarters for Generals Braxton Bragg, H. W. Halleck, and John B. Hood.

Admission Fees: Adults: $1.50; Children: $.50.

Open to Public: Thurs.–Mon.: 1 P.M.–4 P.M.

Visitor Services: Museum; information.

Directions: From I-40 at Jackson, TN.: exit onto Hwy. 45 south; drive to Corinth (50 miles) and exit onto Hwy. 72 (Memphis exit) east. Turn left on Cass St. and proceed under a railroad overpass; proceed to Cruise St. and turn left on Cruise. Follow Cruise to Fillmore St. and turn right. Travel north on Fillmore St. to Childs St. and turn left. Drive one block to the Curlee House at the corner of Childs and Jackson Streets.

---

9 | **Site:** HISTORIC CORINTH WALKING TOUR AND CIVIL WAR VISITORS CENTER, P.O. Box 45, Corinth, MS 38834, 601-287-9501; 601-287-1328

Description: The Historic Corinth Walking Tour follows a route through the historic district of Corinth to illustrate how Corinth appeared at the time of the Siege and Battle and the Union occupation of the town. Wayside exhibits feature Civil War photographs and art with interpretive text and are placed close to their original viewpoints. The tour begins at the Corinth Civil War Visitors Center on the grounds of the historic Curlee House. A video, maps for the self-guided walking tour, and general information about the Siege and Battle of Corinth National Landmark sites are available at the Corinth Civil War Visitors Center.

Admission Fees: Free.

Open to Public: *Walking tour:* Daily: Daylight hours. *Corinth Civil War Visitors Center:* Daily: 9 A.M.–5 P.M.

Visitor Services: Information; visitors center; rest rooms; handicapped access.

Directions: From I-40 at Jackson, TN.: exit onto Hwy. 45 south; drive to Corinth (50 miles) and exit onto Hwy. 72 (Memphis exit) east. Turn left on Cass St. and proceed under a railroad overpass; proceed to Cruise St. and turn left on Cruise. Follow Cruise to Fillmore St. and turn right. Travel north on Fillmore St. to Childs St. and turn left. Drive one block to the Curlee House at the corner of Childs and Jackson Streets. The Corinth Civil War Visitor Center is located at the rear of the Curlee House.

Site: NORTHEAST MISSISSIPPI MUSEUM, 1118 East Fifth St., Corinth, MS 38834, 601-286-6403

Description: The Northeast Mississippi Museum has displays of Civil War artifacts and photographs, a model of the historic railroad crossing, and other information on Civil War Corinth.

Admission Fees: Free.

Open to Public: *Summer:* Mon.–Sat.: 10 A.M.–5 P.M.; Sun.: 2 P.M.–5 P.M. *Winter:* Mon.–Sat.: 10:30 A.M.–4:30 P.M.; Sun.: 2 P.M.–4:30 P.M.

Visitor Services: Museum; gift shop; information; rest rooms.

Directions: From I-40 at Jackson, TN.: exit onto Hwy. 45 south; drive to Corinth (50 miles) and exit onto Hwy. 72 (Memphis exit) east. Turn left on Cass St. and proceed under a railroad overpass; proceed to Cruise St. and turn left on Cruise. Follow Cruise to Fillmore St. and turn right. Travel north on Fillmore St. Turn left on Main St. at the Corinth Library and the First Baptist Church. Follow Main to Polk St. Turn right on Polk and drive three blocks to Fourth St. Turn left on Fourth and the museum is on the left.

Greenwood

Site: FORT PEMBERTON, c/o Greenwood Convention and Visitors Bureau, P.O. Drawer 739, Greenwood, MS 38935-0739, 601-453-9197

Description: Located on Hwy. 82 West on the banks of the Yazoo Pass connecting the Yazoo and Tallahatchie Rivers, Fort Pemberton was a hastily constructed fortification consisting of cotton bales and timber logs. A significant military skirmish occurred here when the Confederate forces successfully drove back three Union ironclads, forcing Grant to seek another route to Vicksburg. A brochure is available at the Convention and Visitors Bureau. The Cottonlandia Museum contains artifacts from Fort Pemberton.

Admission Fees: Free.

Open to Public: Daily: Daylight hours.

Visitor Services: Trails; information.

Directions: From I-55: take Greenwood/Winona exit. Take State Hwy. 82 west to Greenwood. Pick up brochure at Greenwood Convention and Visitors Bureau located on Hwy. 82 at Leflore Ave. on left. To Cottonlandia Museum: Travel west on Hwy. 82; the museum is located on the right, east of Fort Pemberton. To Fort Pemberton: Travel west on Hwy. 82; proceed past Walmart; fort is located on the right, just east of the 49E intersection.

Grenada

Site: GRENADA LAKE, P.O. Box 1045, Grenada, MS 38902-1045, 601-226-5121

Description: Grenada was to be Pemberton's defense line against Grant's approach on the Mississippi Central Railroad against Vicksburg. Eight forts were built here; two of them are restored on Grenada Lake property. Only a skirmish was actually fought because Grant was blocked by Van Dorn's raid.

Admission Fees: Free.

Open to Public: *Forts:* Daily: Daylight hours. *Visitors Center:* Daily: 9 A.M.– Noon and 1 P.M.–5 P.M.

Visitor Services: Lodging; gas; camping; trails; food; museum; gift shop; information; rest rooms; handicapped access.

Regularly Scheduled Events: *Summer:* "Thunder on Water" music festival and boat race.

Directions: From I-55: take Grenada exit for Hwy. 8. Take Hwy. 8 east from Grenada to Scenic Rte. 333 that goes to Grenada Lake.

Holly Springs

13 Site: MARSHALL COUNTY HISTORICAL MUSEUM, 220 East College, P.O. Box 806, Holly Springs, MS 38635, 601-252-3669

Description: The Civil War hit Holly Springs hard. Holly Springs and Marshall County produced 10 Confederate generals, 8 adjutant generals, and 9 members of the Confederate Congress. Holly Springs was chosen as Grant's headquarters and suffered 61 raids. Van Dorn's raid destroyed millions of dollars of Federal supplies.

Admission Fees: $2.

Open to Public: Mon.–Fri.: 10 A.M.–5 P.M.; Sat.: 10 A.M.–2 P.M.

Visitors Services: Museum; gift shop; information; rest rooms; handicapped access.

Regularly Scheduled Events: Annual tours of local Civil War sites: call for schedule.

Directions: From I-55 at Senatobia: travel east on Hwy. 4, 45 miles to Holly Springs and the museum. Located 42 miles southeast from Memphis on U.S. 78.; 60 miles northwest of Tupelo on U.S. 60; 17 miles southwest of Ashland on Hwy. 4; 30 miles north of Oxford on Hwy. 7.

Jackson

14 Site: MANSHIP HOUSE, 420 E. Fortification St., Jackson, MS 39202-2340, 601-961-4724

Description: The Manship House was the home of Charles Henry Manship, the mayor who surrendered Jackson to General Sherman on July 21, 1863.

Admission Fees: Free.

Open to Public: Tues.–Fri.: 9 A.M.–4 P.M.; Sat.: 1 P.M.–4 P.M.

Visitor Services: Museum; information; rest rooms; handicapped access.

Regularly Scheduled Events: *July:* Summer workshops for children.

Directions: From I-55: take Fortification St. exit; continue west on Fortification and turn right (north) onto Congress St. The first driveway on the left belongs to the Manship House parking lot. Visitors should enter the cream-colored visitor center for information and a guided tour.

---

15 **Site:** MISSISSIPPI GOVERNORS' MANSION, 300 Capitol St., Jackson, MS 39201, 601-359-6421

Description: The first occupation of Jackson occurred in May 1863 and then Governor John Pettus abandoned the mansion. He returned in July, only to have to leave again. He moved the capital to Meridian, Macon, and finally, Columbus, where Governor Charles Clark was inaugurated in November 1863. Clark moved the capital to Macon until the legislature reconvened in Jackson in May 1865. The mansion was not occupied until Governor Benjamin Humphreys in October 1965. During the two-and-half-year absence of a governor in the mansion, the house was used as a temporary shelter for wounded soldiers, and Gen. Sherman held a dinner there in July 1863.

Admission Fees: Free.

Open to Public: Tues.–Fri.: 9:30 A.M.–11 A.M.; closed two weeks in Dec. during public school vacation.

Visitor services: Museum; handicapped access.

Regularly Scheduled Events: *First Fri. in Dec.:* Candlelight tour.

Directions: From I-55: take Pearl St. exit (exit 96A). On exit, bear right onto Pearl St. viaduct. Cross South State St.; drive west to the intersection with West St.; turn right. The mansion is at the corner of West and Capitol Streets.

---

16 **Site:** THE OAKS HOUSE MUSEUM, 823 North Jefferson St., Jackson, MS 39202, 601-353-9339

Description: This house museum interprets the life of the James Boyd family from the 1840s to the 1860s. Gen. Grant's troops raided the house, and Gen. Sherman and his troops briefly used the house as a headquarters.

Admission Fees: Adults: $2; Children: $1; Groups (10 or more): $1.25/person.

Open to Public: Tues.–Sat.: 10 A.M.–3 P.M.

Visitor Services: Museum; information.

Directions: From I-55: take High St. exit (96B) west to North Jefferson St. Turn north on Jefferson St.; the museum is #823, on the west side of the street. There is a white picket fence in front of the house.

---

17 **Site:** OLD CAPITOL MUSEUM, Mississippi Department of Archives & History, P.O. Box 571, State St. at Capitol St., Jackson, MS 39205-0571, 601-359-6920

Description: This building was the site of Mississippi's Secession Convention, January 1861. It continued as the seat of state government until May 1863, when it was evacuated before the Battle of Jackson. Vandalized by Federal troops, it remained in Confederate hands, although legislative and state offices were removed to Macon, Mississippi. In October 1864, it served as a Confederate military headquarters.

Admission Fees: Free.

Open to Public: Mon.–Fri.: 8 A.M.–5 P.M.; Sat.: 9:30 A.M.–4:30 P.M.; Sun.: 12:30 P.M.–4:30 P.M.

Visitor Services: Museum; gift shop; information; rest rooms; handicapped access.

Regularly Scheduled Events: *Autumn:* Social studies teachers workshop (annual training session on varied topics for social studies teachers); *Dec.:* Christmas films, period trees, decorations, and electronic train.

Directions: From I-55: take Pearl St. exit to downtown Jackson; turn right at first light onto State St.; pass in front of building; turn right on Amite St. to enter parking lot behind building.

Natchez

18 | **Site:** LONGWOOD, 140 Lower Woodville Rd., Natchez, MS 39120, 601-442-5193

Description: Longwood provides a visitor with eloquent testimony to the devastating impact of the Civil War on the cotton economy of the American South. The tragic story of the hardships of the family who lived there "reared in the lap of luxury and reduced to poverty," has all the tragedy and pathos of *Gone with the Wind* but with a double reverse twist. First, it is true. Second, the family who lost everything was loyal to the Union. Work on the house, begun in 1860, stopped after war was declared in 1861. The northern workmen made their way home to Philadelphia through the blockade that was put on the South, leaving their tools on the workbench, where they remain.

Admission Fees: Adults: $5; Children: $2.50; Groups: $4/person.

Open to Public: *Tours:* Daily: 9 A.M.–5 P.M.; last tour at 4:30 P.M.

Visitor Services: Gift shop; information; rest rooms; handicapped access.

Regularly Scheduled Events: *Three weeks each Oct.:* Natchez Fall Pilgrimage; *Dec.:* Living history.

Directions: From I-120 at Vicksburg, MS: turn south on Hwy. 61; go approximately 75 miles to Natchez. From I-55 at Brookhaven, MS: turn west on Hwy. 84; go approximately 60 miles to Natchez.

19 | **Site:** MELROSE, P.O. Box 1208, Natchez, MS 39121, 601-442-7047

Description: The home of John T. McMurran, Melrose is an excellent

example of an antebellum Greek Revival estate. McMurran was a well-known

Natchez lawyer and planter from the 1830s to 1865, controlling cotton plantations in Mississippi, Arkansas, Louisiana, and Texas. Melrose's story is of the effect of the cotton-based economy on the political and social life of the South and of the Civil War on that economy.

Admission Fees: Admission to the grounds is free; *Guided tours of mansion:* Adults: $5; Children: $2.50; Seniors: $2.50.

Open to Public: Daily: 8:30 A.M.–5 P.M.

Visitor Services: Museum; gift shop; information; rest rooms; handicapped access.

Regularly Scheduled Events: *Mar.:* Spring pilgrimage; *Oct.:* Fall pilgrimage; *Dec.:* Christmas program.

Directions: From I-20 at Vicksburg: take U.S. 61 to Natchez. Turn right on Melrose Pkwy. and follow signs. From I-10 at Baton Rouge: take U.S. 61 to Natchez. Turn left on Melrose Pkwy. and follow signs.

---

20   **Site:** THE WILLIAM JOHNSON HOUSE, P.O. Box 1208, Natchez, MS 39121, 601-442-7047

Description: The home of a free black entrepreneur and diarist in antebellum Natchez, the William Johnson House provides a unique opportunity to glimpse a seldom interpreted part of Southern history. Born a slave, Johnson was freed by his father. He was educated and became a well-known Natchez businessman and slaveholder himself.

Admission Fees: Free.

Open to Public: Mar. and Oct.: Daily; other times as staffing permits: call for information.

Visitor Services: Information.

Directions: From I-20 at Vicksburg: take U.S. 61 to Natchez. Turn right on U.S. 84 toward the bridge. At Canal St. (just before the bridge) turn right. Follow Canal St. to State St. and turn right. Johnson House is on the right. From I-10 at Baton Rouge: take U.S. 61 to Natchez. Turn left on U.S. 84; follow it to Canal St. and turn right. Follow Canal St. to State St. and turn right. Johnson House is on the right.

Port Gibson

---

21   **Site:** GRAND GULF MILITARY MONUMENT, Rte. 2, P.O. Box 389, Port Gibson, MS 39150, 601-437-5911

Description: The river batteries at Grand Gulf were the southernmost leg of the Vicksburg defenses. Grant tried to land his army at Grand Gulf but was driven off by the Confederate batteries. After the Battle of Port Hudson, Grand Gulf became Grant's base of operations.

Admission Fees: Adults: $1.50; Children: $.75; Seniors: $1; Groups: Adults: $1; Children: $.50.

Open to Public: Mon.–Sat.: 8 A.M.–5 P.M.; Sun.: 9 A.M.–6 P.M..

Visitor Services: Camping; trails; museum; gift shop; information; rest rooms; handicapped access.

Regularly Scheduled Events: Civil War artillery demonstrations several times a year.

Directions: From I-20 at Vicksburg: take Hwy 61 south for 22 miles; turn right at Grand Gulf Rd.; proceed 7.5 miles to the site.

---

22 Site: PORT GIBSON BATTLEFIELD, Rte. 2, P.O. Box 389, Port Gibson, MS 39150, 601-437-5911

Description: The Shaifer House was the site of the opening shots in the Battle of Port Gibson. Confederate forces were entrenched at Magnolia Church. Part of the battle was fought on the Bruinsburg Road at Point Lookout.

Admission Fees: Free.

Open to Public: Daily: Dawn to dusk.

Visitor Services: None.

Regularly Scheduled Events: Infantry encampments two or three times a year.

Directions: From I-20 at Vicksburg: go south on Hwy. 61, 28 miles to Port Gibson; turn right on Carol St., proceed 4.5 miles and follow signs.

---

23 Site: WINDSOR RUINS, Department of Archives & History, 400 Jefferson Davis Blvd., Natchez, MS 39120, 601-446-6502

Description: The Windsor mansion was located near the extinct town of Bruinsburg, where Grant's army crossed the Mississippi River during April 30– May 1, 1863, to begin the campaign for the capture of Vicksburg. The mansion was located along the route of Grant's army on its march inland toward Jackson. Windsor Mansion was destroyed by accidental fire in 1890.

Admission Fees: Free.

Open to Public: Daily: Dawn to dusk.

Visitor Services: None.

Directions: From I-20: take the Natchez Trace Pkwy. south to the exit for County Hwy. 552; follow Hwy. 552, past the turnoff for Alcorn State University; follow the signs to the site entrance.

Ocean Springs

24 Site: FORT MASSACHUSETTS, Gulf Islands National Seashore, 3500 Park Rd., Ocean Springs, MS 39564, 601-875-9057

Description: With hostilities underway in 1861, Ship Island and Fort Massachusetts witnessed Confederate occupation; a brief land-naval battle; Federal occupation; creation of western Gulf Union navy headquarters and depot; military prisons, including prisoner-of-war camp; and the staging of 20,000 troops used to capture Confederate New Orleans and Mobile.

Admission Fees: Free.

Open to Public: Fort Massachusetts is normally open from arrival of the first ferryboat to the departure of the last vessel. This includes four hours at midday during spring and autumn and approximately eight hours in summer. Call for schedule.

Visitor Services: Lodging; gas; camping; trails; food; gift shop; information; rest rooms.

Directions: From I-10: take Hwy. 49 south to Gulfport, Mississippi, Small Craft Harbor. Board the ferry to Ship Island via Pan Isles Excursions; approximately one hour.

Raymond

25 Site: RAYMOND DRIVING TOUR, P.O. Box 10, Raymond, MS 39154, 601-857-8041

Description: The Raymond Driving Tour features three structures that stand as a reminder of the Battle of Raymond, fought outside this small community. The Raymond Courthouse, built in 1857–59 by the Weldon Brothers's skilled slave crew, is on the National Register of Historic Places and is an excellent example of Greek Revival architecture. It was used by the Confederate army as a hospital following the three-hour Battle of Raymond. St. Mark's Episcopal Church was organized in 1837, built in 1854, and is still an active church. Used as a hospital for Confederates after the battle, blood stains can still be seen on the floor of the sanctuary. The tour also includes Waverly, used as a temporary headquarters for Gen. Grant, and the Confederate cemetery.

Admission Fees: Free.

Open to Public: Brochure and map available from the city hall: Mon.–Fri.: 8 A.M.–5 P.M. Driving tour: Daily: Daylight hours. Interior tours of church and courthouse by appointment.

Visitor Services: Information.

Regularly Scheduled Events: *First Sat. of May:* 1860s Country Fair (Revival of Southern Culture with food, entertainment, crafts, and history).

Directions: From I-20 at Jackson: take exit 40A (Hwy. 18 south) 8 miles to Raymond. Drive to First St. and turn right. First St. becomes Main St. Turn right at the water tower; then bear left. City hall is a small building behind the courthouse. Park near the water tower; pick up a brochure at city hall.

Tupelo

26 **Site:** TUPELO NATIONAL BATTLEFIELD, Natchez Trace Pkwy., Rural Rte. 1, NT-143, Tupelo, MS 38801, 601-680-4025

Description: Tupelo National Battlefield is a one-acre site off the Natchez Trace Parkway where in July 1864 a battle was fought that served to keep Confederate General Nathan Bedford Forrest from altering the supply line that was essential to the success of Union General William T. Sherman. Neither side could claim victory.

Admission Fees: Free.

Open to Public: Daily: Dawn to dusk. *Gift Shop & Visitor Center:* Daily: 8 A.M.–5 P.M.

Visitor Services: Gift shop; information; rest rooms; handicapped access.

Directions: Take Hwy. 78 to the Natchez Trace Pkwy.; go south on the Natchez Trace Pkwy. for 4 miles to MS Hwy. 6 (Main St.) exit; turn left onto MS Hwy. 6; go 1 mile to battlefield site.

Vicksburg

27 **Site:** BALFOUR HOUSE, 1002 Crawford St., P.O. Box 781, Vicksburg, MS 39181, 601-638-7113 or 800-294-7113

Description: Balfour House was the home of famous siege diarist Emma Balfour. It was also the Union headquarters after the fall of Vicksburg.

Admission Fees: *Tours:* Adults: $5; Children: $2; Seniors: $4; Groups (15 or more): $4.

Open to Public: Mon.–Sat.: 9 A.M.–5 P.M.; Sun.: 1 P.M.–5 P.M.

Visitor Services: Lodging; food; information; rest rooms; handicapped access.

Regularly Scheduled Events: *July 4:* Living history reenactment of 1862; *Dec.:* Christmas ball.

Directions: From I-20 west: take Halls Ferry Rd. exit; turn left; go to Cherry St.; turn right. From I-20 east: take Clay St. exit; proceed to Cherry St.; turn left; go one block to site. Located at corner of Cherry and Crawford Streets.

Balfour House, Vicksburg, MS. (Photograph courtesy of Balfour House.)

THE CAMPAIGN FOR VICKSBURG

Between Cairo, Ill., and the Gulf of Mexico, the Mississippi River meanders over a course nearly 1,000 miles long. During the Civil War, control of this stretch was of vital importance to the Federal government. Command of that waterway would allow uninterrupted flow of Union troops and supplies into the South. It would also have the desired effect of isolating the states of Texas, Arkansas, and most of Louisiana, comprising nearly half the land area of the Confederacy and a region on which the South depended heavily for supplies and recruits.

From the beginning of the war in 1861, the Confederates, to protect this vital lifeline, erected fortifications at strategic points along the river. Federal forces, however, fighting their way southward from Illinois and northward from the Gulf, captured post after post, until by late summer of 1862 only Vicksburg and Port Hudson posed major obstacles to Union domination of the Mississippi. Of the two posts, Vicksburg was the strongest and most important. It sat on a high bluff overlooking a bend in the river, protected by artillery batteries along the riverfront and by a maze of swamps and bayous to the north and south. President Lincoln called Vicksburg "the key" and believed that "the war can never be brought to a close until that key is in our pocket." So far the city had defied Union efforts to force it into submission.

In October 1862, Ulysses S. Grant was appointed commander of the Department of the Tennessee and charged with clearing the Mississippi of Confederate resistance. That same month, Lt. Gen. John C. Pemberton, a West Point graduate and a Pennsylvanian by birth, assumed command of the 50,000 widely scattered Confederate troops defending the Mississippi. His orders were to keep the river open. Vicksburg became the focus of military operations for both men.

During the winter of 1862–63, Grant conducted a series of amphibious operations (often referred to as Bayou Expeditions) aimed at reducing Vicksburg. All of them failed. By spring Grant had decided to march his army of approximately 45,000 men down the west (Louisiana) bank of the Mississippi, cross the river well below Vicksburg, and then swing into position to attack the city from the south.

On March 31, 1863, Grant moved his army south from its encampments at Milliken's Bend, 20 miles northwest of Vicksburg. By April 28 the Northerners were established at Hard Times on the Mississippi above Grand Gulf. On the 29th Adm. David D. Porter's gunboats bombarded the Confederate forts at Grand Gulf to prepare the way for a crossing, but the attack was repulsed. Undaunted, Grant marched his troops a little farther south and, on April 30, stormed across at Bruinsburg.

Striking rapidly eastward to secure the bridgehead, the Northerners met elements of Pemberton's Confederate forces near Port Gibson on May 1. The Southerners fought a gallant holding action, but they were overwhelmed and fell back toward Vicksburg. After meeting and defeating a small Confederate force near Raymond on May 12, Grant's troops attacked and captured Jackson, the state capital, on May 14, scattering the Southern defenders.

Turning his army westward, Grant moved toward Vicksburg along the line of the Southern Railroad of Mississippi. At Champion Hill on May 16 and at Big Black River Bridge on May 17, his soldiers attacked and overwhelmed Pemberton's disorganized Confederates, driving them back into the Vicksburg fortifications. By May 18, advance units of the Federal army were approaching the bristling Confederate defenses.

Believing that the battles of Champion Hill and Big Black River Bridge had broken the Confederate morale, Grant immediately scheduled an assault on the Vicksburg lines. The first attack took place against the Stockade Redan on May 19. It failed. A second attack, launched on the morning of May 22, was also repulsed.

Realizing that it was useless to expend further lives in attempts to take the city by storm, Grant reluctantly began formal siege operations. Batteries of artillery were established to hammer the Confederate fortifications from the land side, while Admiral Porter's gunboats cut off communications and blasted the city from the river. By the end of June, with little hope of relief and no chance to break out of the Federal cordon, Pemberton knew that it was only a matter of time before he must "capitulate upon the best attainable terms." On the afternoon of July 3, he met with Grant to discuss terms for the surrender of Vicksburg.

Grant demanded unconditional surrender; Pemberton refused. The meeting broke up. During the afternoon, the Federal commander modified his demands and agreed to let the Confederates sign paroles not to fight again until exchanged. In addition, officers could retain sidearms and a mount. Pemberton accepted these terms, and at 10 A.M. on July 4, 1863, Vicksburg was officially surrendered.

When Port Hudson surrendered five days later, the great Northern objective of the war in the West—the opening of the Mississippi River and the severing of the Confederacy—was at last realized. For the first time since the war began, the Mississippi was free of Confederate troops and fortifications. As President Lincoln put it, "The Father of Waters again goes unvexed to the sea."

---

28 Site: OLD COURTHOUSE MUSEUM—EVA W. DAVIS MEMORIAL, 1008 Cherry St., Vicksburg, MS 39180, 601-636-0741

Description: During the Siege of Vicksburg in 1863, Union prisoners were housed in this courthouse. The U.S. flag was raised and Grant reviewed his troops. In earlier years (1843) Jefferson Davis launched his political career on the grounds.

Admission Fees: Adults: $2; Children: $1; Seniors: $1.50; Groups (10 or more): Adults: $1.25/person; Children: $.75/person.

Open to Public: Mon.–Sat.: 8:30 A.M.–5 P.M.; Sun.: 1:30 P.M.–5 P.M. NOTE: Oct.–Apr.: closes at 4:30 P.M.

Visitor Services: Museum; gift shop; information; rest rooms; handicapped access.

Directions: From I-20: take Clay St. exit to Cherry St.; turn right.

Site: VICKSBURG NATIONAL MILITARY PARK, 3201 Clay St., Vicksburg, MS 39180, 601-636-0583

Description: Vicksburg National Military Park was established in 1899 to commemorate the Campaign, Siege, and Defense of Vicksburg that took place in 1863. The focus of Union land and naval operations along the Mississippi River, the city fell to General Ulysses S. Grant after a lengthy campaign and 47-day siege on July 4, 1863. The fall of Vicksburg gave the North control of the river, severed a major Confederate supply line that ran east-west through Vicksburg, achieved a major objective of the Anaconda Plan, and effectively sealed the doom of Richmond.

Admission Fees: Cars: $4; School groups: Free.

Open to Public: Daily: 8 A.M.–5 P.M.

Visitor Services: Trails; museum; gift shop; information; rest rooms; handicapped access.

Directions: From I-20: take exit 4B.; follow signs.

Site: THE VICKSBURG CAMPAIGN TRAIL

Points of interest located throughout Mississippi are:

- Big Black Battlefield
- Champion Hill Battlefield
- Confederate Cemetery— Raymond
- Grand Gulf Military Monument Park
- Jackson Battlefield
- Port Gibson Battlefield
- Raymond Battlefield
- Vicksburg National Military Park
- Windsor Ruins

Description: Nationally significant sites associated with Union Major General Ulysses S. Grant's brilliant Campaign and Siege of Vicksburg (April–July 1863).

Directions: Available in "A Guide to the Campaign & Siege of Vicksburg," which provides a self-guided driving tour of these sites. The guide is available free from Mississippi Division of Tourism Development, P.O. Box 1705, Ocean Springs, MS 39566-1705; 1-800-WARMEST. It may be purchased at the sales shops at the following Civil War Discovery Trail sites: Grand Gulf Military Monument Park, Old Capitol Museum, Shiloh National Military Park, and Vicksburg National Military Park.

West Point

31 **Site:** WAVERLEY PLANTATION MANSION, Rte. 2, P.O Box 234, West Point, MS 39773, 601-494-1399

Description: Waverley is a National Historic Landmark Greek Revival home that commemorates the antebellum South. The plantation was a self-sustaining community complete with gardens, orchards, and livestock. In later years, Waverley had its own lumber mill, tannery, and hat-manufacturing operation. Gen. Nathan Bedford Forrest was a friend and frequent visitor of the owner, Col. George Hampton Young. Gen. Forrest spent three weeks recuperating at Waverley during the Civil War. He resided in the Egyptian Room and used the place as a headquarters. The octagonal cupola of the home served as an observation point for watching the river and the prairie for troop movement. Waverley features 20 acres of landscaped gardens with peacocks and black swans.

Admission Fees: Adults: $7.50; Children under 6: Free; Groups (25 or more): $6/person; School groups: $5/person.

Open to Public: *Summer:* Daily: 9 A.M.–6:30 P.M.; *Winter:* Daily: 9 A.M.–5:30 P.M.

Visitor Services: Tours; trails; gift shop; information; rest rooms.

Regularly Scheduled Events: Spring Pilgrimage of Homes and Garden Ball: Call for schedule; *Dec:* Antebellum Christmas.

Directions: Located 15 minutes from Columbus; 1 mile off Hwy. 50 between Columbus and West Point, near the Tenn-Tom Waterway.

Woodville

32 Site: ROSEMONT PLANTATION/HOME OF JEFFERSON DAVIS, P.O. Box 814, Hwy. 24 East, Woodville, MS 39669, 601-888-6809

Description: This is the family home of President Jefferson Davis, built by his parents in 1810 and the family home until 1895.

Admission Fees: Adults: $6; Children: $3.

Open to Public: Mar.–Dec. 15: Mon.–Fri.: 10 A.M.–5 P.M.

Visitor Services: Museum; information; rest rooms.

Directions: One mile off U.S. 61 on Hwy. 24; marked by state highway signs.

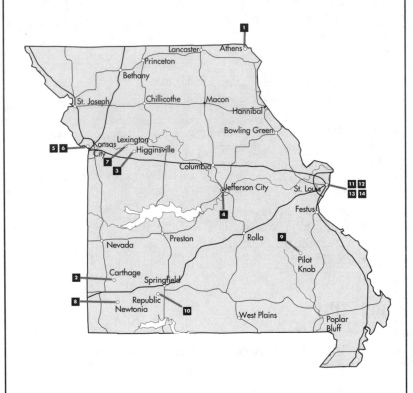

Missouri

Lancaster · Athens · **1**
Princeton
Bethany
St. Joseph
Chillicothe · Macon
Hannibal
Bowling Green
Lexington
5 **6** Kansas City · Higginsville
7
3
Columbia
Jefferson City · St. Louis **11** **12**
13 **14**
4
Festus
Preston · Rolla
Nevada · **9**
Pilot Knob
2 Carthage
Springfield
8 Republic
Newtonia · **10**
West Plains
Poplar Bluff

1 Battle of Athens State Historic Site
2 Battle of Carthage State Historic Site
3 Confederate Memorial State Historic Site
4 Missouri State Capitol and State Museum
5 Battle of Westport
6 Forest Hill Cemetery
7 Battle of Lexington State Historic Site
8 Newtonia Battlefield
9 Fort Davidson State Historic Site
10 Wilson's Creek National Battlefield
11 Bellefontaine Cemetery
12 Calvary Cemetery
13 Jefferson Barracks Historic Site
14 Ulysses S. Grant National Historic Site

MISSOURI

At the outset of the Civil War, Missouri was a peninsula of slavery surrounded on three sides by free states. It was in every sense and at every level a true border state, racked by conflicting loyalties and deep internal divisions. Missouri's star adorned the flags of both sides: While a provisional unionist government ruled from the capital, Jefferson City, an exiled Confederate government held sway first from Arkansas and then from Marshall, Texas. Early in 1861, a specially elected state convention determined that Missouri should remain in the Union but participate in no actions to coerce the seceding states of the South. This hardly settled the issue, and competing secessionist and unionist factions waged a vigorous contest to determine Missouri's eventual loyalties. The North won this contest in the sense of gaining nominal control over the political and military administration of the state, but deep-seated southern loyalties on the part of much of the state's population were never successfully suppressed.

Although the conflict in Missouri was, by and large, a sideshow of the main war being conducted east of the Mississippi, the struggle within the state was a singularly vicious one that included not only large battles on the scale of Wilson's Creek, Pilot Knob, or Westport, but also hundreds of smaller conflicts. With nearly 1,200 battles and skirmishes of record, Missouri ranks third in total number of conflicts behind Virginia and Tennessee. Every year of the war saw armed challenges to Union occupation in the form of Confederate invasions, raiding and recruiting parties launched from Arkansas, and from guerrilla warfare, fought under the black flag with no quarter, that grew more vicious with each passing season.

Sixty percent of Missouri's men of military age marched off to fight for one side or the other. There were 110,000 men, including 8,400 black troops, who fought for the North, while some 30,000 to 40,000—the exact number is not known—donned Confederate gray.

by James M. Denny, Missouri Department of Natural Resources

Athens

Site: BATTLE OF ATHENS STATE HISTORIC SITE, located off State Hwy. 81 on Hwy. CC in Clark Co., mailing address: Revere, MO 63465, 800-334-6946 (state park toll-free number, Mon.–Fri., 8 A.M.–5 P.M.) or 816-877-3871

Description: Site of northernmost Civil War battle west of the Mississippi, fought on August 5, 1861. Thome-Benning House (open to public) was struck by Southern artillery fire during the battle and has since been known as the Cannonball House.

Admission Fees: *Grounds and recreation areas:* Free. *Guided tour:* Adults: $2; Children: $.50.

Open to Public: *Grounds:* Dawn to dusk. *Thome-Benning House:* Mon.–Sat.: 10 A.M.– 4 P.M.; Sun. and holiday hours vary.

Visitor Services: Trails; tours; museum (in Thome-Benning House); information; rest rooms; camping; picnicking; hiking; fishing; boating.

Regularly Scheduled Events: *Every three years:* Major Civil War reenactment of the battle; *Spring and Christmas:* Open house; Annual celebration of the battle and ice-fishing contest: call for schedule. To receive free schedule of Special Events and Programs for parks and historic sites and other information, call 1-800-334-6946, Mon.–Fri.: 8 A.M.–5 P.M.

Directions: From I-70: take State Hwy. 61 (Wentzville) exit (exit 210); proceed north on Hwy. 61 approximately 135 miles to State Hwy. 81 at Canton; proceed north on Hwy. 81 for approximately 40 miles to Highway CC, and follow east 3 miles to Athens.

Carthage

2 Site: BATTLE OF CARTHAGE STATE HISTORIC SITE, located in Carthage on the north side of East Chestnut Street, next to Carter Park; managed by Harry S. Truman Birthplace State Historic Site, 1009 Truman St., Lamar, MO 64759, 800-334-6946 (state park toll-free number, Mon.–Fri., 8 A.M.–5 P.M.) or 417-682-2279.

Description: This 7.4-acre tract was the site of the final confrontation of the Battle of Carthage—a day-long running skirmish that began on July 5, 1861, some 9 miles northeast of Carthage. An interpretative shelter with displays explains the history of this early armed confrontation (it preceded the first Battle of Bull Run by 17 days).

Admission Fees: Free.

Open to Public: Daily: Dawn to dusk.

Visitor Services: Information.

Directions: From I-44: take State Hwy. 71 (Carthage exit), exit 18; proceed north on 71 for 6 miles to Hwy. 571 at Carthage; travel east on Chestnut St. 10 blocks to site.

Higginsville

3 Site: CONFEDERATE MEMORIAL STATE HISTORIC SITE, Route 1, P.O. Box 221-A, Higginsville, MO 64037, 800-334-6946 (state park toll-free number, Mon.–Fri.: 8 A.M.–5 P.M.) or 816-584-2853

Description: 115-acre site contains the grounds of the Confederate veterans home, a historic chapel, and a cemetery containing more than 800 graves. The site serves as a memorial to the 30,000 to 40,000 Missourians who fought for the Stars and Bars. There are picnic tables and several small fishing lakes on the grounds.

Admission Fees: Free.

Open to Public: *Grounds:* Daily: Dawn to dusk. *Chapel and museum:* Mon.–Sat.: 10 A.M.–4 P.M.; Sun. and holiday hours vary: call for schedule.

Visitor Services: Museum; information; rest rooms; picnicking.

Regularly Scheduled Events: To receive free schedule of Special Events and Programs for parks and historic sites and other information call 800-334-6946 (Mon.–Fri.: 8 A.M.–5 P.M.).

Directions: From I-70: take Lexington-Higginsville exit (exit 49); proceed north on State Hwy. 13 for 6 miles to State Hwy. 20; proceed east on Highway 20 for 1 mile to site.

Jefferson City

4 Site: MISSOURI STATE CAPITOL AND STATE MUSEUM, Room B-2, State Capitol, Jefferson City, MO 65101, 800-334-6946 (state park toll-free number, Mon.–Fri.: 8 A.M.–5 P.M.) or 314-751-4127.

Description: The capitol, built between 1913 and 1917, contains the legislative chambers and state offices. Flanking either side of the magnificent rotunda is the Missouri State Museum. The museum features several exhibits on the Civil War and a collection of battle flags as well as other displays pertaining to the state's history and natural resources.

Admission Fees: Free.

Open to Public: Daily: except Jan. 1, Easter, Thanksgiving, and Christmas. Tours are available from 8 A.M.–11:30 A.M. and

1 P.M.–4 P.M., every half hour weekdays and every hour on Sat., Sun., and some holidays. For reservations for group tours, call 314-751-4127.

Visitor Services: Guided tours; museum; information; rest rooms; food; gift shop; handicapped access.

Directions: From I-70: take State Hwy. 63 exit (Jefferson City exit/exit 128a); proceed south on Hwy. 63 to Jefferson City; take first exit after crossing Missouri River; turn east on West Main St. to Capitol.

Kansas City

5 Site: BATTLE OF WESTPORT, c/o Monnett Battle of Westport Fund, Inc. of the Civil War Round Table of Kansas City; 1130 Westport Road, Kansas City, MO 64111, 816-931-6620.

Description: The Battle of Westport, fought on Oct. 21–23, was the largest battle west of the Mississippi River and the decisive battle of Price's 1864 Missouri Campaign. Directions (*see* "Directions" section) guide the visitor to the first of 25 narrative markers on a 32-mile, self-guided automobile tour and a self-guided walking tour of Byram's Ford and the Big Blue Battlefield, where a major part of the battle occurred. Each marker provides directions to the next stop on the tour. A written brochure is available from the address listed above.

Admission Fees: Free.

Open to Public: Daily: Dawn to dusk.

Visitor Services: Self-guided tour; information; guided bus tours are available on request.

Directions: From I-70: take I-435 from west or I-470 from east to State Highway 71; proceed north to Ward Parkway; proceed west on Ward Parkway to Broadway; proceed north on Broadway to Westport Rd.; proceed west on Westport Rd. one block to marker No. 1 at corner of Westport Rd. and Broadway.

---

6   **Site:** FOREST HILL CEMETERY, 6901 Troost Ave., Kansas City, MO 64111, 816-523-2114

Description: This cemetery is on the site of Gen. J. O. Shelby's heroic stand that saved Price's army. A large Confederate monument in the cemetery is surrounded by graves of the Confederate dead, including the celebrated Confederate cavalryman, Gen. J. O. Shelby.

Admission Fees: Free.

Open to Public: Daily: Dawn to dusk.

Visitor Services: None.

Directions: From I-70: take I-435 from west or I-470 from east to State Hwy. 71; proceed north on Hwy. 71 to 75th St.; proceed west on 75th St. to Troost Ave.; proceed north on Troost Ave. to cemetery.

Lexington

7   **Site:** BATTLE OF LEXINGTON STATE HISTORIC SITE, located on 13th St., mailing address: P.O. Box 6, Lexington, MO 64067, 800-334-6946 (state park toll-free number, Mon.–Fri.: 8 A.M.–5 P.M.) or 816-259-4654

Description: Site of the famous "Battle of the Hemp Bales" fought on September 18–20, 1861; victorious Southerners under Gen. Sterling Price besieged and captured a Union garrison. A 106-acre section of the battlefield is preserved as is the Anderson House, a brick mansion that served as a field hospital and was occupied by both sides during the battle.

Admission Fees: *Tour:* Adults: $2; Children: $.50.

Open to Public: *Battlefield grounds:* Daily: Dawn to dusk. *Visitor Center and Anderson House:* Mon.–Sat.: 10 A.M.–4:20 P.M.; Sun. and holiday hours vary.

Visitor Services: Self-guided walking tour of battlefield; tours; museum;

information; gift shop; visitors center; rest rooms; visitor center is handicapped accessible.

Regularly Scheduled Events: *Every three years:* Major Civil War reenactment of the battle; *Apr.:* Kite Day; *Sept.:* Old Homes tour; *Dec.:* Christmas candlelight tour of Anderson House. To receive free schedule of Special Events and Programs for parks and historic sites and other information, call 800-334-6946, Mon.–Fri.: 8 A.M.–5 P.M.

Directions: From I-70: take Lexington-Higginsville exit (exit 49); proceed north on State Hwy. 13 for 20 miles to Lexington; take 13th St. to site.

Newtonia

8 | **Site:** NEWTONIA BATTLEFIELD, P.O. Box 106, Newtonia, MO 64850, 417-451-1040 (ask for Tom Higdon) or 417-451-3415

Description: Two major Civil War battles were fought at Newtonia—one on September 30, 1862, and the other on October 28, 1864. The first battle pitted Brig. Gen. James Blunt against Col. J. O. Shelby. Confederate forces numbered about 4,000; Union forces numbered about 6,500. The 1862 battle was one of the very few Civil War encounters in which Native Americans fought on both sides. Southern forces had Choctaw, Cherokee, and Chickasaw soldiers, while other Cherokee soldiers fought with the North. The 1864 battle was a delaying action by Shelby to protect Gen. Sterling Price's retreat to Arkansas. It was the last battle of the Civil War fought west of the Mississippi.

Admission Fees: Free.

Open to Public: Daily: Daylight hours.

Visitor Services: Trails; information (brochure available at Dillion's store in Newtonia); tours by appointment.

Directions: From I-44: take Alternate 71 south and proceed to Hwy. 86, just south of Granby. Hwy. 86 leads straight into Newtonia. Turn left on County Rd. M.; proceed one block and turn right on Mill. Dillion's is three blocks down on Mill, just past the Ritchey Mansion. Pick up brochure and begin tour.

Pilot Knob

9 | **Site:** FORT DAVIDSON STATE HISTORIC SITE, P.O. Box 509, Pilot Knob, MO 63663, 800-334-6946 (state park toll-free number, Mon.–Fri.: 8 A.M.–5 P.M.) or 314-546-3454

Description: Site of earthwork remnants of Fort Davidson, which was assaulted by the forces of Maj. Gen. Sterling Price on September 27, 1864, during the two day Battle of Pilot Knob. Some 1,200 Confederates fell within an hour in an unsuccessful effort to capture the fort held by General Thomas Ewing Jr. and 1,450 men.

Admission Fees: Free.

Open to Public: *Fort and surrounding grounds:* Daily: Dawn to dusk. *Visitor Center:* Mon.–Sat.: 10 A.M.–4 P.M.: Sun. and holiday hours vary; call for schedule.

Visitor Services: Tours; museum; information; visitors center; rest rooms; handicapped access.

Regularly Scheduled Events: *Every three years:* Major Civil War reenactment of the battle.

Directions: From I-55 at Cape Girardeau: take State Hwy. 72 (exit 99); proceed west approximately 70 miles to Ironton; turn north on State Hwy. 21; proceed 2 miles to Rte. V and turn right to site.

Republic

10 **Site:** WILSON'S CREEK NATIONAL BATTLEFIELD, 6424 West Farm Road 182, Republic, MO 65738, 417-732-2662

Ray House at Wilson's Creek National Battlefield, Republic, MO. (Photograph courtesy of National Park Service and Eastern National.)

Description: The Battle of Wilson's Creek (called Oak Hills by the Confederates) was fought on August 10, 1861. Named for the stream that crosses the area where it took place, the battle was a bitter struggle between Union and Confederate forces for control of Missouri in the first year of the Civil War.

Admission Fees: Adults: $2; Family: $4 maximum.

Open to Public: Daily: 8 A.M.–5 P.M.; call for extended spring and summer hours; Closed Christmas and New Year's Day.

Visitor Services: Trails; tours; museum; information; gift shop; visitors center; rest rooms; handicapped access to the visitors center and the Ray House.

Regularly Scheduled Events: *Open on weekends June–Labor Day:* Historic Ray House; *June:* Civil War music; *Weekends in summer:* Musket and artillery demonstrations; *Aug. 10:* Anniversary celebration; *Weekend in Aug. after the anniversary:* Moonlight Bloody Hill tour.

Directions: From I-44: take exit 70 (MO MM; becomes MO M) south to U.S. 60; cross U.S. 60 and drive three-quarters of a mile to MO ZZ and turn south. The battlefield is located 2 miles south on MO ZZ. From U.S. 60 and U.S. 65: take the James River Expressway to MO FF; turn left (south) on FF; proceed to MO M and turn right (west). Proceed to MO ZZ and turn south; travel 2 miles to the park.

St. Louis

 Site: BELLEFONTAINE CEMETERY, 4947 West Florissant, St. Louis, MO 63115, 314-381-0750

Description: Many Civil War notables are buried in this beautiful cemetery: Edward Bates, Lincoln's attorney general; Union Major Generals Frank P. Blair Jr. and John Pope; Confederate Maj. Gen. Sterling Price; Confederate senator and later U.S. senator George Graham Vest; unionist provisional governor Hamilton Gamble; ironclad boat builder James B. Eads; and many others.

Admission Fees: Free.

Open to Public: *Grounds:* Daily: 8 A.M.– 5 P.M.; *Cemetery office:* Mon.–Fri.: 8 A.M.– 4:30 P.M.

Visitor Services: Information on burial locations available in office.

Directions: From I-70: take West Florissant exit (exit 245B) and proceed north approximately .7 mile to cemetery (next to Calvary Cemetery).

---

12 Site: CALVARY CEMETERY, 5239 West Florissant, St. Louis, MO 63115, 314-381-1313

Description: This Catholic cemetery contains the grave of Gen. William T. Sherman. Several other prominent Civil War personages are interred here, including Thomas Reynolds, Confederate governor-in-exile.

Admission Fees: Free.

Open to Public: *Grounds:* Daily: 8 A.M.– 5 P.M. *Office:* Mon.–Fri.: 8:30 A.M.–4:30 P.M.; Sat.: 8:30 A.M.–12:30 P.M.

Visitor Services: Information on burial locations available in the office.

Directions: From I-70: take West Florissant exit (exit 245B) and proceed north approximately 1.1 miles to cemetery (next to Bellefontaine Cemetery).

---

13 Site: JEFFERSON BARRACKS HISTORIC SITE, 533 Grant Rd., St. Louis, MO 63125-4121, 314-544-5714, 314-544-5790

Description: In 1861, troops from Jefferson Barracks, led by Nathaniel Lyon, participated in the "Camp Jackson Affair," which saved the St. Louis Arsenal from pro-secessionist state forces. In 1862, Jefferson Barracks was turned over to the Medical Department of the U.S. Army and became one of the largest and most important Federal hospitals in the country. Sick and wounded soldiers were brought to Jefferson Barracks by riverboat and railroad car. In 1864, Jefferson Barracks became a concentration point for the defense of St. Louis during "Price's

Raid," the last major Confederate invasion of Missouri. In 1866, a national cemetery was established at Jefferson Barracks.

Admission Fees: Free. NOTE: There may be a small charge for special events and exhibits.

Open to Public: Tues.–Sat.: 10 A.M.–5 P.M.; Sun.: Noon–5 P.M..; Closed Thanksgiving, Christmas, and New Year's Day.

Visitor Services: Trails; tours; museum; information; gift shop; visitors center; rest rooms; camping; improvements for handicapped access underway—call for status.

Regularly Scheduled Events: *Held throughout year:* Native American powwows; *Spring:* World War II weekend; *Dec:* Holiday at Barracks; Other events include Civil War battle reenactments and living history and French Colonial weekend: call for schedule.

Directions: From I-255: exit at Telegraph Rd. and proceed north. At a "Y" intersection, take the right fork (straight) onto Kingston. Follow Kingston to South Broadway and turn right. South Broadway leads to the park. At the park, go through the left opening in the gate and proceed on Grant Rd. to the historic area and the stone buildings that house the museum.

---

14 **Site:** ULYSSES S. GRANT NATIONAL HISTORIC SITE, 7400 Grant Road, St. Louis, MO 63123, 314-842-3298

Description: The Ulysses S. Grant National Historic Site encompasses 5 historic structures from the core of a 1000-acre plantation owned by General Grant. The personal life and the partnership with his wife, Julia Dent Grant, provide the context for understanding his military leadership as Union General during the Civil War and his subsequent Presidency.

Admission Fees: Free.

Open to Public: Daily: 9 A.M.–4:30 P.M.; Closed Thanksgiving, Christmas, and New Year's Day.

Visitor Services: Tours; information; gift shop; visitors center; handicapped access.

Regularly Scheduled Events: *Apr.:* Grant's birthday celebration; *Aug.:* Past residents of White Haven living history; *Dec.:* Christmas and New Year's holiday celebration; *Summer:* Evening programs; call for schedule.

Directions: Located in suburban St. Louis County, immediately across from the Anheuser-Busch "Grant's Farm" attraction. From I-270: exit at Gravois Rd. and go northeast approximately 2.5 miles. Turn left onto Grant Rd. The site is approximately .5 mile down on the left. Enter via the one-lane drive over an abandoned railroad berm. Limited parking for passenger vehicles; drivers of motor homes and buses should call the visitor center concerning access.

NEW MEXICO

$\mathcal{B}$ecause of centuries of colonial isolation under Spanish dominion and its comparatively recent ascension to the United States (in 1846), New Mexico was never outwardly courted by the Union and Confederacy. Also, the territory was poor, and its population was sparse.

New Mexico's role in the Civil War was comparatively minor. However, vital business partnerships with the prosperous North— brought about by the influence of the Santa Fe Trail— were an important factor in rallying sympathy for the North. The territory helped thwart an 1862 invasion by Texas Confederates who were intent on capturing Fort Union, located on the Santa Fe Trail in northeast New Mexico, and then on leaping into Colorado Territory to seize the gold fields for the struggling Confederacy.

At the outbreak of the Civil War, the commander of Fort Union, Henry H. Sibley, resigned his commission and returned to his native Texas. He was placed in command of a force of Texas Confederates, which he then led into New Mexico. The territory's populace, however, did not flock to the Confederate cause. If anything, it stayed away, leaving the invasion force to forage for supplies as it continued up the Rio Grande Valley.

Initially, the Texans defeated a U.S. force at the Battle of Valverde in February, 1862. Shortly afterward, the Confederates seized Albuquerque, then Santa Fe. Meanwhile, a ragtag army of Colorado volunteers marched into New Mexico and strengthened a force of U.S. troops from Fort Union. The combined force then met and defeated the Texas Confederates at the decisive battle of Glorieta Pass in March, 1862. Soon afterward, the Texans retreated south to El Paso, the lone invasion of New Mexico having ended.

Historians regard this as the westernmost campaign of the Civil War.

by Michael E. Pitel, New Mexico Department of Tourism

Pecos

 Site: GLORIETTA BATTLEFIELD, Glorietta Unit, Pecos National Historical Park,
P.O. Drawer 418, Pecos, NM 87552-0418, 505-757-6032

Description: Pecos National Historical Park preserves two sites associated with the Civil War Battle of Glorieta Pass— Apache Canyon (also called Canoncito)

and Pigeon's Ranch. Texan and Colorado volunteers skirmished at Apache Canyon on March 26, 1862. The final encounter took place at Pigeon's Ranch on March 28,

New Mexico

1 Glorietta Battlefield, Glorietta Unit, Pecos National Historical Park
2 Fort Craig

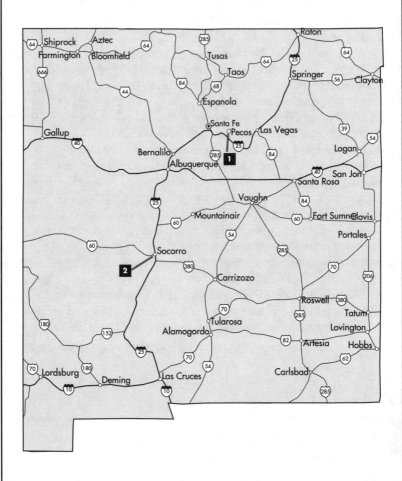

1862. Texan troops withdrew after their supplies were destroyed at Apache Canyon on the 28th. The battle ended the Confederate attempt to gain Federal supplies at Fort Union and the plans to invade Colorado and California. The park also preserves Kozlowski's Ranch—the site of the Union field headquarters during the battle. Much of the Glorietta Battlefield is still in private ownership. The sites are currently closed to public visitation. The visitor center at Pecos National Historical Park contains exhibits and information relating to the battle. Rangers can orient visitors to battle sites. Special talks and tours can also be arranged.

Admission Fees: $2/person.

Open to Public: Visitors Center: Daily: 8 A.M.–5 P.M.; Memorial Day–Labor Day: Open daily until 6 P.M.; closed Christmas.

Visitor Services: Ruins trail; museum; visitors center; rest rooms; ruins trail is 80 percent wheelchair accessible.

Regularly Scheduled Events: *Summer:* Civil War encampment.

Directions: From I-25, southeast of Santa Fe: take exit 290 or 307.

View of Glorietta Battlefield looking northeast from present-day landmark Sharpshooter's Ridge. (Photograph courtesy of Pecos National Historical Park.)

Socorro

2 **Site:** FORT CRAIG, BLM Special Management Area, c/o U.S. Bureau of Land Management, Socorro Resource Area, 198 Neal St., Socorro, NM 87801, 505-835-0412

Description: In February, 1862, the fort supplied U.S. troops to thwart the invasion of Texas Confederates under the command of Gen. Henry H. Sibley. Troops from the fort, under the command of Col. R. S. Canby, bolstered by a contingent of New Mexico volunteers commanded by Kit Carson, engaged Sibley's invasion force at a nearby crossing of the Rio Grande. The day-long Battle of Valverde on Feb. 21, 1862, was a decisive Confederate victory. However, the U.S. troops retreated into the fort, which was never attacked. Sibley's Confederates pressed northward to siege Albuquerque and Santa Fe. Their goal was the capture of Fort Union and the Colorado gold fields. Sibley's troops were defeated one month later, southeast of Santa Fe. Today Fort Craig is in ruins.

Admission Fees: Free.

Open to Public: Daily: Dawn to dusk.

Visitor Services: Trails; tours; information. NOTE: gravel paths; primitive conditions.

Directions: From I-25: take San Marcial exit; take Hwy. 1 and follow the signs. Fort Craig is approximately 10 miles from I-25 and located 32 miles from Socorro and 121 miles from Las Cruces.

NORTH CAROLINA

*A*lthough among the last states to join the Confederacy, North Carolina suffered greatly during the war years. The state served as a vital supply center, furnishing the South's armies with food, arms, and medical equipment. More important, the state also provided 125,000 men, one-sixth of all Confederate soldiers. North Carolina's total loss in battle and from disease was greater than any other Southern state.

Eleven battles and approximately 74 skirmishes were fought on Tar Heel soil. There were four major military operations: the conquest of the sound region, the capture of Fort Fisher and Wilmington, Stoneman's raid, and Sherman's invasion.

The war resulted in 40,000 lost Tar Heel lives, destroyed factories and railroads, and a shattered state economy. At the war's end, the long task of rebuilding was begun in earnest. By 1868 sufficient progress had been made, and the state was readmitted to the Union.

Atlantic Beach

1 **Site:** FORT MACON STATE PARK, P.O. Box 127, Atlantic Beach, NC 28512, 919-726-8598

Description: Construction of this brick fort began in 1826. The fort was garrisoned in 1834 and named after U.S. Senator Nathaniel Macon. At the start of the Civil War, North Carolina seized Fort Macon from Union forces. The Confederate force was later attacked in 1862, and the fort fell into Union hands. For the duration of the war, the fort protected ships recoaling in Beaufort. Fort Macon was a federal prison from 1867 until 1876, garrisoned during the Spanish-American War, and closed in 1903.

Admission Fees: Free.

Open to Public: *Fort:* Daily: 9 A.M.–5:30 P.M. *Park:* Open extended hours; call for schedule.

Visitor Services: Trails; museum; gift shop; information; rest rooms.

Regularly Scheduled Events: *Three times a year:* Reenactment teams.

Directions: From I-40 or I-95: take Hwy. 70 east to Morehead City, NC; turn off Hwy. 70 onto the Atlantic Beach Bridge; follow road to stoplight at the intersection with 58; turn left onto 58 south. Park is at the end of the road.

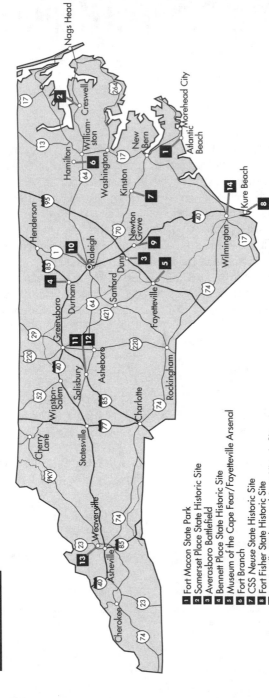

North Carolina

1. Fort Macon State Park
2. Somerset Place State Historic Site
3. Averasboro Battlefield
4. Bennett Place State Historic Site
5. Museum of the Cape Fear/Fayetteville Arsenal
6. Fort Branch
7. CSS Neuse State Historic Site
8. Fort Fisher State Historic Site
9. Bentonville Battleground State Historic Site
10. North Carolina State Capitol
11. Dr. Josephus W. Hall House
12. Salisbury National Cemetery
13. Zebulon B. Vance Birthplace State Historic Site
14. Brunswick Town/Fort Anderson State Historic Site

For North Carolina Tourism information call 1-800-VISIT-NC

Creswell

2 **Site:** SOMERSET PLACE STATE HISTORIC SITE, Rte. 1, P.O. Box 337, Creswell, NC 27928, 919-797-4560

Description: At the dawn of the Civil War, Somerset Place was a wealthy planter's estate and home to more than 300 enslaved men, women, and children. Because of the war, it was transformed into a shadowy war remain that proved home to no one. The stories surrounding that transformation provide a microscopic view of social, emotional, economic, and legal impacts of the war on individual Southerners of different races and genders.

Admission Fees: Free.

Open to Public: Apr. 1–Sept. 30: Mon.–Sat.: 9 A.M.–5 P.M.; Sun.: 1 P.M.–5 P.M.; Oct.1–Apr. 1: Tues.–Sat.:10 A.M.–4 P.M.; Sun.: 1 P.M.–4 P.M.

Visitor Services: Gift shop; information.

Regularly Scheduled Events: Annual Christmas open house program; Biannual Somerset homecomings: call for schedule.

Directions: From I-95: take NC 64 east to Creswell, NC; follow highway signage; 7 miles south to site.

Dunn

3 **Site:** AVERASBORO BATTLEFIELD, P.O. Box 1085, Dunn, NC 28334, 910-892-4113

Description: The site of the 1865 Battle of Averasboro, where Confederate General Hardee sought to check the advance of the left wing of General W. T. Sherman's army as it made its way through eastern North Carolina. The Battle of Averasboro was fought March 15–16, 1865. Although initially successful, the Confederates were no match for the larger Union force and did not slow it enough to prevent the eventual union with the right wing at the Battle of Bentonville, fought 25 miles to the north on March 19–21, 1865.

Admission Fees: Free.

Open to Public: *Cemetery & marker:* Daily: Dawn to dusk.

Visitor Services: None.

Directions: From I-95: take Long Branch Rd. exit and continue east for approximately 4 miles to its intersection with NC Hwy. 82. Turn left on 82 and the site is approximately 4 miles down 82 toward the town of Godwin.

Durham

| 4 | **Site:** BENNETT PLACE STATE HISTORIC SITE, 4409 Bennett Memorial Rd., Durham, NC 27705, 919-383-4345 |

Description: It was at Bennett Farmhouse that Generals Joseph E. Johnston and William T. Sherman met in April 1865 and signed an agreement that surrendered all the Confederate troops in N.C., S.C., Ga., and Fla., almost 90,000 men. This surrender on April 26, 1865, followed General Robert E. Lee's surrender at Appomattox by 17 days and was the largest surrender of the Civil War.

Admission Fees: Free.

Open to Public: Apr.–Oct.: Mon.–Sat.: 9 A.M.–5 P.M.: Sun.: 1 P.M.–5 P.M.; Nov.–Mar.: Tues.–Sat.: 10 A.M.–4 P.M.; Sun.: 1 P.M.–4 P.M.

Visitor Services: Museum; gift shop; information; rest rooms; handicapped access.

Regularly Scheduled Events: *Weekend closest to Apr. 26:* Annual Surrender; *First Sun. in Dec.:* Annual Christmas open house.

Directions: From I-85 north: take exit 170 onto U.S. 70 east; go east on U.S. 70 approximately .5 mile and turn right onto Bennett Memorial Rd. Site is .5 mile down Bennett Memorial Rd. on the right. From I-85 south: take exit 173; follow the signs.

Fayetteville

| 5 | **Site:** MUSEUM OF THE CAPE FEAR/FAYETTEVILLE ARSENAL, 801 Arsenal Ave., P.O. Box 53693, Fayetteville, NC 28305, 910-486-1330 |

Description: The North Carolina Arsenal was under construction by the Federal government from 1838–58. Built in response to woeful national defenses following the War of 1812, the arsenal was originally intended for construction and deposit. The installation was surrendered to a local militia in April 1861 and shortly thereafter became a significant producer of arms and ammunition for the Confederacy. It was destroyed by Sherman's army in March 1865. Today, extant tower and building foundations as well as a 35-foot-high steel facsimile of an original tower represent the focal points of the public presentation.

Admission Fees: Free.

Open to Public: Tues.–Sat.: 10 A.M.–5 P.M.; Sun.: 1 P.M.–5 P.M.

Visitor Services: Museum; gift shop; information; rest rooms; handicapped access.

Regularly Scheduled Events: Military demonstrations throughout the year.

Directions: From I-95: take exit 56 (Hwy. 301) south to Grove St.; turn right onto Grove St.; follow Grove to Bragg Blvd.; turn left on Bragg Blvd.; follow to Hay St.; turn right onto Hay St.; take second left onto Bradford; first street on the right.

Hamilton

6 **Site:** FORT BRANCH, P.O. Box 355, Hamilton, NC 27840, 800-776-8566 or
919-792-6605

Description: Fort Branch protected the Roanoke River Valley farms, the Ram Albemarle construction site, and the Weldon Railroad bridge from destruction by Federal gunboats. The Weldon Railroad bridge was critical to the Army of Northern Virginia in receiving supplies from the port of Wilmington via the Wilmington and Weldon Railroad. Features 7 of the 11 original cannons and well-preserved earthworks.

Admission Fees: Free except on reenactment weekend: $5/car, $10/bus or 15-passenger van.

Open to Public: Apr.–Nov.: Sat.–Sun.: 1:30 P.M.–5:30 P.M.; extended hours for reenactment weekend. Other times by appointment.

Visitor Services: Museum; gift shop; information; rest rooms; handicapped access.

Regularly Scheduled Events: *First full weekend in Nov.:* Annual battle reenactment weekend.

Directions: From I-95: take exit 138 at Rocky Mount; follow U.S. 64 east to Robersonville; take NC 903 north; .5 mile south of Hamilton turn right on the Fort Branch Rd.; go 2 miles; site is on your left.

Kinston

7 **Site:** CSS *NEUSE* STATE HISTORIC SITE, P.O. Box 3043, 2612 West Vernon Ave.,
Hwy. 70 Bus., Kinston, NC 28502-3043, 919-522-2091

Description: The CSS *Neuse* State Historic Site houses and interprets the archaeological remains of the Confederate ironclad, *Neuse,* one of the only three Civil War ironclads on display in the United States. The CSS *Neuse* was an integral factor in preventing Union forces from moving from New Bern to Goldsboro.

Admission Fees: Free.

Open to Public: Apr.–Oct.: Mon.–Sat.: 9 A.M.–5 P.M.; Sun.: 1 P.M.–5 P.M.; Nov.–Mar.: Tues.–Sat.: 10 A.M.–4 P.M.; Sun.: 1 P.M.–4 P.M.

Visitor Services: Museum; gift shop; information; rest rooms; handicapped access.

Regularly Scheduled Events: North Carolina History Bowl competition for eighth-grade students: call for schedule; *Second weekend in Nov.:* Annual living history reenactment.

Directions: From I-95: take Smithfield/ Selma, NC exit; take U.S. 70 east to Kinston approximately 45 miles; in Kinston, take U.S. 70 Bus.; site is .5 mile on right.

Kure Beach

8 | **Site:** FORT FISHER STATE HISTORIC SITE, P.O. Box 169, Kure Beach, NC 28449, 910-458-5538

Description: Fort Fisher was an earthen fort built on New Inlet (Atlantic Ocean inlet to Cape Fear River) to protect it for blockade running into the port of Wilmington. It kept the port open until early 1865. Wilmington fell on February 22, 1865.

Admission Fees: Free.

Open to Public: Apr.–Oct.: Mon.–Sat.: 9 A.M.–5 P.M.; Sun.: 1 P.M.–5 P.M.; Nov.–Mar.: Tues.–Sat.: 10 A.M.–4 P.M.; Sun.: 1 P.M.–4 P.M.

Visitor Services: Trails; museums; gift shop; information; rest rooms; handicapped access.

Regularly Scheduled Events: *Jan.:* Annual commemorative anniversary program; *Summer:* Interpretive program.

Directions: Take I-40 to Wilmington, NC; take U.S. 421 south approximately 20 miles to Kure Beach. Fort Fisher is on the right side of U.S. 421, 4 miles past Kure Beach.

Shepherd's Battery at Fort Fisher, Kure Beach, NC. (Photo courtesy of North Carolina Division of Archives and History.)

Newton Grove

9 | **Site:** BENTONVILLE BATTLEGROUND STATE HISTORIC SITE, P.O. Box 27, Newton Grove, NC 28366, 910-594-0789

Description: Bentonville was the site of the last major battle of the Civil War, March 19–21, 1865, nearly three weeks before Lee's surrender to Grant at Appomattox. The battle is also significant as the largest battle ever fought on North Carolina soil; the last Confederate offensive operation of the war; and the only significant attempt to stop the march of Sherman's army after the fall of Atlanta.

Admission Fees: Free.

Open to Public: Apr.–Oct.: Mon.–Sat.: 9 A.M.–5 P.M.; Sun.: 1 P.M.–5 P.M.; Nov.–Mar.: Tues.–Sat.: 10 A.M.–4 P.M.; Sun.: 1 P.M.–4 P.M.

Visitor Services: Trails; gift shop; information; rest rooms.

Regularly Scheduled Events: *July–Sept.:* Summer seasonal living history program;

Every fifth year: Anniversary commemoration reenactments; *Every year:* Living history.

Directions: From I-95: take exit 90; travel 15 miles south on U.S. 70; left onto State Rte. 1008; travel 3 miles east to site. From I-40: take exit 343; travel 6 miles north on U.S. 701 to State Rte. 1008; travel 3 miles east to site.

Raleigh

10 Site: NORTH CAROLINA STATE CAPITOL (1 East Edenton St.), mail to: 109 East Jones St., Raleigh, NC 27601-2807, 919-733-4994

Description: The building is virtually unaltered from its Civil War–era appearance. Completed in 1840, the capitol's house chamber was the site of the 1861 Secession Convention, and the building served several sessions of the war-era Confederate legislators. The capitol was occupied by staff officers of Sherman's army from April to May 1865 and was peacefully surrendered. The capitol's dome was the site of one of the last U.S. Army signal stations. The legislative chambers contain the original 1840 desks and chairs. The capitol is now being restored to its 1840–65 appearance.

Admission Fees: Free.

Open to Public: Mon.–Fri.: 8 A.M.–5 P.M.; Sat.: 9 A.M.–5 P.M.; Sun: 1 P.M.–5 P.M.; closed New Year's Day, Thanksgiving Day, and Christmas Day.

Visitor Services: Tours; information; rest room; handicapped access.

Regularly Scheduled Events: *First weekend in May:* 1865 occupation of Raleigh Civil War living history; *July:* Traditional July 4 celebration and Civil War encampment.

Directions: From I-40: take Person St. exit into Raleigh. Turn left on Edenton St. Capitol is located at the third block on the left. Parking is available beneath the N.C. Museum of History at the corner of Wilmington and Jones Streets.

Salisbury

11 Site: DR. JOSEPHUS W. HALL HOUSE, P.O. Box 4221, Salisbury, NC 28145-4221, 704-636-0103

Description: A symbol of Old Salisbury, this beautiful house was built in 1820. In 1859, Dr. Hall moved his family into the house. Dr. Hall served as chief surgeon at the Salisbury Confederate Prison during the Civil War. The house was used as headquarters for the Union commander, George Stoneman, following the war.

Admission Fees: Adults: $3; Children $1.

Open to Public: Sat.–Sun.: 2 P.M.–5 P.M.

Visitor Services: Museum; gift shop; rest rooms.

Regularly Scheduled Events: *First or second weekend in Oct.:* Annual tour; *Two weekends before Christmas and on Christmas Eve:* Annual Victorian Christmas at the Hall House.

Directions: From I-85: take exit 76B; travel on Innes St. for about 1 mile; turn left at the Confederate Monument onto Church St.; proceed two blocks and turn right onto West Bank St. The house is in the second block.

---

12 **Site:** SALISBURY NATIONAL CEMETERY, 202 Government Rd., Salisbury, NC 28144, 704-636-2661

Description: Site of the final resting place for the remains of 11,700 Union soldiers who died in the Confederate prison in Salisbury during 1864–65. Cemetery contains the largest number of unknown burials of any of the national cemeteries.

Admission Fees: Free.

Open to Public: *Cemetery:* Daily: Dawn to dusk. *Office and museum:* Mon.–Fri.: 7:30 A.M.–5 P.M.

Visitor Services: Museum; information; rest rooms.

Regularly Scheduled Events: *May:* Memorial Day event; *Nov.:* Veterans Day event.

Directions: From I-85: take exit 76 B; travel west on Innes St. to Long St. Proceed south on Long St. to Monroe St.; turn west on Monroe to Railroad St.; turn south on Railroad St. The cemetery is on the left.

Weaverville

13 **Site:** ZEBULON B. VANCE BIRTHPLACE STATE HISTORIC SITE, 911 Reems Creek Rd., Weaverville, NC 28787, 704-645-6706

Description: This reconstructed log house with six log outbuildings depicts the 1830 farmstead where Civil War governor of North Carolina, Zebulon B. Vance, and his brother, Confederate Brigadier General, Robert B. Vance, were born. Exhibits in visitor center trace their careers.

Admission Fees: Free.

Open to Public: Apr.–Oct.: Mon.–Sat.: 9 A.M.–5 P.M.; Sun.: 1 P.M.–5 P.M.; Nov.–Mar.: Tues–Sat.: 10 A.M.–4 P.M.; Sun: 1 P.M.–4 P.M.

Visitor Services: Museum; gift shop; information; rest rooms.

Regularly Scheduled Events: *Spring:* Pioneer Day; *Autumn:* Pioneer days & Militia encampment; *Dec.:* Christmas open house.

Directions: From I-240: take Weaverville exit onto U.S. 19-23 north; take New Stock Rd. exit and follow signs to site.

Wilmington

14 **Site:** BRUNSWICK TOWN/FORT ANDERSON STATE HISTORIC SITE,
8884 St. Philips Rd., SE, Winnabow, NC 28479, 910-371-6613

Description: Fort Anderson was constructed in March 1862 as part of the overall Cape Fear defense system. This system was to protect the Cape Fear River channel to the port of Wilmington, which was a major supply line to the Confederate forces. On February 19, 1865, a month after Fort Fisher's fall, a severe bombardment by the Union navy and an encircling movement by Union land forces caused the abandonment of Fort Anderson by Confederates who fled northward to Wilmington.

Admission Fees: Free.

Open to Public: Apr.–Oct.: Mon.–Sat.: 9 A.M.–5 P.M.; Sun.: 1 P.M.–5 P.M.; Nov.–Mar.: Tues.–Sat.: 10 A.M.–4 P.M.; Sun.: 1 P.M.–4 P.M.

Visitor Services: Trails; museum; gift shop; information; rest rooms; handicapped access.

Regularly Scheduled Events: *Mid-Feb.:* Civil War encampment.

Directions: Take I-40 into Wilmington; I-40 becomes South College; stay on S. College to the Oleander intersection; turn right on Oleander; travel westbound on U.S. 74-76 until you come to NC 133; take a left off exit; travel southbound on NC 133, approximately 18 miles.

he majority of the battles fought during the Civil War occurred in Confederate territory. Ohio troops, however, fought in every major theater of the war, and 34,591 Ohioans gave their lives. Three out of every five Ohio males between 18 and 45 served in the Union army and navy. A considerable number of Ohioans also served in Confederate armies; seven became Confederate generals.

According to *Ohio and Its People* by George W. Knepper, Ohio supplied the third-largest number of troops to the Union, exceeded only by the more populous states of New York and Pennsylvania. In proportion to state population, Ohio's contribution ranked number one. Distinguished generals, including Ulysses S. Grant, William Tecumseh Sherman, Philip Sheridan, and George McClellan came from Ohio. Five Ohio-born officers in the Union army became president of the United States.

More than 5,000 African American troops from Ohio served in state or federal units, and others served in the units of other states. Ohio stood fourth among the 20 states and the District of Columbia in the number of African Americans serving in the Union army.

Carrollton

1 **Site:** McCOOK HOUSE, P.O. Box 174, Public Square, Carrollton, OH 44615, 216-627-3345

Description: This house is a memorial to the "Fighting McCooks," a nickname given to the family because of their military service. During the Civil War, Daniel McCook's family contributed three major generals, two brigadier generals, one colonel, two majors, and one private to the Union cause. Brother John's side of the McCooks produced one major general, one brigadier general, two lieutenants, and a lieutenant in the navy. Four of Daniel's family, including Daniel himself, lost their lives in the conflict.

Admission Fees: Adults: $2; Children: $.50; Ohio Historical Society members: Free.

Open to Public: Memorial Day weekend–mid-Oct.: Fri.–Sat.: 9 A.M.–5 P.M.: Sun.: 1 P.M.–5 P.M.; tours other times by appointment.

Visitor Services: Museum; information; rest rooms.

Directions: From I-77 south: take Rte. 39 east to Carrollton. From I-77 north: take Rte. 43 from Canton. Located on the west side of the public square in Carrollton, Carroll County.

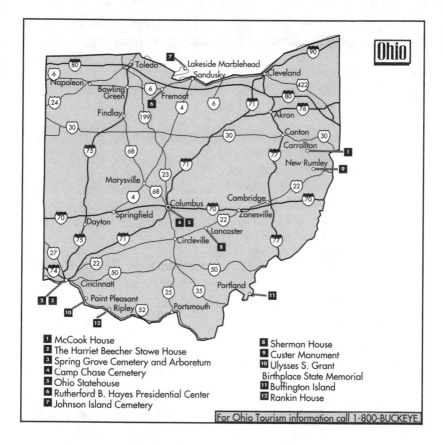

For Ohio Tourism information call 1-800-BUCKEYE.

Cincinnati

2 **Site:** THE HARRIET BEECHER STOWE HOUSE, 2950 Gilbert Ave., Cincinnati, OH 45206, 513-632-5120

Description: The Harriet Beecher Stowe House was built by Lane Seminary in 1833 to serve as the residence of that institution's president. Harriet Beecher Stowe moved to Cincinnati from Connecticut in 1832 with her father, Dr. Lyman Beecher, who had been appointed president of the seminary. During her stay in Cincinnati, she learned of the evils of slavery and expressed it through her book *Uncle Tom's Cabin*. The Stowe House has been restored by youth workers of the Cincinnati Citizens Committee on Youth.

Admission Fees: Free.

Open to Public: Tues.–Thurs.: 10 A.M.–4 P.M.

Visitor Services: Rest rooms; handicapped access.

Regularly Scheduled Events: *May:* Memorial Day sunrise service.

Directions: From I-71 south: take William Howard Taft exit; turn right onto Reading Rd.; travel north to Martin Luther King Dr.; turn right onto Gilbert Ave.

---

3 **Site:** SPRING GROVE CEMETERY AND ARBORETUM, 4521 Spring Grove Ave., Cincinnati, OH 45232, 513-681-6680

Description: Spring Grove Cemetery and Arboretum, celebrating 150 years, encompasses 733 acres. It is known worldwide for its beautiful landscaping and unique "lawn plan." Preserved within this "museum without walls" are exquisite illustrations of art, statuary, and architecture. Among its notable burials are 999 Civil War soldiers; 40 are generals, including General Robert McCook of the "Fighting McCooks" and General Joseph Hooker.

Admission Fees: Free.

Open to Public: Daily: 8 A.M.–6 P.M.

Visitor Services: Information; rest rooms; self-guided walking tour brochure and map. Guided tours available for groups of 20 or more.

Directions: From I-75: take Mitchell Ave. exit; go south on Spring Grove Ave. to entrance.

Columbus

4 **Site:** CAMP CHASE CEMETERY, 2900 Sullivant Ave., Columbus, OH, 614-276-0060

Description: Camp Chase, the largest camp in the area, was used for training Union soldiers. Later, it served as a prison for captured Confederates. There are 2,260 Confederates buried here.

Admission Fees: Free.

Open to Public: Daily: Dawn to dusk.

Visitor Services: None.

Regularly Scheduled Events: *First Sun. in June:* Anniversary of Confederate memorial services.

Directions: From I-70: exit at Broad St.; proceed west on Broad St. to Hague Ave.; turn left on Hague; turn right on Sullivant Ave.; proceed one block to cemetery.

---

5 **Site:** OHIO STATEHOUSE, Corner of Broad and High Streets, Columbus, OH 43215, 614-752-9777

Description: The Ohio Statehouse is the finest example of Greek Revival architecture in the United States. Built between 1839 and 1861, it is a National Historic Landmark. President Abraham Lincoln visited the statehouse three times: first, in 1859, shortly after his involvement with the Lincoln-Douglas debates; second, in 1861, when he spoke to a joint session of the Ohio legislature in the House chamber;

and third, in 1865, when he was laid in state in the rotunda. A monument, These Are My Jewels, pays tribute to seven Ohioans who played key roles in the Civil War, including Ulysses S. Grant, Philip Sheridan, Edwin M. Stanton, James A. Garfield, Rutherford B. Hayes, Salmon P. Chase, and William Tecumseh Sherman.

Admission Fees: Free.

Open to Public: Mon.–Fri., 8 A.M.– 7 P.M.; Sat.–Sun.: 11 A.M.–5 P.M.; Tours can be scheduled by calling 614-752-6350.

Visitor Services: Museum; information; rest rooms; handicapped access.

Regularly Scheduled Events: *Aug.:* Annual G.A.R. Civil War encampment features 1860s baseball game between Ohio Village Muffins and Lady Diamonds and the Ohio legislators.

Directions: From I-71: take Broad St. exit; go west until you reach Third St. Parking is available underground; turn south onto Third St.

Fremont

6 **Site:** RUTHERFORD B. HAYES PRESIDENTIAL CENTER, Spiegel Grove, 1337 Hayes Ave., Fremont, OH 43420, 419-332-2081

Description: This site features a museum, the first presidential library, and the residence of Rutherford B. Hayes, 19th president of the United States. The tomb of the president and his wife, Lucy Webb Hayes, also are located here. Hayes was decorated as a Civil War officer and served twice as governor of Ohio and one term as president. The library contains works of American history from the Civil War to the 20th century.

Admission Fees: *House & museum:* Adults: $7.50; Children: $2; Seniors: $6.50;

House or museum: Adults: $4; Children: $1; Seniors: $3.25.

Open to Public: Mon.–Sat.: 9 A.M.– 5 P.M.; Sun.: Noon–5 P.M.

Visitor Services: Trails; museum; gift shop; information; rest rooms; handicapped access.

Directions: Located at the intersection of Buckland and Hayes Avenues in Fremont, Sandusky County.

Lakeside–Marblehead

7 **Site:** JOHNSON ISLAND CEMETERY, Lakeside-Marblehead, OH 43440, 800-282-5393

Description: This cemetery holds the graves of 206 Confederates who died while imprisoned here.

Admission Fees: Free.

Open to Public: Daily: Dawn to dusk.

Visitor Services: None.

Directions: From I-80/90: take exit 6A north on State Rte. 4 to State Rte. 2 west; take State Rte. 269 north to Danbury & Bay Shore Rd.; travel east on Bay Shore Rd. to Johnson Island entrance.

Lancaster

8 **Site:** SHERMAN HOUSE, 137 E. Main St., Lancaster, OH 43130, 614-687-5891

Description: Sherman House is the birthplace of William Tecumseh Sherman and a museum with war memorabilia and artifacts from the general's collection.

Admission Fees: Adults: $2.50; Children (6–17): $1.

Open to Public: Apr.–Nov.: Tues.–Sun.: 1 P.M.–4 P.M.

Regularly Scheduled Events: *Early Feb.:* Sherman's birthday celebration.

Directions: From I-270: travel south on State Rte. 33 to downtown Lancaster; turn left on State Rte. 22; proceed two blocks to house.

New Rumley

9 **Site:** CUSTER MONUMENT, Ohio Historical Society, 1982 Velma Ave., Columbus, OH 43211-2497, 614-297-2630 or 1-800-BUCKEYE.

Description: This eight-and-one-half-foot bronze statue stands on the site of George Armstrong Custer's birthplace. Custer, born in 1839, became famous as a daring young cavalryman in the Civil War, fighting in the battles of Bull Run, Shenandoah, Waynesboro, Appomattox, and many others.

Admission Fees: Free.

Open to Public: Daily: Dawn to dusk.

Directions: Located on the north side of State Rte. 646, at the west edge of New Rumley, north of Cadiz, in Harrison County.

Point Pleasant

10 **Site:** ULYSSES S. GRANT BIRTHPLACE STATE MEMORIAL, 1591 State Rte. 232, Point Pleasant, OH 45153, 513-553-4911

Description: Ulysses S. Grant, 18th president of the United States was born in this small frame cottage in Point Pleasant, Ohio. Today, Grant's birthplace is restored and open to the public.

Admission Fees: Adults: $1; Children (6–12): $.50; Seniors: $.75; Groups: $10/bus or $.50/person.

Open to Public: Apr.–Oct.: Wed.–Sat.: 9:30 A.M.–Noon & 1 P.M.–5 P.M.; Sun.: Noon–5 P.M.

Visitor Services: Tours.

Directions: Located in the Clermont County Village of Point Pleasant, off State Rte. 52 near the intersection with State Rte. 132.

Portland

 Site: BUFFINGTON ISLAND, Ohio Historical Society, 1982 Velma Ave., Columbus, OH 43211-2497, 614-297-2630 or 1-800-BUCKEYE

Description: Commemorates the only significant Civil War battle that took place on Ohio soil. Here a Union army routed a column of Confederate cavalry commanded by General John Hunt Morgan in 1863.

Admission Fees: Free.

Open to Public: Daily: Dawn to dusk.

Visitor Services: Picnic area; handicapped access.

Directions: The memorial is approximately 20 miles east from Pomeroy, Meigs County, on State Rte. 124, at Portland, OH.

Ripley

 Site: RANKIN HOUSE, P.O. Box 176, Rankin Hill Rd., Ripley, OH 45167, 513-392-1627

The Rankin House, a way station on the "Underground Railroad," Ripley, OH. (Photograph courtesy of the Ohio Historical Society.)

Description: The Rankin House was an important way station on the Underground Railroad by which slaves escaped from the South to freedom. John Rankin was a Presbyterian minister and educator who devoted his life to the antislavery movement. From 1825 to 1865, Rankin and his wife, Jean, with their Brown County neighbors, sheltered more than 2,000 slaves escaping to freedom, with as many as 12 escapees being hidden in the Rankin home at one time. The Rankins prided themselves on never having lost a "passenger."

Admission Fees: Adults: $2; Children (6–12): $.50.

Open to Public: Memorial Day Weekend–Labor Day: Wed.–Sun. and holidays: Noon–5 P.M.; after Labor Day–Oct.: Sat.–Sun.: Noon–5 P.M.

Visitor Services: Tours; rest rooms.

Directions: The entrance road (Race St. or Rankin St.) to the Rankin House runs northeast off of State Rte. 52 at the northwest edge of Ripley, Brown County.

OKLAHOMA

In 1861 the flame of the Civil War sped across Indian Territory, an area that would become the state of Oklahoma 46 years later. And when the war came, it struck with such a fury that left the lands of the Five Civilized Tribes in shambles.

All five tribes—the Cherokee, Creek, Choctaw, Chickasaw, and Seminole—officially sided with the Confederacy in 1861, but in reality, only the Choctaw and Chickasaw were united in their support of the South. All-Indian regiments were formed, and by the end of the war, thousands of Indians would serve on both sides, brother against brother, tribe against tribe.

Located between the unionist states of Kansas and Missouri and the Confederate states of Arkansas and Texas, the Indian Territory was both a crossroads for armies and a source of men, mules, and materiel. From 1861 to 1865 the boys in blue and gray fought 89 battles and skirmishes on the soil that would become Oklahoma. In all, the people of the Five Civilized Tribes suffered more destruction and death per capita than any state of the South, including the states of Virginia, Tennessee, and Missouri.

Today, the remnants of that life and death struggle await the observant traveler.

by Dr. Bob Blackburn, Oklahoma Historical Society

Atoka

1 **Site: CONFEDERATE MEMORIAL MUSEUM, P.O. Box 245, Atoka, OK 74525, 405-889-7192**

Description: Confederates maintained camps nearby along the Middle Boggy River in the Choctaw Nation of Indian Territory. Some died of disease and were buried on the grounds where the museum exists now. The Battle of Middle Boggy was fought on February 13, 1864, when Col. William Phillips and 350 Union troops surprised about 90 Confederates about where the Texas Road crossed the Middle Boggy River. Forty-seven Confederates were killed in the Union victory. The museum includes memorabilia from that Civil War battle. Grounds include cemetery and a section of the Butterfield Mail Route. The Battle of Middle Boggy is reenacted every third year at a nearby site by the Oklahoma Historical Society and Atoka County Historical Society.

Admission Fees: Free. NOTE: Admission fee charged for the reenactment.

Oklahoma

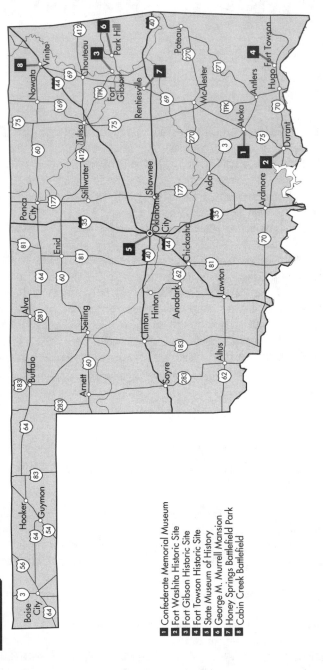

1 Confederate Memorial Museum
2 Fort Washita Historic Site
3 Fort Gibson Historic Site
4 Fort Towson Historic Site
5 State Museum of History
6 George M. Murrell Mansion
7 Honey Springs Battlefield Park
8 Cabin Creek Battlefield

Open to Public: Mon.–Sat.: 9 A.M.–4 P.M.

Visitor Services: Museum; information; gift shop; visitors center; rest rooms; grounds inside stockade and buildings handicapped accessible.

Regularly Scheduled Events: *Second weekend of Feb., every three years, 1997,* *2000, etc.:* Battle of Middle Boggy re-enactment.

Directions: From I-40: travel south on U.S. 69 to Atoka. Museum is located 1 mile north of Atoka on the east side of U.S. 69 with the Oklahoma Travel Information Center.

Durant

2 **Site:** FORT WASHITA HISTORIC SITE, Star Rte. 213, Durant, OK 74701-9443, 405-924-6502

Description: Fort Washita was established in 1842 in the Choctaw Nation of Indian Territory and was used as a staging ground for the Mexican War. Famous Civil War leaders who served earlier at Fort Washita included Randolph B. Marcy, George McClellan, William G. Belknap, and Theophylus H. Holmes. Federal troops abandoned Fort Washita in 1861, and it was occupied by Confederate troops during the Civil War as the headquarters of Brig. Gen. Douglas Cooper. Fort Washita National Historic Landmark today includes ruins, restored barracks, and the parade ground.

Admission Fees: Free.

Open to Public: Mon.–Sat.: 9 A.M.–5 P.M.; Sun.: 1 P.M.–5 P.M.

Visitor Services: Information; gift shop; visitors center; rest rooms; grounds and buildings handicapped accessible.

Regularly Scheduled Events: *Third weekend in Feb.:* Mexican War living history; *First and third weekends of Mar.:* Civil War living history; *First weekend in Apr.:* 1840s Fur Trade Rendezvous (admission charge); *First weekend of Nov.:* Candlelight tours (admission charge); *Mid-Nov.:* Instruction Camp for male reenactors (admission charge); *Dec.:* Mexican and Civil War Christmas living history.

Directions: From I-35: travel east on U.S. 70 to Madill; continue 11 miles East on State Hwy. 199 to Fort Washita Military Park.

Fort Gibson

3 **Site:** FORT GIBSON HISTORIC SITE, P.O. Box 457, Fort Gibson, OK 74434-0457, 918-478-2669

Description: Fort Gibson was established in 1824 in Indian Territory. It was turned over to the Cherokee Nation in 1857, but reactivated by the U.S. Army in 1863. Maj. Gen. James Blunt led 3,000 troops out of Fort Gibson to defeat 6,000 Confederates under Brig. Gen. Douglas Cooper at the Battle of Honey Springs on July 17, 1863. It was the largest battle in Indian Territory and one of the first Civil War battles in which African Americans fought as a unit and the largest in which Native Americans fought on both sides. Col. William Phillips led 1,500 Union troops out of Fort Gibson to invade the Choctaw Nation and won the Battle of Middle Boggy on Feb. 13, 1964. Fort Gibson was operated until 1890. This National Historic Landmark now includes seven original buildings, sections of Civil War entrenchments still visible on the grounds, and a reconstructed log stockade.

Admission Fees: Free. NOTE: Small fees charged for special events such as the Battle of Honey Springs reenactment, Christmas candlelight tours, workshops, seminars, and so forth.

Open to Public: Mon.–Sat.: 9 A.M.–5 P.M.; Sun.: 1 P.M.–5 P.M.

Visitor Services: Tours; museum; information; gift shop; visitors center; rest rooms; grounds inside stockade and buildings are handicapped accessible.

Regularly Scheduled Events: *Every three years in July:* Battle of Honey Springs reenactment; Educational tours on request during school year; *Third weekend in Mar.:* Public Bake Day; *Mid-May:* Military Time Line living history; *Halloween week in Oct.:* Ghost Stories; *Mid-Nov.:* Instruction Camp for female reenactors; *Second weekend in Dec.:* 1848 Christmas candlelight tours; *Third weekend in Dec.:* Community education tours.

Directions: From I-40: travel north at Checotah on U.S. 69 to Muskogee. Go east on U.S. 62 and north on State Hwy. 80 to Fort Gibson Military Park in the town of Fort Gibson.

Fort Towson

4 **Site:** FORT TOWSON HISTORIC SITE, HC 63, Box 1580, Fort Towson, OK 74701-9443, 405-873-2634

Description: Fort Towson was established in 1824 by Col. Matthew Arbuckle near the Red River in Indian Territory. The town of Doaksville was founded one mile away in 1831 and became the capital of the Choctaw Nation during the Civil War. The fort was expanded for the Mexican War but closed by the Federal army in 1854. Confederate Maj. Gen. Sam Bell Maxey established his command post at Fort Towson during the Civil War. The last surrender of the Civil War by a general officer was completed near Doaksville on June 23, 1865, by Brig. Gen. Stand Watie, a Cherokee who commanded the Indian Brigade for the Confederates. Today Fort Towson consists of extensive masonry ruins of barracks, officers' quarters, a bakery, a powder magazine, and other buildings. Archaeological excavations at Doaksville are part of a development plan that will see it intermerged and linked by a trail to Fort Towson by the end of 1997. A sutler's store has been replicated at Fort Towson.

Admission Fees: Free. NOTE: Small fees may be charged for special events, including the Last Surrender Campaign, reenacted every five years to commemorate the last surrender of the Civil War and the Fur Trade Rendezvous.

Open to Public: Mon.–Fri.: 9 A.M.– 5 P.M.; Sat.–Sun.: 1 P.M.–5 P.M.

Visitor Services: Information; gift shop; visitors center; rest rooms; grounds and buildings handicapped accessible.

Regularly Scheduled Events: *First week of Mar.:* 1840s Fur Trade Rendezvous; *Third weekend of June, every five years:* Last Surrender Campaign reenactment.

Directions: From I-35: go east on U.S. 70 through Hugo to town of Fort Towson; go north 2 miles to Fort Towson Military Park. From I-40: go south on Indian Nation Turnpike to Hugo; then go east on U.S. 70 to town of Fort Towson; go north 2 miles to Fort Towson Military Park.

Oklahoma City

5 **Site:** STATE MUSEUM OF HISTORY, 2100 Lincoln Blvd., Oklahoma City, OK 73105, 405-521-2491

Description: The State Museum of History, which is managed by the Oklahoma Historical Society, tells the comprehensive story of Oklahoma from the beginning. It has separate rooms for the Union and the Confederacy to commemorate the Civil War and its impact on Oklahoma. Both rooms include artifacts, relics, paintings, exhibits, and interpretations of the Civil War in Indian Territory and what became the State of Oklahoma. The same building houses the Oklahoma Historical Society Division of Archives and Manuscripts and the Oklahoma Historical Society Research Library, including extensive holdings of Indian units that fought in the Civil War.

Admission Fees: Free.

Open to Public: Mon.–Sat.: 8 A.M.–5 P.M.

Visitor Services: Museum; information; gift shop; visitors center; rest rooms; handicapped access.

Directions: From I-40: travel north on I-235 in the middle of Oklahoma City; exit on Lincoln Blvd. and go north to State Museum in Wiley Post Historical Building on the east side of Lincoln Blvd., just south of the State Capitol. From I-235: exit on NE 23d St.; go east to Lincoln Blvd.; go south on Lincoln to Wiley Post Building as just described.

Park Hill

6 **Site:** GEORGE M. MURRELL MANSION, HC-69, P.O. Box 54, Park Hill, OK 74451-9601, 918-456-2751

Description: George M. Murrell, of Lynchburg, Va., married Minerva Ross, niece of principal chief John Ross of the Cherokee Nation. The Murrells built their home in Park Hill starting in 1844. It became known as Hunter's Home, a social center for Cherokee Nation leaders and Fort Gibson officers. After Minerva died, George married her younger sister, Amanda. During the Civil War, the Cherokee nation split. Murrell, a slave owner with strong family ties in Virginia and Louisiana, was married into the Ross family, which was led by strong unionists. The Murrell home was occupied by both armies during the war and was one of the few in Indian Territory not burned by one side or the other. The homes of John Ross, leader of the pro-Union faction, and Gen. Stand Watie of the Confederates were both burned, as were 75 percent of the homes of the Cherokees. Restoration of the Murrell Mansion is underway.

Admission Fees: Free. NOTE: A small fee is charged for the Ghost Story sessions during Halloween week.

Open to Public: Wed.–Sat.: 10 A.M.–5 P.M.; Sun.: 1 P.M.–5 P.M.

Visitor Services: Trails; information; visitors center; rest rooms; grounds and lower floor of mansion are handicapped accessible.

Regularly Scheduled Events: *First week of June:* 1858 Lawn Social living history; *Mid-Aug.:* Civil War living history encampment; *First weekend of Sept.:* Civil War surrender of Chief Ross; *Oct., Halloween week:* Ghost Stories.

Directions: From I-40: go north on U.S. 69 to Muskogee; then east on U.S. 62 to 4 miles short of Tahlequah; then south on State Hwy. 82 to Park Hill. From I-44: travel south on U.S. 69; proceed east on U.S. 62; go south on State Hwy. 82 to Park Hill.

Rentiesville

7 **Site:** HONEY SPRINGS BATTLEFIELD PARK, c/o Oklahoma Historical Society, 2100 Lincoln Blvd., Oklahoma City, OK 73105, 405-522-5241

Reenactment at Honey Springs Battlefield in Oklahoma. (Photograph by Jeff Briley, courtesy of Oklahoma Historical Society.)

Description: On July 17, 1863, 3,000 Union troops under Maj. Gen. James Blunt defeated 6,000 Confederates under Brig. Gen. Douglas Cooper in the Battle of Honey Springs. It was one of the first Civil War battles in which African Americans fought as a unit—the First Regular Kansas Volunteers (Colored). They carried the day, defeating two Texas cavalry units. It was also the largest battle in which Native Americans fought on both sides, and it was a turning point of the war in Indian Territory. The Union controlled the Cherokee Nation, the upper Arkansas River, and most of Indian Territory for the rest of the war. The current site includes monuments to the battle and woods and pastures with a few structures. A project to develop a visitors center is underway and scheduled for completion by 1998.

Admission Fees: Free. NOTE: An admission fee is charged for the reenactment of the battle, held every three years in mid-July.

Open to Public: Daily: Daylight hours.

Visitor Services: Information.

Regularly Scheduled Events: *Mid-July, every three years, 1996, 1999, and so forth:* Battle of Honey Springs reenactment; *Mid-July:* Battle of Honey Springs memorial service.

Directions: From I-40: go north on U.S. 69 four miles to exit marked Rentiesville; go 2 miles east to Rentiesville; just after Rentiesville, at the edge of town, turn north (left) to the monuments and battle site.

Vinita

---

8 **Site:** CABIN CREEK BATTLEFIELD, c/o Oklahoma Historical Society, 2100 Lincoln Blvd., Oklahoma City, OK 73105, 405-522-5241

Description: Two Civil War battles were fought at Cabin Creek—both Confederate raids on Union supply wagon trains moving from Fort Scott toward Fort Gibson. On July 1, 1863, Stand Watie and the Confederates failed to stop the wagon train as it crossed Cabin Creek about 10 miles south of what is today Vinita. It was one of the first battles in which African Americans fought as a unit west of the Mississippi River. On September 18, 1864, Watie and the Confederates won the Second Battle of Cabin Creek, capturing 740 mules, 130 wagons, and more than $1 million in supplies. Monuments to the leaders and soldiers of both sides were erected by the United Daughters of the Confederacy and are maintained by the Oklahoma Historical Society and the Friends of Cabin Creek at the battle site.

Admission Fees: Free.

Open to Public: Daily: Daylight hours.

Visitor Services: Information; handicapped access.

Regularly Scheduled Events: *Last weekend in Sept., every three years, 1998, 2001, and so forth:* Battle of Cabin Creek reenactment.

Directions: From I-44: exit at Vinita onto U.S. 60/State Hwy. 82. Proceed east for 3 miles until these roads split; turn right and continue to follow Hwy. 82 for another 10 miles south to State Hwy. 28. Turn right onto Hwy. 28 and proceed 5 miles to Pensacola. Turn right onto a county road and proceed about 2.5 miles to the monument site.

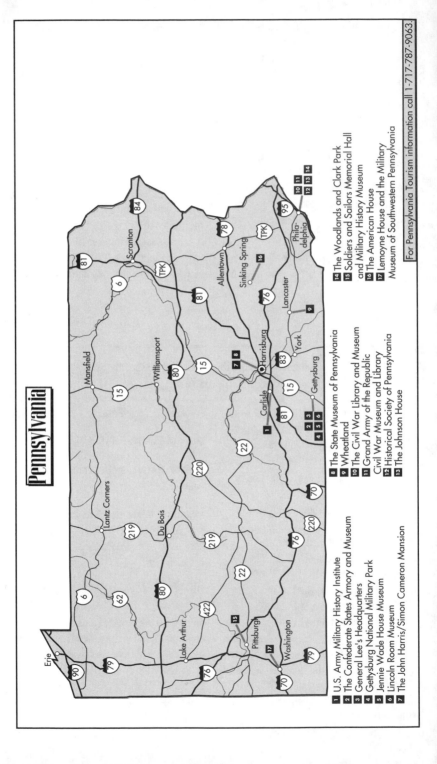

Pennsylvania

1. U.S. Army Military History Institute
2. The Confederate States Armory and Museum
3. General Lee's Headquarters
4. Gettysburg National Military Park
5. Jennie Wade House Museum
6. Lincoln Room Museum
7. The John Harris/Simon Cameron Mansion

8. The State Museum of Pennsylvania
9. Wheatland
10. The Civil War Library and Museum
11. Grand Army of the Republic
    Civil War Museum and Library
12. Historical Society of Pennsylvania
13. The Johnson House

14. The Woodlands and Clark Park
15. Soldiers and Sailors Memorial Hall
    and Military History Museum
16. The American House
17. Lemoyne House and the Military
    Museum of Southwestern Pennsylvania

For Pennsylvania Tourism information call 1-717-787-9063.

PENNSYLVANIA

*G*eographic, political, and economic circumstances placed a reluctant Pennsylvania in the forefront of the Union coalition of states during the Civil War.

Because of Pennsylvania's geographic location and advanced railroad network, a transportation estuary was developed for the campaigns in Virginia and Maryland and, via the Ohio River and railroad extensions, for the west operations as well. In the end, Pennsylvania supplied one-sixth of the combatants and a leading share of the metal, textile, fuel, and food products. The relatively small Confederate forays to Chambersburg in August 1862 and July 1864 and the climactic Gettysburg campaign of June and July 1863 were the only periods of fighting on Pennsylvania soil. At Gettysburg one-third of the Union army was from Pennsylvania, commanded by two Pennsylvanians—John F. Reynolds and George G. Meade.

Politically, at the outset of the Civil War, there was less than a consensus in Pennsylvania for abolition, but political leaders from the newly arisen Republican Party convinced the public that the Union must be preserved. Later, ghastly casualties and the failures of the army, even as reorganized by the Pennsylvanian Gen. George B. McClellan, swelled antiwar sentiment. The possibility of a negotiated peace allowing Confederate independence haunted the North's wartime government. Pennsylvania's Congressmen Thaddeus Stevens led the Congressional Radical Republicans, who prosecuted the war vigorously. Stevens worked uncompromisingly for the equality of African Americans.

Economically, Philadelphia banker Jay Cooke was commissioned to float government loans to finance the war. Free-enterprise economics prevailed, although political pressure forced private business into cooperating with military goals.

The Gettysburg and Vicksburg victories of July 1863 did not destroy the Confederacy; Pennsylvanians served on through Grant's Virginia campaigns, and Sherman's march through Tennessee, Georgia, and South Carolina. Former army commander George McClellan of Philadelphia was the Democratic candidate for president. Although reputed to be popular with the common soldiers, the soldiers as well as a slim Pennsylvania civilian majority voted for Lincoln, who carried the state by a mere 3.5 percent.

by Louis M. Waddell, Division of History,
Pennsylvania Historical and Museum Commission

Carlisle

1 **Site:** U.S. ARMY MILITARY HISTORY INSTITUTE, Upton Hall, Bldg. 22, Carlisle
Barracks, Carlisle, PA 17013-5008, 717-245-4134

Description: Carlisle Barracks was a recruiting depot, particularly for cavalry. It
was occupied briefly in June and July 1863
by portions of Lee's Army of Northern Virginia. The Union troops reoccupied the post
on July 2. In July 1864 Union troops were
marched from the barracks in response to
the Confederate raid on and burning of
Chambersburg, Pennsylvania.

Admission Fees: Free.

Open to Public: Weekdays: 8 A.M.–
4 P.M.; closed on weekends.

Visitor Services: Museum; information;
rest rooms; handicapped access.

Regularly Scheduled Events: *One evening
a month, Sept.–May:* Guest lecturer speaks
on a military history topic.

Directions: From I-81: take exit 17; proceed south on U.S. 11 about 3 miles. At the
fourth signal light, turn left; Upton Hall is
on the right.

Gettysburg

2 **Site:** THE CONFEDERATE STATES ARMORY AND MUSEUM, 529 Baltimore St.,
Gettysburg, PA 17325, 717-337-2340

Description: The museum features a large
collection of rare and original Confederate
small arms, edged weapons, and memorabilia as well as some Union weapons. Each
artifact displayed is carefully and accurately
described, and a tour through the facility is
truly an educational experience.

Admission Fees: Adults: $3; Children
(6–12): $2; Seniors: $2; Groups: $1.50–
$2/person.

Open to Public: Mon.: Noon–8 P.M.; Wed.–
Sun.: Noon–8 P.M.

Visitor Services: Museum; gift shop.

Directions: From Rte. 15: take Baltimore
Pike exit; travel 2-3 miles; museum is on
the right, across from the Holiday Inn.

For More Information

For Gettysburg visitor information, contact Gettysburg Convention and Visitors Bureau, Dept. 702, 35 Carlisle
St., Gettysburg, PA 17325; 717-334-6274

3 **Site:** GENERAL LEE'S HEADQUARTERS, 401 Buford Ave., Gettysburg, PA 17325, 717-334-3141

Description: This stone house was used by General Robert E. Lee as his personal headquarters July 1, 1863, during the Battle of Gettysburg.

Admission Fees: Adults: $1; Children: Free.

Open to Public: *Summer:* Daily: 9 A.M.– 9 P.M.; *Winter:* Daily: 9 A.M.–5 P.M.

Visitor Services: Museum; gift shop; rest rooms.

Directions: Located 23 miles east of I-81 on U.S. 30.

4 **Site:** GETTYSBURG NATIONAL MILITARY PARK, 97 Taneytown Rd., Gettysburg, PA 17325, 717-334-1124

Description: Gettysburg National Military Park is the site of a major battle of the Civil War. The three days of fighting on July 1, 2, and 3, 1863, are considered a turning point in the war and marked the second and final invasion of the North by the Confederate forces.

Admission Fees: Free; Orientation Map is $2.

Open to Public: *Battlefield:* Daily: 6 A.M.– 10 P.M.; *Visitors Center:* 8 A.M.–5 P.M.

Visitor Services: Civil War Explorer; museum; bookstore; information; rest rooms; handicapped access.

Regularly Scheduled Events: *June 15– Sept. 1:* Ranger-guided walks; *Mar.:* Battle seminar.

Directions: Located 78 miles north of Washington D.C.; take I-270 west to Frederick, MD; take U.S. 15 north directly to the park. From Harrisburg, PA: take U.S. 15 south for approximately 36 miles directly into the park.

Little Round Top, Gettysburg National Military Park. (Photograph courtesy of Gettysburg Convention and Visitors Bureau.)

THE BATTLE OF GETTYSBURG

On June 3, 1863, a month after his dramatic victory at Chancellorsville, Confederate General Robert E. Lee began marching his Army of Northern Virginia westward from its camps around Fredericksburg, Virginia. Once through the gaps of the Blue Ridge Mountains, the Southerners trudged northward into Maryland and Pennsylvania. They were followed by the Union Army of the Potomac under General Joseph Hooker, but Lee, whose cavalry under J. E. B. Stuart was absent on a brash raid around the Federal forces, had no way of knowing his adversary's whereabouts.

The two armies touched by chance at Gettysburg on June 30. The main battle opened on July 1 with Confederates attacking Union troops on McPherson Ridge west of town. Though outnumbered, the Federal forces (now commanded by General George G. Meade) held their position until afternoon, when they were finally overpowered and driven back to Cemetery Hill south of town. The Northerners labored long into the night over their defenses while the bulk of Meade's army arrived and took up positions.

On July 2 the battle lines were drawn up in two sweeping arcs. The main portions of both armies were nearly one mile apart on parallel ridges: Union forces on Cemetery Ridge; Confederate forces on Seminary Ridge to the west. Lee ordered an attack against both Union flanks. James Longstreet's thrust on the Federal left turned the base of Little Round Top into a shambles, left the Wheatfield strewn with dead and wounded, and overran the Peach Orchard. Farther north, Richard S. Ewell's evening attack on the Federal right at East Cemetery Hill and Culp's Hill, though momentarily successful, could not be exploited to Confederate advantage.

On July 3 Lee's artillery opened a two-hour bombardment of the Federal lines on Cemetery Ridge and Cemetery Hill. This for a time engaged the massed guns of both sides in a thundering duel for supremacy, but did little to soften up the Union defensive position. Then, in a desperate attempt to recapture the partial success of the previous day, some 12,000 Confederates under George E. Pickett advanced across the open fields toward the Federal center. Only one Southerner in three retired to safety.

With the repulse of Pickett's assault, the Battle of Gettysburg was over. The Confederate army that staggered back into Virginia was physically and spiritually exhausted. Never again would Lee attempt an offensive operation of such magnitude. And Meade, though criticized for not pursuing Lee's troops, would forever be remembered as the man who won the battle that has come to be known as the "High Watermark of the Confederacy."

by Julie K. Fix, The Civil War Trust

5 Site: JENNIE WADE HOUSE MUSEUM, 548 Baltimore St., Gettysburg, PA 17325, 717-334-4100

Description: During the Battle of Gettysburg, 20-year-old Mary Virginia Wade along with her mother stayed at the home of her sister, Mrs. J. Lewis McClellen, who had just given birth to her first child. While baking bread for the Union troops, a stray bullet passed through two doors striking and killing Jennie Wade. Jennie Wade became Gettysburg's heroine. The 1863 home is now a museum that tells the story and life of Jennie Wade.

Admission Fees: Adults: $5.25; Children: $3.25; Seniors: $4.75; Groups (10 or more): Adults: $3/person; Children: $1.50/person.

Open to Public: Mar.–May: Daily: 9 A.M.–5 P.M.; end of May & June: 9 A.M.–7 P.M.; July–Aug.: 9 A.M.–9 P.M.; Sept.–Oct.: 9 A.M.–7 P.M.; End of Oct. & Nov.: 9 A.M.–5 P.M.; closed Dec.–Feb.

Visitor Services: Museum; gift shop; information.

Directions: Located along Baltimore St. (Rte. 97 South).

6 Site: LINCOLN ROOM MUSEUM, 12 Lincoln Square, Gettysburg, PA 17325, 717-334-8188

Description: The "Lincoln Room" is located in the historic Wills House, where President Lincoln stayed the night before he gave his Gettysburg Address on November 19, 1863. The house was used as a hospital site after the Battle of Gettysburg. The actual bedroom is preserved, and an audio program is presented to visitors. In addition, there is an area displaying items of Lincoln's and period artifacts.

Admission Fees: Adults: $3.25; Children: $1.75; Seniors: $3; Groups: 15 percent off regular admission.

Open to Public: Daily: 9 A.M.–5 P.M.

Visitor Services: Museum; gift shop; information.

Regularly Scheduled Events: *Nov. 19:* Anniversary of the Gettysburg Address.

Directions: In the center of the Borough of Gettysburg at the corner of Rte. 30. At the intersection of York St. & Baltimore St.

Harrisburg

7 Site: THE JOHN HARRIS/SIMON CAMERON MANSION, 219 South Front St., Harrisburg, PA 17104, 717-233-3462

Description: From 1863 to 1889, this was the home of Simon Cameron, Lincoln's first secretary of war. Cameron was a controversial figure who had proposed arming blacks in the war effort and was forced to resign as a result. He also established Harrisburg as a central location for the movement of Union troops and materiel.

Admission Fees: Adults: $3.50; Children: $1.50; Seniors: $2.50; Groups: $.50 discount.

Open to Public: May–Dec.: Mon.–Fri.: 11 A.M.–3 P.M.; Sat.: 10 A.M.–4 P.M.

Visitor Services: Museum; gift shop; rest rooms.

Regularly Scheduled Events: *Late autumn:* Civil War encampment; *Sept.–May:* Lecture series.

Directions: From I-83: take the Second St. exit. Get in the left lane and turn left on Washington St.; turn right into the parking lot just after River St.

---

8 **Site:** THE STATE MUSEUM OF PENNSYLVANIA, P.O. Box 1026, Harrisburg, PA 17108-1026, 717-787-4980

Description: Among the museum's collections is a large and important collection of Civil War materials, many of which are exhibited in a second-floor gallery, "Keystone of the Union," which illustrates the role of the Commonwealth in the war. The collection includes flags, uniforms, firearms, swords, accoutrements, and soldiers' personal gear.

Admission Fees: Free.

Open to Public: Tues.–Sat.: 9 A.M.–5 P.M.; Sun: Noon–5 P.M.

Visitor Services: Museum; gift shop; information; rest rooms; handicapped access.

Directions: From I-83 south: take Second St. exit; turn right on North St.; proceed two blocks to Third & North; museum is on opposite corner. From I-81: take exit 22 (Front St.); turn left on North St.

Lancaster

9 **Site:** WHEATLAND, 1120 Marietta Ave., Lancaster, PA 17603, 717-295-8825

Description: Home of President James Buchanan, 15th president of the United States, 1857–61.

Admission Fees: Adults: $5.50; Children: $1.75; Seniors: $4.50; Groups (15 or more by reservation): $3.50/person.

Open to Public: Apr. 1–Nov. 30: Daily: 10 A.M.–4 P.M.

Visitor Services: Food; museum; gift shop; information; rest rooms.

Regularly Scheduled Events: *May–June:* Old-Fashioned Sunday; *Oct.:* Halloween tours; *Dec.:* Christmas candlelight tours.

Directions: Located 1.5 miles west of Lancaster on Rte. 23 (Marietta Ave.) near the intersection of President Ave.

Philadelphia

10 **Site:** THE CIVIL WAR LIBRARY AND MUSEUM, 1805 Pine St., Philadelphia, PA 19103, 215-735-8196

Description: Founded in 1888, the Civil War Library and Museum is the oldest Civil War museum in the country. Three floors of exhibits include extensive George G. Meade, Ulysses S. Grant, and John F. Reynolds collections. Research library includes more than 2,000 photographs, microform, manuscripts, and 12,000 books.

Admission Fees: Adults: $3; Children under 12: Free; Seniors: $2; Groups (up to 30 by reservation): $1/person.

Open to Public: Mon.–Sat.: 10 A.M.–4 P.M.; Sun.: 11 A.M.–4 P.M.

Visitor Services: Museum; gift shop; information; rest rooms; limited handicapped access.

Regularly Scheduled Events: Special changing exhibits at least twice a year; *Second Thurs. of the month:* Meeting place of Civil War Round Table.

Directions: From I-76 east: take South St. exit (left-hand exit). At the top of the ramp turn left; follow South St. to 18th; turn left; follow 18th St. two blocks to the corner of 18th & Pine St. From I-95 north or south: take I-676 (Vine St. Expressway); follow I-676 to merge with the Schuylkill Expressway, I-76; follow I-76 east, get into the left lane; take the South St. exit, as before.

11 **Site:** GRAND ARMY OF THE REPUBLIC CIVIL WAR MUSEUM AND LIBRARY, 4278 Griscom St., Philadelphia, PA 19124-3954, 215-289-6484

Description: The museum contains an extensive collection of Civil War artifacts, battle relics, personal memorabilia, paintings, documents, and photographs that were initially assembled by the veterans who formed Post 2 of the Grand Army of the Republic.

Admission Fees: Free.

Open to Public: Third Mon. of every month: 7 P.M.–9 P.M.; Second Tues. of every month:

7 P.M.–9 P.M.; First Sun. of every month and by appointment.

Visitor Services: Museum; gift shop; rest rooms; handicapped access.

Regularly Scheduled Events: Programs are presented the first Sun. of every month: call for schedule.

Directions: From I-95: exit at Bridge St.; go west on either Bridge or Wakeling St.; follow to Griscom St., turn left to museum.

12 **Site:** HISTORICAL SOCIETY OF PENNSYLVANIA, 1300 Locust St., Philadelphia, PA 19107, 215-732-6201

Description: Contains an extensive collection of Civil War artifacts and documents; collection of Underground Railroad artifacts; and the papers and diary of William Still, founder of the abolition movement in Philadelphia.

Admission Fees: Adults: $2.50; Children: $1.50; Seniors: $1.50.

Open to Public: Tues., Thurs., Fri. & Sat.: 10 A.M.–5 P.M.; Wed.: 1 P.M.–9 P.M.

Visitor Services: Museum; information; rest rooms; handicapped access.

Directions: From I-95: take I-676 (Vine St. Expressway) exit; go south on 15th St. After five blocks, turn left onto Locust St.; museum is located on 13th & Locust Streets.

---

13 **Site:** THE JOHNSON HOUSE, 6133 Germantown Ave., Philadelphia, PA 19144, 215-843-0943

Description: The Johnson House was a station on the Underground Railroad. At this time the Johnson House is the only site in Philadelphia that interprets the Underground Railroad.

Admission Fees: Adults: $3; Children: $1.50; Seniors: $1.50.

Open to Public: Apr.–Oct.: Sat.: 1 P.M.–4 P.M. All other times by appointment. Call to confirm reservation.

Visitor Services: Museum; gift shop; information.

Directions: From Pennsylvania Turnpike: exit 25 at Norristown; follow Germantown Pike east for 8 miles. From I-76: take the Lincoln Dr. exit. Just beyond the second stoplight, turn onto Harvey St. and follow to the end; turn left onto Germantown Ave.

---

14 **Site:** THE WOODLANDS AND CLARK PARK, The Woodlands: 4000 Woodland Ave., Philadelphia, PA 19104, 215-386-2181; Clark Park: located in downtown Philadelphia.

Description: The Woodlands cemetery comprises the memorials of abolitionists, generals, volunteer nurses, authors, and even Confederate sympathizer, the Reverend Fleming James. The graves of other veterans also recall the war experience as do a number of original GAR Meade Post #1 markers. The grounds overlook the convergence of the Schuylkill River and Mill Creek, used to transport the Union wounded at Gettysburg to nearby Satterlee Hospital, the largest U.S. Army hospital in the Civil War. Clark Park is located on the former hospital site. A stone from the battlefield at Gettysburg was placed in the park in 1916 to commemorate the Satterlee Hospital; a plaque rests at the base of the stone.

Admission Fees: *The Woodlands:* Guided tour of grounds & mansion: $3. *Clark Park:* Free.

Open to Public: *The Woodlands:* Daily: 9 A.M.–5 P.M. *Clark Park:* Daily: Daylight hours.

Visitor Services: *At The Woodlands:* Trails; museum; information; rest rooms. *At Clark Park:* Handicapped access.

Regularly Scheduled Events: *Apr.:* At The Woodlands: Adopt-a-Grave picnic and walkabout; *Nov.:* At Clark Park: Veterans Day commemoration.

Directions: To The Woodlands: From I-76: exit at University Ave.; turn left on Balti- more Ave.; turn left on Woodland Ave.; proceed left through gates at 40th St.; follow white arrows. To Clark Park: From I-76: exit on University Ave. Proceed straight for about three blocks to the first large intersection. Turn left onto Baltimore Ave. and continue from 38th St. to 43d St. Clark Park and the Gettysburg stone are on the left between 43d St. and 44th St.

Pittsburgh

15 **Site:** SOLDIERS AND SAILORS MEMORIAL HALL AND MILITARY HISTORY MUSEUM, 4141 Fifth Ave., Pittsburgh, PA 15213, 412-621-4253

Description: Soldiers and Sailors Memorial Hall was built in 1910 to honor Allegheny veterans who served in the Civil War. The museum holds the finest Civil War relics in the area: muskets and rifles, pistols, sabers and bayonets, cannons, and other personal and battlefield memorabilia. In addition, there are photographs and paintings depicting the Civil War battles and leaders. It also has the most comprehensive Civil War library in the area.

Admission Fees: Free.

Open to Public: Mon.–Fri.: 9 A.M.–4 P.M.; Weekends: 1 P.M.–4 P.M.

Visitor Services: Museum; gift shop; information; rest rooms; handicapped access.

Directions: From Pennsylvania Turnpike: take I-376 west to Oakland exit; continue in right lane up hill to second traffic light; turn left; then turn right at next light onto Forbes Ave.; turn left on Bigelow. From I-79: take exit I-279 to I-376; take Forbes Ave. exit; turn left on Bigelow Blvd.

Sinking Spring

16 **Site:** THE AMERICAN HOUSE, 737 Fritztown Rd., Sinking Spring, PA 19608, Berks County Visitors Bureau: 610-375-4085 or 800-439-7687

Description: The American House operated under the proprietorship of Civil War veteran, John J. K. Gittelman. Upon the outbreak of the war, Gittelman, on October 19, 1862, became Corporal of Company E, 17th Pennsylvania Volunteer Cavalry, Second Brigade, First Division, Army of the Potomac. Today, the American House contains specialty shops, featuring a crafts gallery, gift shop, a restaurant, and an ice-cream parlor.

Admission Fees: Free.

Open to Public: Tues.–Sat.: 10 A.M.–8 P.M.; Sun.: Noon–8 P.M.; hours vary on Mon.

Visitor Services: Food; ice-cream parlor; retail specialty shops; information; rest rooms.

Regularly Scheduled Events: Annual Civil War encampment weekend: call for dates.

Directions: From Pennsylvania Turnpike: take exit 22 (Morgantown); take I-176 north to Rte. 422 west. At traffic light, Sinking Springboro Hall, fork to left off 422 west onto Columbia Ave. (which turns into Fritztown Rd.); American House is located 1.8 miles on the right.

Washington

17 **Site:** LEMOYNE HOUSE AND THE MILITARY MUSEUM OF SOUTHWESTERN PENNSYLVANIA, Washington County Historical Society, 49 East Maiden St., Washington, PA 15301, 412-225-6740

Description: The LeMoyne House is the 1812 home of Dr. F. Julius LeMoyne, a physician, abolitionist, and humanitarian. This house was a stop on the Underground Railroad. Dr. LeMoyne was a candidate for governor of Pennsylvania on the platform of antislavery. His son, Dr. Frank LeMoyne, was a surgeon for the Union during the Civil War. The military museum occupies one room within the LeMoyne House. The core collection contains Civil War artifacts, including military equipment and uniforms and a military history library.

Admission Fees: Adults: $3; Children: $1.50; Groups: $2.50/person.

Open to Public: Wed.–Fri.: Noon–4 P.M.; Sun.: 2 P.M.–4 P.M.; closed mid-Dec.–Jan.

Visitor Services: Museum; gift shop; information.

Regularly Scheduled Events: *Third weekend in May:* National Pike festival (museum open extended hours); *Dec.:* Christmas tours (first person interpretation; extended hours).

Directions: Located 25 miles south of Pittsburgh, at the intersection of interstates 70 and 79. From I-70/79: exit at Rte. 19 south. Turn right at Rte. 40 west. LeMoyne House is in the first block on the right.

SOUTH CAROLINA

$\mathcal{S}$outh Carolina played a major role in the Civil War from the beginning—indeed, in the more than 30 years of tension between the North and South before the war. When Abraham Lincoln was elected president in 1860, many South Carolinians were among the most prominent and most enthusiastic proponents of secession from the Union. The South Carolina General Assembly called a secession convention and on December 20 became the first state to secede.

Three Federal forts in Charleston Harbor—Fort Sumter, Fort Moultrie, and Castle Pinckney—were crucial to the interests of both the United States and the new republic of South Carolina. When Major Robert Anderson moved a small Federal garrison from Fort Moultrie to Fort Sumter in late December, the South Carolinians responded by taking Castle Pinckney and Fort Moultrie, making war a distinct possibility. In March 1861, Lincoln decided to send provisions to Fort Sumter. In the early morning of April 12, Confederate troops demanded the surrender of Fort Sumter and ordered the artillery bombardment that began the Civil War. Anderson surrendered the next day after a prolonged bombardment.

The Palmetto State was not a major battleground during the Civil War, though it did see a few major campaigns and several minor engagements. Most notable were the occupation of the Sea Islands; the long siege of Charleston, which lasted until the end of the war; and the march of Federal troops commanded by General William T. Sherman from Savannah to Columbia and into North Carolina in early 1865. The Federal blockade of Southern ports was headquartered at Port Royal after its capture by a large naval expedition in November 1861. Sea Islands were used for the training and education of thousands of ex-slaves whom the Federal authorities considered to be freed by virtue of the military occupation of the area.

Federal attempts to capture Charleston began in June 1862 at Secessionville, on James Island, and continued through the bloody assault on Battery Wagner in July 1863. Fort Sumter withstood three major bombardments and only surrendered in February 1865 after the city was evacuated by Confederate troops. After Sherman captured Savannah in December 1864, he marched his Federals into South Carolina. Sherman's march left considerable devastation and lasting bitterness that lingered for years.

One of the more obvious costs of the war was the 12,000 lives lost or ruined. Perhaps the most significant consequence of Union victory, however, was the emancipation of 400,000 slaves and their subsequent attempt to adjust to their new place in South Carolina society. As in so much of the South, the end of the war raised as many new questions as the old ones it had been fought to answer.

by J. Tracy Power, South Carolina Department of Archives and History

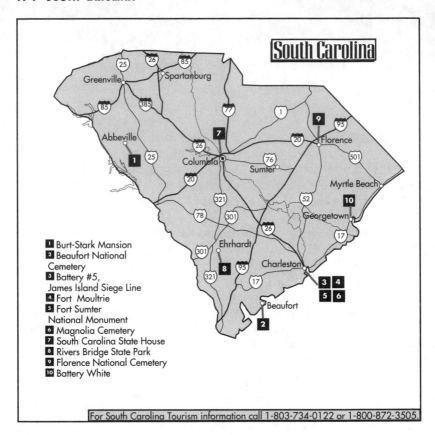

South Carolina

1 Burt-Stark Mansion
2 Beaufort National Cemetery
3 Battery #5, James Island Siege Line
4 Fort Moultrie
5 Fort Sumter National Monument
6 Magnolia Cemetery
7 South Carolina State House
8 Rivers Bridge State Park
9 Florence National Cemetery
10 Battery White

For South Carolina Tourism information call 1-803-734-0122 or 1-800-872-3505.

Abbeville

Site: BURT-STARK MANSION, 306 North Main St. at Greenville St., Abbeville, SC 29620, 864-459-4600

Description: This house was the site of the last Council of War held by Confederate President Jefferson Davis, on May 2, 1865. Davis, along with a few members of his cabinet and several Confederate generals, was on his way south after the fall of Richmond and hoped to rally support. Though Davis still clung to the hope of military success, he was persuaded by subordinates that further resistance was futile, and the war was over.

Admission Fees: $4

Open to Public: Fri.–Sat.: 1 P.M.–5 P.M.; any day by appointment.

Visitor Services: Tours.

Directions: From I-26 east or west: take exit 54, then take SC Hwy. 72, 3 miles west to Clinton; 24 miles SW to Greenwood; 24 miles west to Abbeville; turn right onto South Main St., travel around square;

follow signs on North Main St. to house. From I-85: take exit 27; then take SC Hwy. 81 South to Anderson; SC Hwy. 28, 30 miles to Abbeville. SC Hwy 28 becomes North Main St. in Abbeville; follow signs on North Main St. to house.

Beaufort

2 **Site:** BEAUFORT NATIONAL CEMETERY, 1601 Boundary St., Beaufort, SC 29902, 803-524-3925

Description: This national cemetery was established in 1863 for the burial of Union soldiers who died during the Federal occupation of Beaufort and for the reinterment of Union soldiers' remains from various locations in South Carolina, Georgia, and Florida. More than 9,000 Union soldiers or veterans are buried here—4,400 of them unknown—including 2,800 prisoners of war from the camp at Millen, Georgia, as well as 1,700 black Union soldiers. There are 117 Confederate soldiers buried here.

Admission Fees: Free.

Open to Public: *Office:* Mon.–Fri.: 8 A.M.–4:30 P.M. *Cemetery:* Daily: Dawn to dusk.

Visitor Services: None.

Directions: From I-95: take exit 33 to Beaufort; take U.S. Hwy. 21 south through Pocotaligo, Sheldon, and Garden's Corner; proceed past the U.S. Marine Corps Air Station on left; cemetery is on left approximately 2 miles after air station.

Charleston

3 **Site:** BATTERY #5, JAMES ISLAND SIEGE LINE, South Carolina Battleground Trust, 1251 Marsh View Dr., Charleston, SC 29412, 803-762-3563

Description: Battery #5, a Confederate earthwork constructed in 1863 under the direction of General P. G. T. Beauregard, commander of the Departments of South Carolina, Georgia, and Florida, was the eastern terminus of the James Island Siege Line. Intended to anchor the Confederate defenses of James Island and overlooking Seaside Creek and the Secessionville peninsula, this battery is an excellent intact example of a Civil War earthwork.

Admission Fees: Free.

Open to Public: Daily: Dawn to dusk.

Visitor Services: None.

Directions: From I-26: take exit for U.S. Hwy. 17 south toward Savannah; cross over Ashley River; take Hwy. 171 for 5 miles; turn left onto Burclair Dr. to Secessionville Rd. to Seaside Plantation; second road on the right.

4 Site: FORT MOULTRIE, a unit of Fort Sumter National Monument, 1214 Middle St., Sullivan's Island, SC 29484, 803-883-3123

Description: Fort Moultrie is administered by the Fort Sumter National Monument. Fort Moultrie's history covers 171 years of seacoast defense, from the first decisive victory in the American Revolution to protecting the coast from U-boats in World War II. The present fort, built in 1809, was occupied by Major Robert Anderson and 85 Federal soldiers before they moved to Fort Sumter. During the first battle of the Civil War, (April 12–13, 1861), Confederates at Fort Moultrie fired upon Union troops in Fort Sumter. Confederate forces successfully used both forts to protect Charleston from a combined Union navy and army seige from 1863–65.

Admission Fees: Free.

Open to Public: Daily: 9 A.M.–5 P.M.; closed Christmas Day.

Visitor Services: Orientation film; museum; rest rooms; bookstore; information; handicapped access.

Directions: From Charleston: take U.S. 17 north toward Mount Pleasant. Just over the Cooper River Bridge, turn right onto U.S. Hwy 703. Stay on this road to Sullivan's Island; at the stop sign turn right onto Middle St.; the Fort is 1.5 miles from this intersection.

5 Site: FORT SUMTER NATIONAL MONUMENT, 1214 Middle St., Sullivan's Island, SC 29482, 803-883-3123. Accessible by private boat or through Fort Sumter Tours, 803-722-1691.

Description: Fort Sumter National Monument includes Fort Sumter, a coastal fortification that began construction in 1829 but was still not completed by the time the Civil War began here in April 1861. Confederate and South Carolina troops under the direction of General P. G. T. Beauregard bombarded the Union garrison commanded by Major Robert Anderson for 34 hours on April 12–13 until Major Anderson surrendered the fort. Fort Sumter was occupied by a Confederate garrison for most of the war. During the Siege of Charleston, 1863–65, Fort Sumter was reduced to one-third of its original size. After the war, Fort Sumter was repaired but never rebuilt to its original height.

Admission Fees: Free.

Tour Boat Fees: Adults: $10; Children (6–12): $5.50; Seniors and military: $1 discount.

Open to Public: Daily: except Christmas. Easter weekend and April–Labor Day: 10 A.M.–5:30 P.M.; Dec. 26–Jan. 1, Mar., and the day after Labor Day through Feb.: 10 A.M. –4 P.M.; Dec.–Feb.: 2 P.M.–4 P.M.

Visitor Services: Museum; museum shop; rest rooms; information; handicapped access.

Directions: To the City Marina: take I-26 to Charleston; take U.S. Hwy. 17 south toward Savannah; turn left onto Lockwood Blvd.; turn right at the first traffic light; City Marina is on the right. To Patriots

Point: take I-26 to Charleston; take U.S. Hwy. 17 north toward Mt. Pleasant; just over the Cooper River Bridge, turn right onto U.S. Hwy. 703 (Coleman Blvd.); at first traffic light turn right into Patriots Point. For private boaters: Fort Sumter is 3.3 miles from Charleston at the harbor entrance.

Fort Sumter, Charleston, SC. (Photograph courtesy of the National Park Service, Fort Sumter National Monument.)

---

6 **Site:** MAGNOLIA CEMETERY, 70 Cunnington Ave., Charleston, SC 29405, 803-722-8638

Description: Magnolia Cemetery, established in 1850, includes the graves of several prominent Confederate civilian and military leaders. Captain Horace Hunley and the crew of the CSS *H.L. Hunley*, the Confederate submarine that was the first to sink a warship, are also buried here. A monument to South Carolina's Civil War dead stands in the Confederate section of the cemetery, which contains the graves of many officers and enlisted men, many of whom died during the siege of Charleston.

Admission Fees: Free.

Open to Public: *Grounds:* Winter: 8 A.M.–5 P.M.; Summer: 8 A.M.–6 P.M.; *Office:* Mon.–Fri. 9 A.M.–4 P.M.

Visitor Services: None.

Directions: From I-26: take exit 219B (Meeting St.); turn left at second light; then turn right at Cunnington Ave. Cemetery is at the end of the block.

Columbia

---

7 **Site:** SOUTH CAROLINA STATE HOUSE, Gervais St. and Main St., Columbia, SC 29201, 803-734-2430

Description: The South Carolina State House, begun in 1855 and unfinished until after the Civil War, witnessed the Federal occupation of Columbia on February 17–18, 1865. Union artillery batteries seeking to find their range fired on this building from across the Congaree River, and bronze stars mark the places where their shells hit the state house. General William T. Sherman's Federals also raised the United States flag over the unfinished building, looted the existing state house, and repealed the Ordinance of Secession. Several Civil War–related monuments are on the state house grounds.

Admission Fees: Free.

Open to Public: Closed for renovations until 1998.

Visitor Services: None.

Directions: From I-26, which becomes Elmwood Ave: turn right onto Main St., which dead-ends at the state house at Gervais St. From I-77: travel south to 277, which becomes Bull St.; take Bull St. to Gervais St.; turn right on Gervais St.; proceed three blocks and turn onto Main St. The state house is on the left at the end of Main St.

Ehrhardt

8 **Site:** RIVERS BRIDGE STATE PARK, Rte. 1, Ehrhardt, SC 29081, 803-267-3675

Description: The only significant engagement in South Carolina during General William T. Sherman's advance through the state in early 1865 took place on February 2 and 3 at the still-intact earthworks overlooking Rivers Bridge, on the Salkehatchie River. Sherman's Federals, some 8,000 troops, were delayed briefly by 900 Confederates under the overall command of General Lafayette McLaws. They soon outflanked the Confederate position upstream at Buford's Bridge and downstream at Broxton's Bridge, forcing a Confederate withdrawal and clearing the way for a Federal advance to Columbia.

Admission Fees: Free.

Open to Public: Daily: 9 A.M.–9 P.M.

Visitor Services: Camping; trails; museum; rest rooms; handicapped access.

Regular Scheduled Events: Annual battle reenactment and living history exhibit.

Directions: From I-95: take exit 47, SC Hwy. 641, 20 miles west to Ehrhardt and follow signs to Rivers Bridge State Park.

Florence

9 **Site:** FLORENCE NATIONAL CEMETERY, 803 East National Cemetery Rd., Florence, SC 29501, 803-669-8783

Desciption: This national cemetery was established in 1865 and is associated with the nearby Union prisoner-of-war camp, Florence Stockade, which held as many as 12,000 prisoners between September 1864 and February 1865. The prisoner cemetery formed the nucleus of the new national cemetery. Some 3,000 Union soldiers who died in the prison, as many as 2,000 of them unknown, are buried here.

Admission Fees: Free.

Open to Public: *Office:* Mon.–Fri.: 8 A.M.–5 P.M.; *Cemetery:* Daily: Dawn to dusk.

Visitor Services: None.

Directions: From I-95: travel on U.S. 52 (Lucas St.) to North Irby St. and turn right; North Irby St. becomes South Irby St.; continue on South Irby St.; turn left onto National Cemetery Rd.

Georgetown

10 **Site:** BATTERY WHITE, Belle Isle Yacht Club, Georgetown, SC 29440, 803-546-1423

Description: Battery White, a Confederate earthwork constructed in 1862 under the direction of General John C. Pemberton, commander of the Departments of South Carolina and Georgia, was built on Mayrant's Bluff to defend the entrance to Winyah Bay and the Santee River. It is an excellent intact example of a Civil War earthwork.

Admission Fees: Free.

Open to Public: Daily: Dawn to dusk.

Visitor Services: None.

Directions: From I-95: take Rt. 521, at Alcolu, east for 50 miles and cross the Santee River; follow signs to Belle Isle Garden.

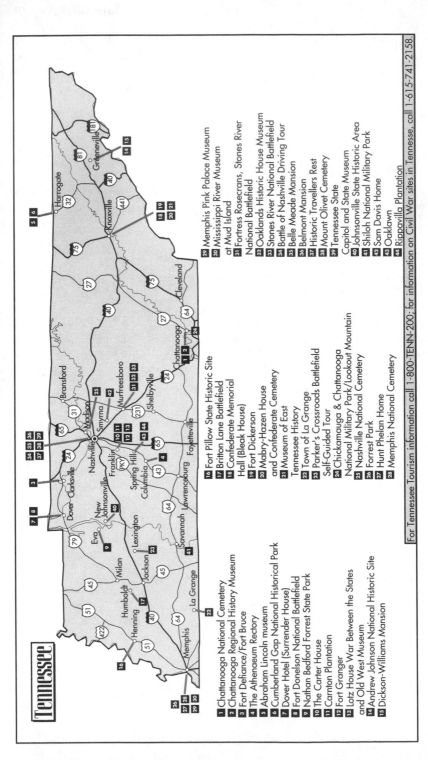

Tennessee

1 Chattanooga National Cemetery
2 Chattanooga Regional History Museum
3 Fort Defiance/Fort Bruce
4 The Athenaeum Rectory
5 Abraham Lincoln museum
6 Cumberland Gap National Historical Park
7 Dover Hotel (Surrender House)
8 Fort Donelson National Battlefield
9 Nathan Bedford Forrest State Park
10 The Carter House
11 Carnton Plantation
12 Fort Granger
13 Lotz House War Between the States and Old West Museum
14 Andrew Johnson National Historic Site
15 Dickson-Williams Mansion

16 Fort Pillow State Historic Site
17 Britton Lane Battlefield
18 Confederate Memorial Hall (Bleak House)
19 Fort Dickerson
20 Mabry-Hazen House and Confederate Cemetery
21 Museum of East Tennessee History
22 Town of La Grange
23 Parker's Crossroads Battlefield Self-Guided Tour
24 Chickamauga & Chattanooga National Military Park/Lookout Mountain
25 Nashville National Cemetery
26 Forrest Park
27 Hunt Phelan Home
28 Memphis National Cemetery

29 Memphis Pink Palace Museum
30 Mississippi River Museum at Mud Island
31 Fortress Rosecrans, Stones River National Battlefield
32 Oaklands Historic House Museum
33 Stones River National Battlefield
34 Battle of Nashville Driving Tour
35 Belle Meade Mansion
36 Belmont Mansion
37 Historic Travellers Rest
38 Mount Olivet Cemetery
39 Tennessee State Capitol and State Museum
40 Johnsonville State Historic Area
41 Shiloh National Military Park
42 Sam Davis Home
43 Oaklawn
44 Rippavilla Plantation

For Tennessee Tourism information call 1-800-TENN-200; for information on Civil War sites in Tennessee, call 1-615-741-2158.

Tennessee

*T*he outcome of the Civil War was decided in the heartland of the Confederacy, known as the Western Theater. Tennessee, one of the strongholds of this region, was the last of the Southern states to secede from the Union, yet it would become the second most embattled, with more than 1,462 military encounters on its soil. One of the reasons for such intense fighting within Tennessee's borders was its strategic importance for the new Confederacy. Besides being an important defensive perimeter state, Tennessee was a leader among other Southern states in production of raw materials, manufacturing facilities, and agricultural goods, and it was the secondmost populated state in the Confederacy. Tennessee was a major link in the South's overall transportation system with more than a dozen railroads and four major rivers essential to the Confederacy for the placement of troops and materiel.

Splitting the Confederacy and destroying the South's natural resources were two of the Federal government's major war objectives. These could only be accomplished by gaining control of the Mississippi, Tennessee, and Cumberland rivers. The eventual capture of Tennessee's river and rail systems and the Federal occupation of its major cities thwarted Confederate hopes for victory.

by Fred M. Prouty, Administrator, Tennessee Wars Commission

Chattanooga

 Site: CHATTANOOGA NATIONAL CEMETERY, 1200 Bailey Ave., Chattanooga, TN 37404, 423-855-590

Description: Chattanooga National Cemetery was established during the Civil War in December 1863 by an order from Gen. George Thomas to provide a proper burial for Union soldiers killed in battles around Chattanooga. Eight Andrews' Raiders are buried in the cemetery, four of whom were the first to receive the Medal of Honor.

Admission Fees: Free.

Open to Public: Daily: 24 hours.

Visitor Services: Information; rest rooms; handicapped access.

Regularly Scheduled Events: *May:* Memorial Day ceremony; *Nov.:* Veterans Day ceremony.

Directions: From I-24: take the Fourth Ave. exit. Turn right at the first traffic light; turn left at the next traffic light. Turn right at Holtzclaw Ave. and continue to the main entrance of the cemetery. Proceed into the cemetery and turn right to the cemetery office to pick up brochure.

---

2   **Site:** CHATTANOOGA REGIONAL HISTORY MUSEUM, 400 Chestnut St., Chattanooga, TN 37402, 423-265-3247

Description: The Chattanooga Regional History Museum has an extensive Civil War collection numbering more than 500 pieces, including: a mountain howitzer; Grant's headquarter's chair; dozens of muskets, rifles, swords, knives, and pistols; projectiles; minié balls; various accouterments; uniforms; original photographs taken by R. M. Linn, George N. Bernard, and others; diaries and letters; and veterans' and National Park memorabilia. These artifacts are on display in the museum's permanent collection or stored in its archives.

Admission Fees: Adults: $2.50; Children: $1.50; Seniors: $1.75; Groups (10 or more): $1.50/person.

Open to Public: Mon.–Sat.: 10 A.M.–4:30 P.M.; Sun.: 11 A.M.–4:30 P.M.

Visitor Services: Museum; gift shop; information; rest rooms; handicapped access.

Regularly Scheduled Events: Programs on Civil War history: call for schedule.

Directions: From I-24: take exit 178 to I-124 north; take exit 1C; turn right on Chestnut St.; take first left turn into museum parking lot.

Clarksville

---

3   **Site:** FORT DEFIANCE/FORT BRUCE, 200 South Second St., Clarksville, TN 37040, 615-648-0001

Description: During the capture of Clarksville, Fort Defiance was burned and abandoned by Confederate forces, leading to the fall of Fort Donelson. The recapture of the city by Confederate troops in August 1862, renewed interest in the fort. During the remainder of the war, the fort was commanded by Colonel Sanders D. Bruce, of Kentucky, for whom it was renamed.

Admission Fees: Free.

Open to Public: Daily: 8 A.M.–5 P.M.

Visitor Services: For tours, call Clarksville-Montgomery Co. Historical Museum at 615-645-2507.

Directions: From I-24 west from Clarksville: take exit 4; turn left onto Hwy. 79; cross bridge to Craft St.; turn right (41A north) across bridge; turn left onto B St.; then turn left onto Walker St.; turn left at A St.

Columbia

---

4   **Site:** THE ATHENAEUM RECTORY, 808 Athenaeum St., Columbia, TN 38401, 615-381-4822

Description: The Athenaeum Rectory was headquarters for Generals Negley and Schofield during the Civil War. Gen. Nathan Bedford Forrest was a frequent visitor. The owner of the house, the Reverend F. G. Smith, the rector of a girls' school, outfitted a company of Confederate soldiers, the Maury Rifles. The Reverend Smith also designed a submarine and worked on a hot air balloon for the South.

Admission Fees: Adults: $2; Children: $1; Seniors: $1.

Open to Public: Tues.–Sat.: 10 A.M.–4 P.M.; Sun.: 1 P.M.–4 P.M.

Visitor Services: Tours; museum; gift-shop; rest rooms; handicapped access.

Regularly Scheduled Events: *First full week after the Fourth of July:* Girls' 1861 summer school; *Autumn:* Tour of homes, by special reservation.

Directions: From I-65 South: take Saturn Pkwy. to Hwy. 315 (take Columbia exit from Saturn Pkwy). Travel approximately 8 miles into Columbia to West Seventh St. and turn right. Proceed three blocks to West Seventh St. Church of Christ. Turn left immediately past the church on Athanaeum St. The house is at the end of the street and is designated by a blue sign.

Cumberland Gap/Harrogate

5 **Site:** ABRAHAM LINCOLN MUSEUM, Lincoln Memorial University, Harrogate, TN 37752, 615-869-6235

Description: From his humble birth in rural Kentucky to the dramatic years of the Civil War and his tragic death, Lincoln's life is recounted at the Abraham Lincoln Museum. You are invited to experience the events of his time—the events that shaped the future of this country in its fight for an identity amid the problems of slavery and sectionalism. The Abraham Lincoln Museum is a monument to regional and national history that allows visitors to get a glimpse of the Great Emancipator.

Admission Fees: Adults: $2; Children (6–12): $1; Seniors (60 and over): $1.50.

Open to Public: Mon.–Fri.: 9 A.M.–4 P.M.; Sat.: 11 A.M.–4 P.M.; Sun.: 1 P.M.–4 P.M.

Visitor Services: Gift shop; rest rooms; information.

Directions: From I-81: take Hwy. 25E exit; travel south through Middlesboro, KY on Hwy. 25E. The museum is located on the campus of Lincoln Memorial University.

6 **Site:** CUMBERLAND GAP NATIONAL HISTORICAL PARK, U.S. 25E South, P.O. Box 1848, Middlesboro, KY 40965, 606-248-2817

Description: Cumberland Gap is the historic mountain pass on the Wilderness Road that opened the pathway for westward migration. During the Civil War,

Cumberland Gap was first held by the South, then captured by Union troops. Each side held the Gap twice.

Admission Fees: Free.

Open to Public: *Mid-June–Labor Day:* Daily: 8 A.M.–6 P.M.; *Labor Day–mid-June:* Daily: 8 A.M.–5 P.M.

Visitor Services: Gift shop; rest rooms; trails; museum; information; camping; handicapped access.

Directions: From I-75 at the Caryville exit: take Hwy. 63 to 25E. Turn left on 25E; travel 5 miles to the park.

Dover

7 **Site:** DOVER HOTEL (SURRENDER HOUSE), P.O. Box 434, Dover, TN 37058, 615-232-5348

Description: The Dover Hotel was the site where Gen. Ulysses S. Grant accepted the Confederate surrender of Gen. Simon Bolivar Buckner after the Battle of Fort Donelson in February 1862. The house is the only original surrender structure remaining from the Civil War.

Admission Fees: Free.

Open to Public: June–Sept.: Daily: Noon–4 P.M.

Visitor Services: Information; rest rooms; handicapped access.

Directions: From I-24: exit onto Hwy. 79 south at Clarksville; continue 35 miles to Dover; turn left at Petty St.; the hotel is two blocks down on the left.

8 **Site:** FORT DONELSON NATIONAL BATTLEFIELD, P.O. Box 434, Dover, TN 37058, 615-232-5348

Description: Fort Donelson was built by the Confederates to control the Cumberland River. The fort was captured in February 1862 by the Union army under the command of General Grant, and victory secured Union control of the Cumberland River, Nashville, Clarksville, and most of middle Tennessee.

Admission Fees: Free.

Open to Public: Daily: 8 A.M.–4:30 P.M.

Visitor Services: Trails; museum; gift shop; information; rest rooms; handicapped access.

Directions: From I-24: take Rte. 79 to Dover; follow signs.

Eva

9 **Site:** NATHAN BEDFORD FORREST STATE PARK, Star Rte., Eva, TN 38333, 901-584-6356

Description: The park was named for Gen. Nathan Bedford Forrest, the intrepid Confederate cavalry leader who on November 4, 1864 attacked and destroyed the Federal supply and munitions depot at (old) Johnsonville at the mouth of Trace Creek. His operations were concentrated along the river near the park and the town of Eva. The park features a monument to Gen. Forrest and a map delineating the action at Johnsonville.

Admission Fees: Free.

Open to Public: *Park:* Daily: 24 hours; *Museum:* Apr.–Nov.: 8 A.M.–4:30 P.M.

Visitor Services: Camping; trails; museum; gift shop; information; rest rooms; handicapped access.

Regularly Scheduled Events: *Third Sat. in Sept.:* Civil War reenactment; *Second Sat. in Oct.:* Folklife festival.

Directions: Located north of I-40 on the Tennessee River. From I-40: take exit 126; travel north on Hwy. 641 (15 miles) to Hwy. 70 in Camden; go around courthouse; take Hwy. 191 north for 9 miles to the park. There are signs from Camden.

Franklin

10 **Site:** THE CARTER HOUSE, 1140 Columbia Ave., Franklin, TN 37065, 615-791-1861

Description: Built in 1830, the Carter House was the location of the 1864 Battle of Franklin. Serving as a federal command post before the battle and as a hospital after, the house and grounds are today preserved on 10 acres. In this night battle lasting only five hours, more Confederate soldiers, including six generals, were lost than in Pickett's Charge at Gettysburg.

Admission Fees: Adults: $5; Children 12 and under: $1.50; Seniors: $4; Groups (25 or more): $1 off each.

Open to Public: Apr.–Oct.: Mon.–Sat.: 9 A.M.–5 P.M.; Sun.: 1 P.M.–5 P.M.; Nov.–Mar.: Mon.–Sat.: 9 A.M.–4 P.M.; Sun.: 1 P.M.–4 P.M.

Visitor Services: Museum; gift shop; film; rest rooms.

Regularly Scheduled Events: *First weekend in Dec.:* Candlelight tour of homes.

Directions: From I-65: take exit 65; take Hwy. 96 into Franklin; at Courthouse Sq., turn left on Main St.; turn left on Columbia Ave (State Rte. 31 South). Entrance off Fowlkes St.

11 **Site:** CARNTON PLANTATION, 1345 Carnton Lane, Franklin, TN 37064, 615-794-0903

Description: Carnton was built in 1826 by Randal McGavock, a former mayor of Nashville. On November 30, 1864, Confederate troops moved through the grounds of Carnton to engage well-entrenched Federal troops to the northwest. The resulting battle left more than 6,000 Confederate casualties, many of which were taken to

Carnton, which served as a hospital. Also visit the McGavock Confederate Cemetery, the largest private Confederate cemetery in the nation and a National Historic Landmark. It adjoins the Carnton property and is maintained by Franklin UDC; call 615-794-5056 for more information.

Admission Fees: Adults: $5; Children (4–12): $1; Seniors: $4.

Open to Public: Apr.–Oct.: Mon.–Sat.: 9 A.M.–5 P.M.; Sun.: 1 P.M.–5 P.M.; Nov.–Mar.: Mon.–Sat.: 9 A.M.–4 P.M.; Sun.: 1 P.M.–4 P.M.

Visitor Services: Museum; gift shop; rest rooms.

Directions: From I-65: take exit 65 (Hwy. 96) to MacHatcher By-Pass, turn left to Lewisburg Ave. (431); turn left on Carnton Ln.

---

12 **Site:** FORT GRANGER, P.O. Box 305, Franklin, TN 37065, 615-791-3217

Description: In February 1863, General Rosecrans, in command of the Federal troops in middle Tennessee, ordered Major General Gordon Granger to fortify Franklin. On November 30, 1864, Confederate General Hood attacked. The fort was abandoned when the Federals withdrew to Nashville during the night, but was reoccupied two weeks later as Hood's defeated army withdrew from the state.

Admission Fees: Free.

Open to Public: Daily: 8 A.M.–5 P.M.

Visitor Services: Tours may be arranged through the Carter House Museum by calling 615-791-1861.

Directions: From I-65: take Franklin exit (Hwy. 96) west toward downtown Franklin for 2.5 miles. Turn right into Pinkerton Park and follow the signs to the fort. (The park is on the right just before the bridge over the Harpeth River, before you get into downtown Franklin.)

---

13 **Site:** LOTZ HOUSE WAR BETWEEN THE STATES AND OLD WEST MUSEUM, 1111 Columbia Ave., Franklin, TN 37064, 615-791-6533

Description: The Lotz House features rare Confederate and Union artifacts as well as Old West and Native American items. The house was built in 1858 by German woodworker Albert Lotz and still features much of his handiwork. Lotz House was used as a hospital after the Battle of Franklin.

Admission Fees: Adults: $5; Children: $1.50; Seniors: $4; Groups (25 or more): $3/ person.

Open to Public: Mon.–Sat.: 9 A.M.– 5 P.M.; Sun.: Noon–5 P.M.

Visitor Services: Museum; gift shop.

Regularly Scheduled Events: *June 3:* Confederate Memorial Day celebration; *Nov. 30:* Commemoration of the Battle of Franklin.

Directions: From I-65: take exit 65; travel west on Hwy. 96 to Franklin's town square; turn left (around square) on Main St. and proceed to the second light. Travel south approximately .25 mile on Hwy. 31 (Columbia Ave.) to 1111 Columbia Ave. House is on the left; look for signs and a cannon on the front porch.

Greeneville

14 Site: ANDREW JOHNSON NATIONAL HISTORIC SITE, P.O. Box 1088, Greeneville, TN 37744-1088, 423-638-3551 or 423-638-1326

Description: This 16-acre site preserves two homes, the tailor shop, and cemetery where President Andrew Johnson lived, worked, and was buried. When Tennessee seceded from the Union, Johnson became an avid opponent of seccession and was appointed military governor of Tennessee by President Lincoln in 1862.

Admission Fees: Tours of the Homestead: 18 or older: $2.

Open to Public: Daily: 9 A.M.–5 P.M.; Closed Thanksgiving, Christmas, and New Year's Day.

Visitor Services: Rest rooms; museum.

Directions: From I-81: follow 11E north if traveling north or TN 172 if traveling south. Follow directional signs to the visitor center, located at the corner of College and Depot Streets in Greeneville. Ranger will direct visitors to the homestead and national cemetery.

15 Site: DICKSON-WILLIAMS MANSION, Church and Irish Streets, Greeneville, TN 37745, 423-787-7746

Description: This mansion, built between 1815 and 1821, hosted many notables: Marquis de Lafayette, Henry Clay, and presidents Jackson and Polk. During the war, it served as headquarters for both Union and Confederate officers while they were in Greeneville. It was in this house that Gen. John Hunt Morgan, the "Rebel Raider," spent his last night, before he was killed in the garden on September 4, 1864. The room where Gen. Morgan slept contains the original furniture from when he occupied the room.

Admission Fees: Adults: $3; Children: $1.

Open to Public: By appointment: call 423-638-4111.

Visitor Services: Tours.

Regularly Scheduled Events: *Oct.:* Reenactment of Battle of Blue Springs; *Dec.:* Christmas tours.

Directions: From I-81 northbound: take exit 23; turn right onto 11-E (4-lane) and continue for 12 miles; take Greeneville Business exit (exit right). Turn right on Summer St.; at the fourth traffic light, turn left onto Irish St. The mansion is two blocks down on the right at Church and Irish Streets. From I-81 southbound: take exit 36; turn left onto Baileyton Rd. (State Rd. 172); proceed 10–11 miles to the first traffic light and turn right onto Main St.; continue on Main St. through one traffic light; turn right at the second traffic light onto Church St.; the mansion is one block down on the left.

Henning

 Site: FORT PILLOW STATE HISTORIC SITE, Rte. 2, P.O. Box 109-D, Henning, TN 38041, 901-738-5581

Description: Federal forces captured this important Confederate river defense in 1862. On April 12, 1864, Confederate General N. B. Forrest attacked the fort and demanded immediate surrender of the garrison, but he was refused. The fort was then stormed and captured. Because of high Union casualties and the presence of black troops, controversy surrounding this battle still exists today.

Admission Fees: Free.

Open to Public: *Grounds:* Daily: 8 A.M.–10 P.M.; *Visitors Center:* Mon.–Fri.: 8 A.M.–4:30 P.M.

Visitor Services: Camping; trails; information; museum; gift shop; rest rooms; handicapped access.

Regularly Scheduled Events: *Every second weekend in Apr.:* Living History Weekend; *First weekend in Nov.:* Civil War lectures.

Directions: From I-40: take Brownsville exit, Hwy. 19 to Hwy. 51.; travel south; turn left to Hwy. 87 west. Follow signs to the park.

Humboldt

17 **Site:** BRITTON LANE BATTLEFIELD, c/o 461 Sanders Bluff Rd., Humboldt, TN 38343, 901-784-4227; 901-935-2209

Description: On September 1, 1862, Confederate Col. William H. Jackson's 7th Tennessee Cavalry, Forrest's Brigade, attacked the 20th and 30th U.S. Infantry, Cavalry, and Artillery under the command of Col. Dennis, near Jackson, Tennessee. The Battle of Britton's Lane resulted in the capture of a large Union wagon train, two pieces of artillery, and 213 prisoners. Monuments mark the site along with a mass grave of Confederates killed in the action. An extant cabin on the site was used as a Federal and a Confederate hospital site. After the battle, 87 Union prisoners were imprisoned in the Denmark Presbyterian Church near Britton Lane Battlefield. The

structure still contains graffiti left by the Union prisoners.

Admission Fees: Free.

Open to Public: Daily: 24 hours.

Visitor Services: Trails; museum; information; handicapped access.

Regularly Scheduled Events: *Throughout the year:* Reenact-ments, living history, gun shows, Civil War church services: call for information.

Directions: From I-40: take exit 76 (Hwy. 223 south); travel on Hwy. 223 south 9 miles to Denmark. Turn left at Denmark Church onto Britton Lane Rd.

Knoxville

18 **Site:** CONFEDERATE MEMORIAL HALL (BLEAK HOUSE), P.O. Box 15012, Knoxville, TN 37901, 800-727-8045, 423-523-2316

Description: Bleak House is a Victorian mansion built in 1858 by prominent Knoxvillian Robert H. Armstrong, using slave labor to mold the bricks on site. During the Siege of Knoxville and the Battle of Fort Sanders in November and December 1863, the home served as headquarters for Confederate generals James Longstreet and Lafayette McLaws. Three soldiers using the house's tower as a sharpshooters post were killed here by Federal cannon fire. A comrade sketched their likenesses on the wall of the tower. Two cannonballs are still embedded in the walls. Artillery also used the lawn to fire on the Federals.

Admission Fees: Adults: $2.50; Children: $.50; Seniors: $1.50.

Open to Public: Tues.–Fri.: 1 P.M.–4 P.M.; Group tours by appointment.

Visitor Services: Museum; tours; gift shop; rest rooms.

Regularly Scheduled Events: *Dec.:* Christmas open house; *Apr.:* Extended hours and gardens open during Knoxville dogwood arts festival.

Directions: From I-40: take Kingston Pike exit; turn right (west) on Kingston Pike. Confederate Memorial Hall is on left at 3148 Kingston Pike.

19 **Site:** FORT DICKERSON, P.O. Box 15012, Knoxville, TN 37901, 800-727-8045, 423-523-2316

Description: Fort Dickerson was one of 16 earthen forts and battery emplacements built by the Federal army to protect Knoxville during the Civil War. The fort, atop a 300-foot-high ridge across the Tennessee River from Knoxville, was begun in November 1863 and completed in January or February 1864. The position was attacked by Confederate cavalry under Gen. Joseph Wheeler on November 15, 1863, but the assault was canceled due to the formidable terrain, artillery, and unex-pected strong force guarding the approaches to Knoxville. There is only a highway marker at the fort; future plans call for this to be a part of a Knoxville Civil War driving tour.

Admission Fees: Free.

Open to Public: Daily: Daylight hours.

Visitor Services: None.

Directions: From I-40: take the Downtown or Hwy. 441 exit; go south on Hwy. 441 (Chapman Hwy.)/Henley St.; cross the Henley St. bridge and continue for approximately 1 mile. There is a Gulf gas station on the left; the drive to the fort is on the right and is marked by a sign.

20 **Site:** MABRY-HAZEN HOUSE AND CONFEDERATE CEMETERY, 1711 Dandridge Ave., Knoxville, TN 37915, 423-522-8661

Description: The Mabry-Hazen House was occupied by Union and Confederate troops alternately. From 1861 to 63, Knoxville was occupied by Confederate troops under Gen. Felix Zollicoffer, who set up headquarters in the home. In 1863, Knoxville and the Mabry home were taken over by Union troops while the family continued to live upstairs. The grounds were fortified, and Mrs. Mabry's sketch of the trenches surrounding the house survives. Hundreds of artifacts help create a personal picture of family life during the Civil War and Reconstruction. The Knoxville Confederate Cemetery contains the remains of 1,600 Confederate troops plus 60 Union soldiers killed between 1861 and 1864. The centerpiece of the cemetery is a 12-foot-square, 48-foot-high monument dedicated in 1891.

Admission Fees: Adults: $3; Children: $1.50; Seniors: $2.50; Groups: $2.50/person.

Open to Public: Mon.–Fri.: 10 A.M.–5 P.M.; Sat.: 1 P.M.–5 P.M.; Open Sun. for holidays and special events only.

Visitor Services: Museum; gift shop; information; rest rooms; limited handicapped access.

Regularly Scheduled Events: *Spring:* Civil War reenactment weekend; *June:* Confederate Memorial Day observance; *Dec.:* Christmas tour (Victorian holiday decor).

Directions: From I-40: take exit 388 to James White Pkwy. Take first exit off Pkwy.; turn left on Summit Hill Dr.; at second traffic light Summit Hill Dr. becomes Dandridge Ave; turn left on Rosedale; take first gravel drive to the right.

---

21 Site: MUSEUM OF EAST TENNESSEE HISTORY, P.O. Box 1629, 600 Market St., Knoxville, TN 37910, 423-544-4262

Description: The museum interprets and preserves the history of East Tennessee and its people. The museum dedicates a section of "The East Tennesseeans" permanent exhibit to the crucial role the Civil War played in this region's history. A Union stronghold in a secessionist state, East Tennessee has a unique story to tell. The historical society attempts to give a balanced presentation relating the events and debate of the time, while focusing on the East Tennessee men, women, and children who lived during the period.

Admission Fees: Adults: $3; Children: $2; Seniors: $2.50; Groups: $2/person.

Open to Public: Tues.–Fri.: 10 A.M.–4 P.M.; Sun.: 1 P.M.–5 P.M.

Visitor Services: Museum; gift shop; information; rest rooms; handicapped access.

Regularly Scheduled Events: The East Tennessee Historical Society holds lectures once a month, brown bag lunches in summer, and evening events in autumn and spring; call for details.

Directions: From I-40 east or west through downtown Knoxville: take James White Pkwy. exit; then take first exit off Pkwy. onto Summit Hill Dr.; turn left on Locust Ave. Proceed to Union Ave. and turn left. Travel two blocks and turn right on Market St. Proceed two blocks to museum on the right.

La Grange

22 **Site:** TOWN OF LA GRANGE, P.O. Box 621, La Grange, TN 38046, 901-878-1246

Description: La Grange was occupied by Federal troops from 1862 until the Civil War ended. In 1863, Grierson's Raid originated here. Immanuel Episcopal Church was a hospital. See the birthplace of Lucy Holcombe Pickens, the "Queen of the Confederacy," and many antebellum homes. Pick up brochure for the driving and walking tour.

Admission Fees: Free; brochure costs $3.

Open to Public: Daily: Daylight hours. Pick up driving tour brochure at Cogbill's Store and Museum (901-878-1235) or at city hall (901-878-1246). Cogbill's Store and

Museum is open Thurs.–Sun. except in winter, when it is open only on Sun. 1 P.M.–5 P.M.; call ahead for schedule.

Visitor Services: In town: gas; food; museum (in Cogbill's Store); gift shop.

Directions: From I-40: take exit 56; drive south toward Somerville on TN Hwy. 76, which intersects TN Hwy. 57 in Moscow. Turn east onto TN Hwy. 57; drive approximately 10 miles to La Grange. Hwy. 57 becomes Main St.; Cogbill's Store and the city hall are located on the corner of Main St. and La Grange Rd.

Lexington

23 **Site:** PARKER'S CROSSROADS BATTLEFIELD SELF-GUIDED TOUR, 273 North Broad St., Lexington, TN 38351, 901-968-5533

Description: The Battle of Parker's Crossroads was fought on December 31, 1862. Union forces sought to capture Confederate troops on their return from their "First West Tennessee Raid." When Confederate General Forrest found himself caught between two Union forces at Parker's Crossroads, each roughly the size of his own, he ordered his troops to "Charge both ways," and made a successful escape.

Admission Fees: Free.

Open to Public: Daily: Dawn to dusk.

Visitor Services: Rest rooms.

Regularly Scheduled Events: *Every two years in June 1996, 1998, and so forth:* Reenactment of the Battle of Parker's Crossroads.

Directions: The site is traversed by I-40. Starts at I-40 and Hwy. 22. at exit 108.

Lookout Mountain (see Chattanooga)

24 **Site:** CHICKAMAUGA & CHATTANOOGA NATIONAL MILITARY PARK/LOOKOUT MOUNTAIN, Point Lookout Visitor Center, Lookout Mountain, TN 37350, 615-821-7786

Description: The Lookout Mountain district of Chickamauga & Chattanooga NMP preserves land on which the Battle of Lookout Mountain was fought, November 24, 1863, as part of the Battles for Chattanooga.

Admission Fees: Free.

Open to Public: Daily: 8 A.M.–4:45 P.M.; Summer: 8 A.M.–5:45 P.M.

Visitor Services: Museum; gift shop; rest rooms; handicapped access.

Regularly Scheduled Events: *Anniversary of the Battles for Chattanooga:* Living history regiment demonstrations; Special tours of Missionary Ridge and other battle sites: Call for schedule.

Directions: From I-24: take exit 74; turn onto U.S. 41 east, then onto State Hwy. 148 up Lookout Mountain. After ascending approximately 3 miles, turn right onto East Brow Rd. At the end of East Brow Rd. is Point Park.

Madison

25 **Site:** NASHVILLE NATIONAL CEMETERY, 1420 Gallatin Road South, Madison, TN 37115-4619, 615-327-5360

Description: In 1867, 16,489 interments were brought from all over the area and reinterred in the Nashville National Cemetery. Of these, 4,156 are unknown. In the battle of Franklin, south of Nashville, on November 30, 1864, the Union suffered 2,000 casualties, and the Confederates lost 6,000 men.

Admission Fees: Free.

Open to Public: *Office:* Mon.–Fri.: 8 A.M.–4:30 P.M. *Grounds:* Daily: Daylight hours.

Visitor Services: Information; rest rooms.

Directions: From I-65 at Nashville: take I-65 north; exit at Briley Pkwy. Follow Briley Pkwy. 2 miles to Gallatin Rd. Take second exit (Gallatin Rd. North, Madison). The national cemetery is located .25 mile on the left.

Memphis

26 **Site:** FORREST PARK, P.O. Box 24813, Memphis, TN 38124, 901-576-4500 (ask for county historian)

Description: Park in downtown Memphis is the site where Gen. Nathan Bedford Forrest is buried. The park features a large, bronze, equestrian statue of the general that was erected in 1905 as well as the granite monument that serves as the grave marker for the general and his wife, Mary Montgomery Forrest. After the Civil War,

Gen. Sherman said of Forrest, "He was the most remarkable man our Civil War produced on either side." Gen. Lee, when asked to identify the greatest soldier under his command, said, "a man I have never seen sir . . . Forrest." The monument is located two blocks from the scene of Forrest's death in 1877.

Admission Fees: Free.

Open to Public: Daily: 24 hours.

Visitor Services: Trails; handicapped access.

Regularly Scheduled Events: *Sun. closest to July 13:* Forrest's birthday celebration.

Directions: From I-240 north: take the Union Ave. westbound exit. Forrest Park is on the north side of Union between Dunlap and Manassas Streets. From I-240 south and I-40: take the Madison St. westbound exit. Forrest Park is on the south side of Madison between Dunlap and Manassas Streets.

---

27 Site: HUNT PHELAN HOME, 533 Beale St., Memphis, TN 38104, 901-344-3166

Description: Built from 1828–32 by slaves and Chickasaw Indians, this home hosted many well-known Tennesseans, including President Andrew Jackson, President Jefferson Davis, and Gen. Nathan Bedford Forrest. During the Civil War, Confederate Gen. Leonidas Polk planned the Battle of Corinth, Mississippi, in the home. Later, Union Gen. Ulysses S. Grant used the home as his headquarters and planned the Battle of Vicksburg in the library. After the war, the first school in the county for African Americans was built on the property by the Freedmen's Bureau. A large family archive contains many Civil War–related papers and books.

Admission Fees: Adults: $10; Children (5–12): $6; Children under 5: Free; Seniors and Students: $9; Groups: call for rates.

Open to Public: *Summer:* Daily: 9 A.M.–6 P.M.; *Autumn–Spring:* Daily: 10 A.M.–5 P.M. Call for specific dates.

Visitor Services: Museum; gift shop; information; rest rooms; handicapped access to first floor of home and gardens.

Directions: Located at 533 Beale St., on the corner of Beale and Lauderdale. From I-240: take Union St. exit and proceed west on Union St. to Lauderdale St.; turn left on Lauderdale St. and continue to Beale St.; turn right on Beale St., and the home is on the left.

---

28 Site: MEMPHIS NATIONAL CEMETERY, 3568 Townes Ave., Memphis, TN 38122, 901-386-8311

Description: Strong Union land and river forces captured Memphis on June 6, 1862, and with the surrender, the city became the location of several Federal hospitals serving the Western theater of war. The dead from these hospitals were buried in private cemeteries and in 1866 were reinterred in the Mississippi National Cemetery. In 1867 the name was changed to the Memphis National Cemetery. Of the 13,965 soldiers buried at this site, 8,866 are unknown. Other burials include those from the U.S.S.

Sultana, which sank in April, 1865 and ranks as one of the nation's deadliest maritime disasters with 1,700 soldiers and crew lost.

Admission Fees: Free.

Open to Public: *Office:* Mon.–Fri.: 8 A.M.–4:30 P.M.; *Grounds:* Daily: 24 hours.

Visitor Services: Information; rest rooms.

Regularly Scheduled Events: *May:* Memorial Day program; *Nov:* Veterans Day program.

Directions: From I-240: take exit 8B/Jackson Ave. Travel south approximately 2 miles; after crossing railroad viaduct, take first left onto Townes Ave. Cemetery gate is at the intersection of Jackson and Townes Avenues.

Site: MEMPHIS PINK PALACE MUSEUM, 3050 Central Ave., Memphis, TN 38111-3399, 901-320-6320

Description: The Civil War exhibit displays artifacts, documents, and photographs of civilian Memphis; arms and equipment; and currency. It provides material on the war around Memphis; the battle of Memphis; Gen. Nathan Bedford Forrest; and Confederate veterans. A vignette of an artillery crew serving an ordnance rifle is the centerpiece of the exhibit. The Civil War exhibit is part of a larger museum.

Admission Fees: Adults: $5.50; Children: $3.50; Groups: call for rates.

Open to Public: Memorial Day–Labor Day: Mon.–Wed.: 9 A.M.–5 P.M.; Thurs.–Sat.: 9 A.M.–9 P.M.; Sun.: Noon–5 P.M.; day after Labor Day–day before Memorial Day: Mon.–Wed.: 9 A.M.–4 P.M.; Thurs.: 9 A.M.–8 P.M.; Fri.–Sat.: 9 A.M.–9 P.M.; Sun.: Noon–5 P.M.

Visitor Services: Food; museum; gift shop; information; rest rooms; handicapped access.

Directions: From I-40: take Sam Cooper Blvd. to the Highland exit. Travel south on Highland for 2 miles to the Central Ave. intersection. Turn west on Central and continue for 1 mile. The museum is located on the north side of Central Ave.

Site: MISSISSIPPI RIVER MUSEUM AT MUD ISLAND, 125 North Front St., Memphis, TN 38103-1713, 901-576-7232

Description: Within the Mississippi River Museum are five galleries dedicated to the significant role of the Mississippi River in the Civil War. A life-size replica of a Union City ironclad gunboat is featured. Also included are a half-dozen boat models, displays of Civil War uniforms, field equipment, weapons, and personal items.

Admission Fees: Adults: $6; Children: $4; Seniors: $4.

Open to Public: *Spring:* Tues.–Sun.: 10 A.M.–5 P.M.; *Summer:* Daily: 10 A.M.–8 P.M.; *Autumn:* Tues.–Sun.: 10 A.M.–5 P.M.; closed Nov.–early Apr.; call for dates.

Visitor Services: Museum; gift shop; information; rest rooms; handicapped access.

Directions: From I-40 east: take Front St. exit; turn right (south) and proceed two blocks.

Murfreesboro

31 **Site:** FORTRESS ROSECRANS, STONES RIVER NATIONAL BATTLEFIELD, 3501 Old Nashville Hwy., Murfreesboro, TN 37129-3094, 615-893-9501

Description: After the Confederates had withdrawn from Murfreesboro at the conclusion of the Battle of Stones River in January, 1863, the Federal army, under General William Rosecrans, began fortifying Murfreesboro. Fortress Rosecrans became one of the Union's largest earthen fortifications of the Civil War. The features that remain include Redoubt Brannan, Lunettes Palmer and Thomas, and Curtain Wall #2.

Admission Fees: Free.

Open to Public: Redoubt Brannan is being readied for visitor access. Lunette Thomas is not open. Lunette Palmer and Curtain Wall #2 are open during daylight hours.

Visitor Services: Trail; exhibits; handicapped access.

Directions: From I-24: take exit 78B, turn left on Golf Ln. into the Old Fort Park of Murfreesboro.

---

32 **Site:** OAKLANDS HISTORIC HOUSE MUSEUM, 900 North Maney Ave., Murfreesboro, TN 37130, 615-893-0022

Description: Oaklands was one of the largest plantations in Rutherford County during the Civil War. It was the home of the Maney family, one of the wealthiest families in the county. The plantation was used by the Union army in June of 1862 as a camp. On July 13, 1862, Confederate Gen. Nathan Bedford Forrest and his cavalry raided the city of Murfreesboro and recaptured it. The surrender was negotiated at Oaklands.

Admission Fees: Adults: $4; Children: $2.50; Seniors: $3; Groups: $3/person.

Open to Public: Tues.–Sat.: 10 A.M.–4 P.M.; Sun.: 1 P.M.–4 P.M.

Visitor Services: Museum; gift shop; information.

Regularly Scheduled Events: *May:* Annual antique show; *Dec.:* Candlelight tour of homes.

Directions: From I-24: take exit 81B; proceed to third traffic light; turn right on Broad St. Proceed to next traffic light and turn left on Maney Ave.; follow Maney Ave. to Oaklands.

---

33 **Site:** STONES RIVER NATIONAL BATTLEFIELD, 3501 Old Nashville Hwy., Murfreesboro, TN 37129, 615-893-9501

Description: A fierce midwinter battle took place here between December 31, 1862 and January 2, 1863. After this battle, the Union army controlled middle Tennessee and constructed Fortress Rosecrans, a large earthen supply depot.

Admission Fees: Free.

Open to Public: Daily: 8 A.M.–5 P.M.

Visitor Services: Museum; gift shop; information; rest rooms; handicapped access.

Regularly Scheduled Events: *May:* Memorial Day ceremony; *Weekend following July 4*: Artillery encampment weekend; *Weekend closest to Dec. 31 and Jan. 1–2:* Anniversary programs.

Directions: From I-24: take exit 78B onto Hwy. 96; take Hwy. 96 to intersection with Hwy. 41/70; turn left on Hwy. 41 north. Travel about 2 miles to Thompson Lane; turn left; exit onto Old Nashville Hwy.; follow signs.

Nashville

| 34 | **Site:** BATTLE OF NASHVILLE DRIVING TOUR, c/o Metropolitan Historical Commission, 209 Tenth Ave. South, Ste. 414, Nashville, TN 37203, 615-862-7970 |

Description: Historians have called the Battle of Nashville one of the most decisive of the Civil War. Union forces had held this strategically important city since February 1862. After losing Atlanta to Sherman, Gen. John Bell Hood moved his Army of Tennessee north, hoping to reclaim Nashville. On December 15–16, 1864, the Confederacy's last offensive action ended in the loss of the Army of Tennessee as an effective fighting force. The driving tour visits the main points of the Union defenses of Nashville, including Fort Negley and the Confederate lines of battle. The tour brochure includes a map and pertinent background information.

Admission Fees: Free.

Open to Public: Daily: Daylight hours.

Visitor Services: Information.

Directions: Write or call for brochure at the address listed above or pick up a brochure at the Cumberland Science Museum. To Cumberland Museum and Fort Negley: From I-65: take Wedgewood Ave. exit. Proceed west on Wedgewood Ave. and turn right onto Eighth Ave. South; proceed to the next traffic light and turn right on Chestnut; cross over the interstate to Ft. Negley Blvd. and turn left onto Ft. Negley Blvd. Fort Negley is on the right; continue to curve around on this road, and the Cumberland Science Museum is just past Fort Negley on the right.

| 35 | **Site:** BELLE MEADE MANSION, 5025 Harding Rd., Nashville, TN 37205, 615-356-0501 |

Description: The Belle Meade plantation house was built in 1853 by William J. Harding. When Tennessee entered the Civil War, Governor Isham G. Harris appointed Harding to the Military and Financial Board. During the Battle of Nashville in December of 1864, Confederate Gen. James R. Chalmers made his headquarters at Belle Meade. Bullet scars from a cavalry skirmish on the front lawn are visible on the limestone columns of the front porch. After the war, Belle Meade became one of the nation's first stables for thoroughbred horses.

Admission Fees: Adults: $7; Children: $2; Seniors: $6.50; Groups: $6/person.

Open to Public: Mon.–Sat.: 9 A.M.–5 P.M.; Sun.: 1 P.M.–5 P.M.

Visitor Services: Tours; museum; gift shop; information; rest rooms; handicapped access on first floor.

Regularly Scheduled Events: *Third weekend in Sept.:* Fall Fest (antiques, music, crafts, food, children's activities); *Last weekend in Oct.:* Dunham Station Rendezvous (reenactment camp of frontier life from 1780s to 1850s).

Directions: From I-440: take 70S exit; proceed approximately 4 miles on 70S; Belle Meade is on the left.

---

36 Site: BELMONT MANSION, 1900 Belmont Blvd., Nashville, TN 37212, 615-386-4459

Description: Belmont Mansion was built by Joseph and Adelicia Acklen in 1853 and enlarged in 1859–60. During the Civil War, the house served as headquarters for Gen. Stanley and for Gen. Thomas J. Wood, commander of the Fourth Army Corps. At Belmont, Wood gave orders to all division commanders for the first day of the Battle of Nashville.

Admission Fees: Adults: $5; Children: $2; Children under 6: Free; Seniors: $4.50; Groups: $4.50/person.

Open to Public: June–Aug.: Mon.–Sat.: 10 A.M.–4 P.M.; Sun: 2 P.M.–5 P.M.; Sept.–May: Tues.–Sat.: 10 A.M.–4 P.M.

Visitor Services: Tours; gift shop; rest rooms; handicapped access.

Regularly Scheduled Events: *Day after Thanksgiving–Dec.:* Christmas at Belmont.

Directions: From I-65: take Wedgewood exit. Travel west on Wedgewood Ave. Turn left on Magnolia; turn left onto 18th Ave.; turn left onto Acklen.

---

37 Site: HISTORIC TRAVELLERS REST, 636 Farrell Pkwy., Nashville, TN 37220, 615-832-8197

Description: One of the oldest residences in Nashville built in 1799 by Judge John Overton. In the Civil War, Union troops camped on the grounds during the Federal occupation of Nashville. For two weeks before the Battle of Nashville, Travellers Rest was the headquarters of Confederate Commander Gen. John Bell Hood. Riding from Murfreesboro to confer with Hood, Gen. Nathan Bedford Forrest spent the night on December 11, 1864. During the second day of the Battle of Nashville, December 16, 1864, Federal forces charged the Confederate right flank on Peach Orchard Hill, located on the Overton property and within sight of the house. It was the scene of several charges by the U.S. Colored Infantry.

Admission Fees: Adults: $5; Children: $3.

Open to Public: Tues.–Sat.: 10 A.M.–5 P.M.; Sun.: 1 P.M.–5 P.M.

Visitor Services: Gift shop; information; rest rooms.

Regularly Scheduled Events: *June:* Summer Solstice and Celtic Festival; *Sept.:* Country Fair; *Dec.:* Twelfth Night.

Directions: From I-65: take Harding exit; turn left onto Franklin Rd.; proceed 1 mile; turn left onto Farrell Rd.; turn right onto Farrell Pkwy. Entrance is on the left.

38 **Site**: MOUNT OLIVET CEMETERY, 1101 Lebanon Rd., Nashville, TN 37210, 615-255-4193

Description: This cemetery is the final resting place of nearly 1,500 Confederate soldiers. The Confederate Circle Monument marks the remains of individuals of all ranks. Mount Olivet is also the burial place for seven generals.

Admission Fees: Free.

Open to Public: Daily: Dawn to dusk.

Visitor Services: Information.

Regularly Scheduled Events: Annual tour of cemetery with living history: call for schedule.

Directions: From I-40: exit at Fesslers Ln.; proceed north on Fesslers Ln. until it dead-ends into Hermitage Ave./Lebanon Rd.; turn right onto this road and continue to Mount Olivet Cemetery which is on the right, past Calvary Cemetery.

39 **Site**: TENNESSEE STATE CAPITOL AND STATE MUSEUM, 505 Deaderick Street, Nashville, TN 37243-1120, 615-741-2692

Description: The capitol was completed in 1859. The fortifications around the capitol consisted of four earthworks connected by a stockade with loopholes. The Tennessee State Museum traces the history of the state from prehistoric Indians until the early 1900s, including a large section on the Civil War. This section includes descriptions and artifacts from each major battle in Tennessee, audio-visual presentations, firearms, uniforms, paintings of notable soldiers, and a large collection of battle flags.

Admission Fees: Free.

Open to Public: *State Museum:* Tues.–Sat.: 10 A.M.–5 P.M., Sun.: 1 P.M.–5 P.M.; *State Capitol:* Mon.–Fri.: 9 A.M.–4 P.M.

Visitor Services: *State Museum:* museum; gift shop; information; rest rooms; handicapped access.

Directions: From I-40: take Broadway exit; travel toward downtown. From Broadway, turn left onto Fifth Ave.; after third intersection, museum is on left at Fifth and Deaderick. State Capitol is located one block away at Sixth and Charlotte.

Tennessee State Capitol, known as Fort Andrew Johnson during the War. Photograph circa 1864. (Photograph courtesy of The National Archives.)

New Johnsonville

40 **Site:** JOHNSONVILLE STATE HISTORIC AREA, Rte. 1, P.O. Box 37-4, New Johnsonville, TN 37134, 615-535-2789

Description: On November 4, 1864, at Johnsonville, General N. B. Forrest's cavalry took up artillery positions on the west bank of the Tennessee River. The Confederates destroyed the Federal depot at Johnsonville.

Admission Fees: Free.

Open to Public: Daily: 8 A.M.–sunset.

Visitor Services: Trails; museum; information; rest rooms; handicapped access.

Regularly Scheduled Events: *Every other year:* Reenactment; Living history: call for schedule.

Directions: From I-40 at Memphis: travel to Hwy. 13; go north to Waverly, to Hwy. 70 west; follow signs.

Shiloh

41 **Site:** SHILOH NATIONAL MILITARY PARK, Rte. 1, P.O. Box 9, Shiloh, TN 38376, 901-689-5275

Description: General Albert Sidney Johnston's Army of the Mississippi (C.S.A.), marching north from its base at Corinth, attacked and partially overran Ulysses S. Grant's Federal Army of the Tennessee. Shiloh was the first large-scale battle of the Civil War, and the magnitude of casualties shocked the nation. There were 65,000 Federal troops at Shiloh and 13,000 casualties. Confederate troop strength was 44,700 with 10,700 casualties.

Admission Fees: Adults: $2; Families: $4.

Open to Public: Daily: 8 A.M.–5 P.M.

Visitor Services: Trails; museum; bookstore; information; rest rooms; handicapped access.

Regularly Scheduled Events: *First weekend in Apr.:* Living history weekend:

Directions: From I-40 at Parkers Cross Roads: travel south on Hwy. 22, 57 miles south to Shiloh Park entrance; follow signs.

Smyrna

42 **Site:** SAM DAVIS HOME, 1399 Sam Davis Rd., Smyrna, TN 37167, 615-459-2341

Description: The Sam Davis Home is the family home and farm of Tennessee's "Boy Hero of the Confederacy," Sam Davis. The land consists of 168 acres of the original 1,000-acre plantation. Sam Davis was serving as a member of the Coleman Scouts when he was captured by the Union army and accused of being a spy. He was executed at age 21.

Admission Fees: Adults: $4; Children: $2.50; Seniors: $3.50; Groups (10 or more): $.50 discount.

Open to Public: June–Aug.: Mon.–Sat.: 9 A.M.–5 P.M.; Sun.: 1 P.M.–5 P.M.; Sept.–

May: Mon.–Sat.: 10 A.M.–4 P.M.; Sun: 1 P.M.–4 P.M.

Visitor Services: Museum; gift shop; information; rest rooms; handicapped access.

Regularly Scheduled Events: *May:* Days on the Farm/living history demonstrations; *June:* Civil War Expo; *mid-Oct.:* Heritage Days.

Directions: From I-24 east: take exit 66B; go approximately 5.5 miles to Sam Davis Rd. From I-24 west: take exit 70; proceed approximately 5 miles to Sam Davis Rd.

Spring Hill

43 **Site:** OAKLAWN, 3331 Denning Lane, Spring Hill, TN 37174, 615-486-9037; 800-381-1865

Description: By the evening of November 29, 1864, Confederate Gen. John Bell Hood had managed to put his troops between U.S. Gen. John Schofield's army and the town of Spring Hill. While Gen. Hood slept in his temporary headquarters at Oaklawn, the Federal army slipped by Confederate pickets and made its escape to the strong fortifications in Franklin. Hood never forgave his officers for missing the opportunity to utterly rout and destroy the Federal army. The Battle of Spring Hill was fought across the grounds of Oaklawn.

Admission Fees: Adults: $5; Children: $3; Seniors: $4; Groups: $4/person.

Open to Public: Mon.–Sat.: 10 A.M.–4 P.M.; Sun.: 1 P.M.–4 P.M.

Visitor Services: Tours; information.

Regularly Scheduled Events: *Apr. and Dec.:* Home Pilgrimage.

Directions: From I-65: 25 miles south of Nashville take Saturn Pkwy.; travel on Saturn Pkwy.; take Columbia exit. Turn left immediately at the end of the ramp to Rippavilla Plantation; tour of Oaklawn originates here.

44 **Site:** RIPPAVILLA PLANTATION, P.O. Box 1076, Columbia, TN 38402, 615-486-9037; 800-381-1865

Description: Rippavilla Plantation was completed in 1853. Early in the Civil War its owner, Confederate Maj. Nathaniel Cheairs, had carried the white flag of surrender to Gen. Ulysses S. Grant at Fort Donelson. On November 30, 1864, Maj. Cheairs welcomed Confederate Gen. Hood and his ranking officers to breakfast. It was here that Hood angrily accused his staff of letting the entire Federal army escape to Franklin. Five Confederate generals at that breakfast were dead by evening in the bloody Battle of Franklin.

Admission Fees: Adults: $5; Children: $2; Groups: $4/person.

Open to Public: Mon.–Sat.: 10 A.M.–4 P.M.; Sun.: 1 P.M.–4 P.M.

Visitor Services: Museum; gift shop; information; rest rooms; handicapped access.

Regularly Scheduled Events: *Apr. and Dec.:* Home Pilgrimage; *Oct.:* Balloon Festival; Civil War reenactments: ongoing—call for schedule.

Directions: From I-65: 25 miles south of Nashville take Saturn Pkwy.; travel on Saturn Pkwy.; take Columbia exit. Turn left immediately at the end of the ramp; Rippavilla Plantation is located 100 yards on the left.

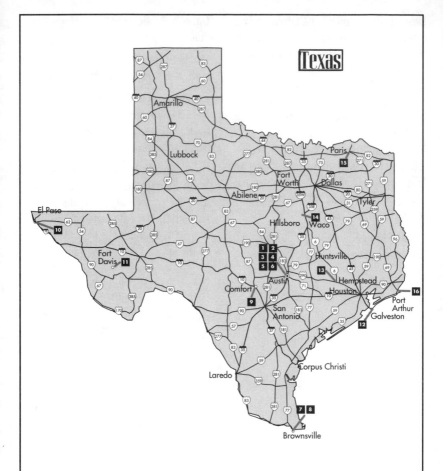

Texas

1 Confederate Soldiers Monument
2 George Armstrong Custer Residence
3 Lorenzo de Zavala State Archives and Library Building
4 State Cemetery
5 Texas Governor's Mansion
6 Texas Historical Commission
7 Fort Brown and Historic Brownsville Museum
8 Palmito Ranch Battlefield
9 Treüe der Union Monument
10 U.S. Army Museum of the Noncommissioned Officer
and Fort Bliss Museum
11 Fort Davis National Historic Site
12 The Rosenburg Library and Texas History Center
13 Liendo Plantation
14 Confederate Research Center and Museum
15 Samuel Bell Maxey House
16 Sabine Pass State Historical Park

TEXAS

A mere 16 years after Texas had given up its status as an independent nation and joined the Union, the American Civil War erupted. Despite the efforts of then Governor Sam Houston to keep Texas in the Union or at least to reestablish a neutral republic, voters overwhelmingly approved an ordinance of secession, and the state formally joined the Confederacy in early March 1861. On February 16, Ben McCulloch, a veteran Texas Ranger, captured the commander of the U.S. troops in Texas and took possession of a string of frontier forts from Ft. Bliss in El Paso to Ft. Brown in Brownsville. Although the great majority of Texans supported the Southern cause, there were notable exceptions as evidenced by the killing of 30 German settlers from the Comfort area of the Texas Hill Country who were caught as their party attempted to flee to Mexico in August 1862.

Although the largest battles of the war took place in theaters to the east, Texas saw some significant actions primarily related to the defense of its borders and ill-fated attempts to expand Confederate dominance into New Mexico and Arizona. Of the 90,000 Texans to see service in the war, only one-third were in action east of the Mississippi; however, these were represented by such distinguished units as Benjamin F. Terry's Texas Rangers and John Bell Hood's Texas Infantry Brigade of whom Lee once remarked, "I never ordered the Brigade to hold a place, that they did not hold it."

The Texas coast was the object of much Federal attention with a blockade beginning in July 1861. The major port city of Galveston was captured on October 4, 1862 and held until New Year's Day, 1863, when General John B. Magruder recaptured it. Sabine Pass was also held for a short time by Union troops in late 1862, but a second major Union attack was repulsed by Lt. Richard W. Dowling and a handful of artillerymen on September 8, 1863. The Federals then focused their attention on southern Texas and the mouth of the Rio Grande, the major supply route to Mexico. Brownsville was captured in November 1863 but retaken by troops under the command of Rip Ford in the summer of 1864. Federal troops managed to hold Brazos Island at the mouth of the Rio Grande but were again defeated by Ford's troops on May 13, 1865, at Palmito Ranch near Brownsville, more than a month after Lee's surrender in Virginia, in what proved to be the last battle of the Civil War.

General Edmund Kirby Smith, commander of the Trans-Mississippi Department and headquartered in Marshall, Texas, formally surrendered on board a Union ship in Galveston Bay on June 2, 1865, bringing an end to the Civil War.

by Stanley O. Graves, AIA, Texas Historical Commission

Austin

1 **Site:** CONFEDERATE SOLDIERS MONUMENT, 112 East 11th, Austin, TX 78701, 512-305-8400

Description: The Confederate Soldiers Monument, located at the Texas State Capitol's south entrance, was erected in 1901. It consists of five bronze figures representing the infantry, cavalry, Confederate states, and battles fought between 1861 and 1865. Pompeo Coppini executed the bronze figures, and Frank Teich erected the monument.

Admission Fees: Free.

Open to Public: Mon.–Fri.: 9 A.M.–5 P.M.; Sun.: 10 A.M.–5 P.M.

Visitor Services: Museum; information; gift shop; visitors center; rest rooms; handicapped access.

Directions: From I-35: take 11th St. exit to downtown Austin. Proceed west on 11th St. about .5 mile to capitol.

---

2 **Site:** GEORGE ARMSTRONG CUSTER RESIDENCE (State School for the Blind), c/o Urban Issues Program, Univ. of Texas/Austin, Austin, TX 78712, 512-471-7903

Description: After the Civil War, reconstruction was the next item of business for the Union. In Texas, General George Armstrong Custer was the Federal military commander for the Union in charge of a division of cavalry. Originally built for the State School for the Blind, the building constructed in 1865 is a two-story limestone Italianate-style residence. The building served as Custer's headquarters for a few months after the Civil War from late 1865 to early 1866. The ever-ambitious Custer did not stay long in Texas, eventually transferring up north, where he gained fame in his last stand at the Little Big Horn.

The renamed Arno Nowotny Building now houses the University's Urban Issues Program. It does not contain any of Custer's belongings, but does have furniture of the period.

Admission Fees: Free.

Open to Public: Mon.–Fri.: 8 A.M.–4 P.M.; tours must be arranged in advance.

Visitor Services: Tours; information; rest rooms.

Directions: From I-35: take Martin Luther King Blvd. (MLK). Travel west on MLK. The Custer residence is at the southwest corner of I-35 and MLK.

---

3 **Site:** LORENZO DE ZAVALA STATE ARCHIVES AND LIBRARY BUILDING, P.O. Box 92927, Austin, TX 78711, 512-463-5455

Description: The Texas State Archives contain Civil War records related to the State of Texas. These records consist primarily of Confederate pension applications and records of Texas state troops and militias.

Admission Fees: Free.

Open to Public: Mon.–Fri.: 8 A.M.–5 P.M.

Visitor Services: Information; rest rooms; handicapped access.

Directions: From I-35: take 12th St. exit in downtown Austin. Proceed west on 12th St. for about .25 mile. The State Archives Building is located directly east of the Texas State Capitol.

---

4 **Site:** STATE CEMETERY, Navasota St., Austin, TX 78702, 512-463-0605, http://www.gsc.state.tx.us/statecemetery

Description: The State Cemetery was established in 1851 with the burial of Edward Burleson. The southeast section of the cemetery has historically been referred to as "The Confederate Plat." More than 2,047 Confederate veterans and their wives are buried and marked by row after row of simple white marble tablets. Each tablet contains the name of the soldier, with most also including the date of birth and death and the company with which he fought. The Confederates were first buried in the State Cemetery in 1871. In that year the sexton was authorized by the state legislature to procure suitable monuments as long as the cost did not exceed $40 each. In 1867 the state legislature authorized funds for the removal of General Albert Sidney Johnston's remains from the State of Louisiana to the Texas State Cemetery. General Johnston was the strategic force behind the Confederate offensive at Shiloh, but he chose to lead the charge and was fatally wounded. Elisabet Ney, noted sculptor, carved in white marble a recumbent statue of the general in 1902 and designed a metal Gothic-style tomb, located west of The Confederate Plat.

Admission Fees: Free.

Open to Public: Daily: 8 A.M.–5 P.M. NOTE: The State Cemetery will be closed from Jan. 1996–Jan. 1997 for restoration.

Visitor Services: Internet access to biographies, photos, and Confederate records; trails; gift shop; visitors center; rest rooms; handicapped access at ßComal St. gate.

Directions: From I-35: drive south of Austin; take Eighth St. exit; drive on frontage road; turn left on Seventh St.; drive under freeway three blocks to Navasota St.; turn left and drive past turn-of-century caretaker's cottage. Visitors center is on the right.

General Albert Sidney Johnston's Tomb, carved by noted sculptor Elisabet Ney; State Cemetery, Austin, TX. (Photograph courtesy of the Texas Historical Commission.)

5   **Site:** TEXAS GOVERNOR'S MANSION, 1010 Colorado, Austin, TX 78701,
512-463-5518

Description: The Greek Revival house was built in 1856 and every Texas governor since has lived in the mansion. Abraham Lincoln reputedly offered Governor Sam Houston a commission in the United States army during the secession crisis to keep Texas in the Union. Houston burned Lincoln's letter in a mansion fireplace. He was forced from office in March 1861 for refusing to sign an oath of allegiance to the Confederacy and replaced by Lt. Governor Edward Clark. Clark was succeeded by Governor Francis R. Lubbock who later resigned his office to join the Confederate army, becoming an aide-de-camp to Jefferson Davis.

Admission Fees: Free.

Open to Public: Mon.–Fri.: 10 A.M.– 11:40 A.M.; tours every 20 minutes. Call first to check availability; group reservations required.

Visitor Services: Tours; handicapped access.

Directions: From I-35: take State Capitol exit.

6   **Site:** TEXAS HISTORICAL COMMISSION, P.O. Box 12276, Austin, TX
78711-2276, 512-463-6100

Description: Many of Texas's 11,500 historical markers are Civil War related. A high percentage of the historical marker files, which are located in the Carrington-Covert House, contain documented narratives supporting the historical significance of the subject matter of each marker.

Admission Fees: Free.

Open to Public: Mon.–Fri.: 8 A.M.–5 P.M.

Visitor Services: Information; rest rooms; the main floor and library are handicapped accessible; files are hand-delivered to the public.

Directions: From I-35: take the 15th St. exit in downtown Austin. Proceed west on 15th St. for approximately .5 mile to Colorado St. Turn right onto Colorado and proceed one city block to 16th St. The Texas Historical Commission is housed in the Carrington-Covert House at the southeast corner of Colorado and 16th.

Brownsville

7   **Site:** FORT BROWN AND HISTORIC BROWNSVILLE MUSEUM, c/o Historic
Brownsville Museum, 641 East Madison St., Brownsville, TX 78520,
210-548-1313

Description: Fort Brown, established in 1846, housed Federal troops during the Mexican War. In 1861, Texas state troops occupied the fort. With the southern Atlantic coast blockaded, Brownsville became an important Confederate port, with cotton and war materiel flowing back and forth. To eliminate the trade, a Union army landed at the mouth of the Rio Grande in November 1863, occupying Fort Brown and Brownsville. Eight months later a strong Confederate army drove out Federal forces and held the fort until the end of the war. The original hospital building is now the administration building for Texas Southmost College. Other extant buildings include post headquarters, a medical laboratory, guardhouse, and morgue. The Historic Brownsville Museum houses materials related to Brownsville's long military history.

Admission Fees: *Grounds:* Free. *Museum:* Adults: $2; Children: $.50.

Open to Public: Mon.–Fri.: 10 A.M.–4:30 P.M.; Sat.: 9 A.M.–1 P.M.; Sun.: 2 P.M.–5 P.M. (closed Sun. in summer).

Visitor Services: Tours; museum; information; rest rooms.

Directions: Fort Brown/Texas Southmost College is at the terminus of Taylor Ave. in Brownsville. Historic Brownsville Museum is in the restored Southern Pacific Depot at 601 E. Madison St.

---

8 **Site:** PALMITO RANCH BATTLEFIELD, c/o Brownsville Convention and Visitors Bureau, 650 Farm-to-Market 802, Brownsville, TX 78520, 800-626-2639

Description: . More than one month after Lee's surrender to Grant at Appomattox, the battle at Palmito Beach represented the last-known engagement fought as part of the Civil War and the ongoing conflict between the Confederacy's Trans-Mississippi Department and the Union army. Fought May 12 and 13, 1865, the Confederates were protecting the center of their lucrative and secretive cotton shipping operation with Mexico and European mills. The battle was the Union's last unsuccessful attempt to seize control of the Lower Rio Grande region.

Admission Fees: Free.

Open to Public: Daily: Dawn to dusk. Visitors can drive or bicycle along Hwy. 4, Boca Chica Hwy., and view the battlefield and related historical markers. However, most of the property is private, and trespassing is strongly discouraged.

Visitor Services: None.

Directions: From Brownsville: follow Hwy. 4 to the Gulf of Mexico.

Comfort

9 **Site:** TREÜE DER UNION MONUMENT (German for "True to the Union"), c/o The Comfort Heritage Foundation, Box 433, Comfort, TX 78013, 210-995-3131(Chamber of Commerce); 210-995-2398 (public library)

Description: The oldest Civil War monument in Texas (dedicated August 10, 1866), this limestone obelisk by an unknown German stonecutter is inscribed with the names of the 36 men captured and killed in the *Nueces* Massacre in August of 1862.

Admission Fees: Free.

Open to Public: Daily: 24 hours.

Visitor Services: Information.

Regularly Scheduled Events: *Aug. 10, 1996:* 130th anniversary to be held; thereafter call for schedule. Rededication ceremonies on major anniversaries.

Directions: The town of Comfort is approximately 30 miles northwest of San Antonio, just off I-10. Proceed through Comfort on Hwy. 27 west, toward the towns of Center Point and Kerrville. The monument is on the left (south) side of the road, just past the intersection of High St. and Hwy. 27.

El Paso

10 Site: U.S. ARMY MUSEUM OF THE NONCOMMISSIONED OFFICER AND FORT BLISS MUSEUM; Fort Bliss Museum mailing address and telephone: Attn.: ATZC-DPD-M, Fort Bliss, TX 79916, 915-568-2804 or 915-568-6940. Noncommissioned Officer Museum mailing address and telephone: Attn.: ATSS-S-M, USASMA, Fort Bliss,TX 79918-5000, 915-568-8646

Description: Fort Bliss, a U.S. Army post established in 1848 to assert authority over lands acquired after the Mexican War, served as headquarters for Confederate forces in the Southwest during the Civil War. The U.S. Museum of the Noncommissioned Officer traces the history of the U.S. NCO Corps with some artifacts that pertain to the Civil War. The Fort Bliss Museum is an exact replica of the original adobe fort that was part of the frontier military era. The museum includes a small Civil War exhibit that focuses on Sibley's campaign into New Mexico to establish the Confederate Territory of New Mexico.

Admission Fees: Free.

Open to Public: *Fort Bliss Museum:* Daily: 9 A.M.–4:30 P.M.; *U.S. Army Museum of the*

Noncommissioned Officer: Mon.–Fri.: 9 A.M.–4 P.M.; Sat.–Sun.: Noon–4 P.M.

Visitor Services: Museum; information.

Directions: To Fort Bliss Museum: From I-10: go north on U.S. 54 to Pershing Dr. and turn right; proceed to Sheridan Rd. and turn right; the museum is at Sheridan Rd. and Pleasanton. To NCO Museum: From I-10: go north on U.S. 54 to Fred Wilson Rd. and turn right; proceed to Sergeant Major Blvd. and turn left; proceed to Biggs St. and turn left; travel to Simms St. and turn right; the museum is three blocks down on the right.

Fort Davis

11 | **Site:** FORT DAVIS NATIONAL HISTORIC SITE, P.O. Box 1456, Fort Davis, TX 79734, 915-426-3224

Description: Fort Davis, established in 1854, was the first military post to guard the route westward and offer haven by the precious waters of Limpia Creek. Colonel John R. Baylor's Confederate cavalry brigade reached Fort Davis on April 13, 1861, and Union troops withdrew in compliance with orders already received from Brig. Gen. David E. Twiggs, commanding the Eighth United States Military District. The Confederates remained a few months, then vacated the post. Federal troops returned in June 1867, but little of value remained and construction ensued.

Admission Fees: $2/person or $4/vehicle; Free admission with Golden Passport.

Open to Public: Daily: 8 A.M.–5 P.M.; Closed on Christmas.

Visitor Services: Trails; tours; museum; information; gift shop; visitors center; rest rooms.

Directions: From I-10: take Hwy. 17 south; this joins Hwy. 118; the site is located just before the town of Fort Davis. Fort Davis is approximately 39 miles from I-10.

Galveston

12 | **Site:** THE ROSENBURG LIBRARY AND TEXAS HISTORY CENTER, 2310 Sealy, Galveston, TX 77550, 409-763-8854

Description: The Rosenburg Library contains Civil War artifacts in a museum-like setting. The Galveston and Texas History Center contains Civil War Muster Rolls, Civil War–era Galveston newspapers, Civil War maps, and a manuscript collection, which includes letters and diaries written by Civil War participants from Galveston.

Admission Fees: Free.

Open to Public: *Rosenburg Library:* Mon.–Thurs.: 9 A.M.–9 P.M.; Fri.–Sat.: 9 A.M.–6 P.M.; Sun: open Sept.–May from 1 P.M–5 P.M.

Galveston and Texas History Center: Tues.–Sat.: 9 A.M.–5 P.M.

Visitor Services: Museum; information; rest rooms; handicapped access.

Directions: From I-45 (southeast from Houston): merge into Broadway Ave. in Galveston. Continue east on Broadway to 24th St.; turn left (north) on 24th and proceed about two city blocks; The Rosenburg Library and the History Center are located just past Ashton-Villa Historic House Museum.

Hempstead

13 **Site:** LIENDO PLANTATION, P.O. Box 454, Hempstead, TX 77445, 409-826-4400, 800-826-4371

Description: This Greek Revival-style home was built by Leonard Waller Groce and is among the most famous and historic plantations in Texas. Liendo was built by slave labor and completed in 1853. During the Civil War, Camp Groce was established at Liendo, where cavalry, artillery, and infantry were recruited. Converted to a prisoner-of-war camp, it housed troops captured at the Battle of Galveston. From September 1 to December 1, 1865, the plantation was the camp for Lt. Col. G. A. Custer and his command.

Admission Fees: $5.

Open to Public: First Sat. of each month: Tours given at 10 A.M., 11:30 A.M., and 1 P.M.; open to group tours with advance reservations.

Visitor Services: Tours; information.

Directions: From Hwy. 290: take the FM 1488 exit; travel 1 mile northeast and turn right on Wyatt Chapel Rd. The plantation is .5 mile on the right on Wyatt Chapel Rd.

Hillsboro

14 **Site:** CONFEDERATE RESEARCH CENTER AND MUSEUM, Hill College, 112 Lamar Dr., Hillsboro, TX 76645, 817-582-2555

Description: The research center houses an extensive collection of archival materials and books, microfilm, and vertical files on the Civil War, with emphasis on Confederate military history. The museum displays a collection of military art, guns, photographs, original battle flags, and artifacts.

Admission Fees: Free.

Open to Public: Mon.–Fri.: 8 A.M.–Noon and 1 P.M.–4 P.M.; closed on college holidays.

Visitor Services: Tours; museum; information; gift shop; visitor center; rest rooms; handicapped access.

Regularly Scheduled Events: *First Sat. in Apr.* (except on Easter weekend): Confederate History Symposium. NOTE: Reservations should be made before Mar. 1 because space is limited.

Directions: Located .5 mile east of I-35 at Hillsboro on the Hill College campus, south of Dallas.

Paris

15 **Site:** SAMUEL BELL MAXEY HOUSE, 812 S. Church St., Paris, TX 75460, 903-785-5716

Description: The Samuel Bell Maxey House, a two-story residence, was constructed in 1866–67 by Gen. Maxey on his return to Paris, Texas, after the Civil War. The home, with a rear ell, is an excellent example of a late Greek Revival–style residence foreshadowing the Victorian era. Gen. Maxey, born in Kentucky on March 30, 1825, graduated from West Point Military Academy, and went on to fight in the Mexican War with Gen. Zachary Taylor. After resigning from the military to study law in 1849, he married and moved to Texas. Advocating secession, Maxey headed to the field to fight for the Confederacy. In the spring of 1865, he was promoted to Major General; but the war was coming to a close, and his army disbanded in May 1865. He returned to Paris, where he practiced law and later served in the United States Senate. He died on August 16, 1895 in Eureka Springs, Arkansas, where he had gone to recover after a period of ill health. Some of Gen. Maxey's Civil War items are on temporary and permanent display at his home.

Admission Fees: Adults: $2; Children: $1; Children under 6: Free.

Open to Public: Fri. and Sun.: 1 P.M.–5 P.M.; Sat: 8 A.M.–5 P.M.; Open by appointment on Wed. and Thurs. for large groups.

Visitor Services: Tours; museum; information; gift shop; rest rooms; handicapped access to grounds and first floor only.

Regularly Scheduled Events: *Sept.:* Civil War reenactment; *Dec.:* Christmas open house.

Directions: From I-30: exit on State Hwy. 24 north; proceed to Paris. In Paris, State Hwy. 24 becomes Church St.; proceed approximately 1 mile past the railroad tracks; the Samuel Bell Maxey House is on the left.

Port Arthur

16 **Site:** SABINE PASS STATE HISTORICAL PARK, c/o Texas Parks and Wildlife Dept., Attn.: Cultural Resources Program, Public Lands Division, 4200 Smith School Rd., Austin, TX 78744, 512-389-4000, 512-389-4736

Description: Two naval engagements, or battles, of the Civil War occurred at Sabine Pass. The first took place September 24–25, 1862, and the second on September 8, 1863. Sabine Pass was a major Confederate center for the shipment and trade of cotton in exchange for supplies and arms, and the Union forces attempted to blockade harbors and disrupt shipping along the Gulf coast. To protect Sabine Pass from Union incursions, the Confederates first constructed Fort Sabine, and then constructed Fort Griffin, both earthworks along the Pass. Twice the Union forces attempted to overrun Confederate fortifications, briefly but successfully in 1862 in preparation for the invasion of Galveston and Houston, and then unsuccessfully in 1863. The 1863 engagement that repulsed the Union forces (22 ships and troops) is commemorated by a monument to Confederate Lt. Richard W. ("Dick") Dowling and his men. Through time and erosion, there is no visible evidence of Confederate Forts Sabine and Griffin at the Sabine Pass State Historical Park.

Admission Fees: Free.

Open to Public: Mon.–Sat.: 8 A.M.–5 P.M.

Visitor Services: Trails; rest rooms; camping.

Regularly Scheduled Events: *Sept. 8:* Dick Dowling commemoration.

Directions: Sabine Pass State Historical Park is about 22 miles south of I-10, from either Orange or Beaumont. From I-10 at Orange: take State Hwy. 87 exit south through Beaumont to the Park. From I-10 at Beaumont: take the U.S. 69 exit south to State Hwy. 87 in Port Arthur (11 miles); follow State Hwy. 87 to the Park, about .5 mile south of the small town of Sabine Pass on FM 3322.

VIRGINIA

*V*irginians voted to secede from the Union on May 23, 1861. Before the vote, former U.S. President John Tyler, a native Virginian, chaired a peace conference in Washington, D.C., with the goal of resolving the nation's sectional crisis. Delegates to a convention called by the Virginia General Assembly had been leaning toward preserving the Union, but after the Washington Peace Conference failed and Virginians reacted negatively to President Abraham Lincoln's inaugural address, public opinion changed. Edmund Ruffin, a Virginian, fired one of the first shots of the Civil War on April 12 at Fort Sumter, South Carolina, and when Lincoln called for troops to put down the Southern forces, the convention quickly voted for secession on April 17. The convention's action was ratified in a referendum on May 23.

The western Virginia counties opposed to secession formed a new state, West Virginia, which was admitted to the Union in 1863. Westerner Francis H. Pierpont, head of the pro-Union Restored Government of Virginia, established offices in Alexandria in 1863 and eventually moved to Richmond after the Union victory in 1865.

For four long years, the Union army's chief goal was to capture Richmond. Consequently, more of the major battles of the Civil War were fought in Virginia than in any other state. In 26 major battles and hundreds of smaller engagements, more men fought and died in Virginia than in any other state. Recently, the Civil War Sites Advisory Commission reported to Congress that one-third of the nation's most important battlefields are in Virginia. More Civil War sites are open to the public in Virginia than in any other state.

From 1861 to 1865, the Confederate strategy was essentially defensive. Until 1864, when Grant took command of Union forces, the Southern troops fighting in Virginia repulsed Northern attacks.

Many of the Civil War's greatest ironies unfolded in Virginia. Robert E. Lee was offered command of the Union army but refused before he accepted command of the Army of Northern Virginia. Fighting raged on the same bloody ground where the nation won its freedom from England at Yorktown. More African-Americans were awarded the Medal of Honor in Virginia for their valor during the Civil War than in any other state. The Congress of the Confederate States of America took up residence in Virginia's State Capitol, meeting place of the oldest legislative body in the Western Hemisphere.

Perhaps one of the greatest ironies of all is the story of Wilmer McLean, who fled Northern Virginia where the first major land battle of the war was fought in July, 1861, at Manassas, to find peace at Appomattox Court House. On April 9, 1865, in McLean's home there, Confederate General Robert E. Lee surrendered to Ulysses S. Grant.

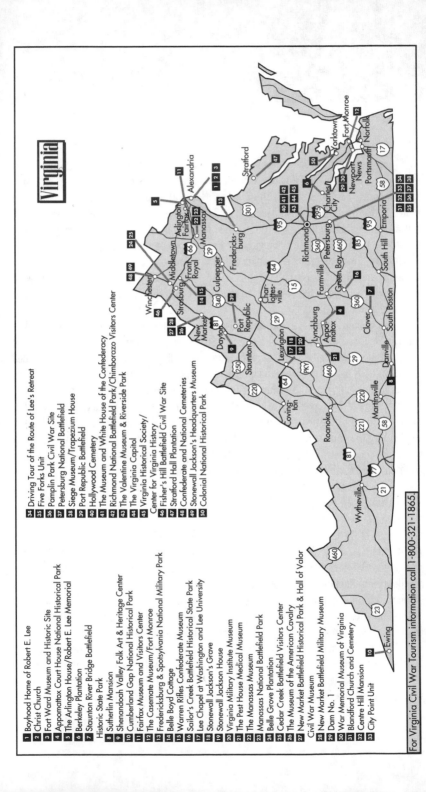

Virginia

1 Boyhood Home of Robert E. Lee
2 Christ Church
3 Fort Ward Museum and Historic Site
4 Appomattox Court House National Historical Park
5 The Arlington House/Robert E. Lee Memorial
6 Berkeley Plantation
7 Staunton River Bridge Battlefield Historic State Park
8 Sutherlin Mansion
9 Shenandoah Valley Folk Art & Heritage Center
10 Cumberland Gap National Historical Park
11 Fairfax Museum and Visitors Center
12 The Casemate Museum/Fort Monroe
13 Fredericksburg & Spotsylvania National Military Park
14 Belle Boyd Cottage
15 Warren Rifles Confederate Museum
16 Sailor's Creek Battlefield Historical State Park
17 Lee Chapel at Washington and Lee University
18 Stonewall Jackson's Grave
19 Stonewall Jackson House
20 Virginia Military Institute Museum
21 The Pest House Medical Museum
22 The Manassas Museum
23 Manassas National Battlefield Park
24 Belle Grove Plantation
25 Cedar Creek Battlefield Visitors Center
26 The Museum of the American Cavalry
27 New Market Battlefield Historical Park & Hall of Valor Civil War Museum
28 New Market Battlefield Military Museum
29 Dam No. 1
30 War Memorial Museum of Virginia
31 Blandford Church and Cemetery
32 Centre Hill Mansion
33 City Point Unit

34 Driving Tour of the Route of Lee's Retreat
35 Five Forks Unit
36 Pamplin Park Civil War Center
37 Petersburg National Battlefield
38 Siege Museum/Trapezium House
39 Port Republic Battlefield
40 Hollywood Cemetery
41 The Museum and White House of the Confederacy
42 Richmond National Battlefield Park/Chimborazo Visitors Center
43 The Valentine Museum & Riverside Park
44 The Virginia Capitol
45 Virginia Historical Society/ Center for Virginia History
46 Fisher's Hill Battlefield Civil War Site
47 Stratford Hall Plantation
48 Confederate and National Cemeteries
49 Stonewall Jackson's Headquarters Museum
50 Colonial National Historical Park

For Virginia Civil War Tourism information call 1-800-321-1865.

Alexandria

1 Site: BOYHOOD HOME OF ROBERT E. LEE, 607 Oronoco St., Alexandria, VA 22314, 703-548-8454

Description: Lee lived here from age five until he entered West Point. The house is a splendid example of Federal architecture. The site interprets Lee's early life.

Admission Fees: Adults: $3; Children (11–17): $1.

Open to Public: Mon.–Sat.: 10 A.M.–4 P.M.; Sun.: 1 P.M.–4 P.M.; closed Dec.15–Feb.1.

Visitor Services: Guided tours.

Directions: From I-395: take exit 1B (Rte. 1 north) to Old Town Alexandria. Turn right on Oronoco St.

2 Site: CHRIST CHURCH, 118 North Washington St., Alexandria, VA 22314, 703-549-1450

Description: Lovely English-style church built 1767–73 and attended by George Washington and Robert E. Lee. Lee's pew is marked, as is the communion rail where he was confirmed.

Admission Fees: Free.

Open to Public: Mon.–Sat.: 9 A.M.–4 P.M.; Sun.: 1 P.M.–3 P.M.

Visitor Services: Gift shop.

Directions: From I-395: take exit 1B (Rte. 1 north) to Old Town Alexandria; turn right onto King St.; turn left onto Columbus. Church is on the right, at the corner of Cameron and North Washington Streets.

3 Site: FORT WARD MUSEUM AND HISTORIC SITE, 4301 West Braddock Rd., Alexandria, VA 22304, 703-838-4848

Description: One of the 68 major forts built to protect Washington, D.C., during the Civil War. The museum features a Civil War collection and a reference library.

Admission Fees: Free.

Open to Public: *Museum:* Tues.–Sat.: 9 A.M.–5 P.M.; Sun.: Noon–5 P.M. *Park:* Daily: 9 A.M.–sunset.

Visitor Services: Rest rooms; gift shop; handicapped access; trails; picnic area.

Regularly Scheduled Events: *Second Sat. of Aug.:* Union Army Garrison Day.

Directions: From I-395: take Seminary Rd. exit east. Follow signs to the fort (near Alexandria Hospital).

SURRENDER AT APPOMATTOX COURT HOUSE

Guillaume's painting of "The Surrender of Gen. Lee to Gen. Grant," Appomattox Court House National Historical Park, Appomattox, Virginia. (Photograph courtesy of the National Park Service.)

Generals Lee and Grant were well-matched adversaries who skillfully led their troops against each other in the last year of the Civil War. Robert E. Lee's greatest strengths were aggressiveness and an ability to assess his opponents. Ulysses S. Grant knew how to exploit his opponent's weaknesses to his own best advantage.

When Lee and Grant sat down in the parlor of Wilmer McLean's home in Appomattox Court House, Virginia, Grant asked only that the Confederates pledge not to take up arms against the United States. Officers were allowed to keep their sidearms, and any man who owned a horse was allowed to take it home with him.

At Appomattox Court House on April 9, 1865, Robert E. Lee, commanding general of the Army of Northern Virginia, surrendered his men to Ulysses S. Grant, general-in-chief of all United States forces. Though several Confederate armies under different commanders remained in the field, Lee's surrender signaled the end of the Southern states' attempt to create a separate nation. Three days later the men of the Army of Northern Virginia marched before the Union army, laid down their flags, stacked their weapons, and then began their journey back to their homes. For them it was an ending, but for the nation it was a new beginning.

Lee's capitulation did not bring an immediate end to the Confederate States of America, for other armies were still in the field. It wasn't until Joseph E. Johnston surrendered to William T. Sherman in North Carolina on April 26 and Edmund Kirby Smith hauled down the flag in Galveston, Texas, on June 2 that the Confederacy ceased to exist.

Appomattox

4   **Site:** APPOMATTOX COURT HOUSE NATIONAL HISTORICAL PARK, State Rte. 24, Appomattox, VA 24522, 804-352-8987

Description: General Robert E. Lee surrendered to Lt. General Ulysses S. Grant here on April 9, 1865. The historic meeting of Lee and Grant at the McLean house is captured in the picturesque village of Appomattox Court House, which still reflects its 1865 appearance.

Admission Fees: Adults: $2; Children under 16: Free.

Open to Public: June–Aug.: Daily: 9 A.M.–5:30 P.M.; rest of year: 8:30 A.M.–5 P.M.

Visitor Services: Rest rooms; handicapped access; bookstore.

Directions: From I-81 at Lexington: travel east on VA Rte. 60 to VA Rte. 24 south; approximately one and a half hours. Located on VA 24, 3 miles northeast of Appomattox.

Arlington

5 **Site:** THE ARLINGTON HOUSE/ROBERT E. LEE MEMORIAL, Arlington Cemetery, Arlington, VA 22211, 703-557-0613

Description: Home of General Lee and Mary Custis Lee, a great-granddaughter of Martha Washington. The Union seized the estate, converting it into a training center and later a cemetery.

Admission Fees: Free; hourly parking fee for cemetery.

Open to Public: Apr.–Oct.: Daily: 9:30 A.M.–6 P.M.; Oct.–Mar.: Daily: 9:30 P.M.–4:30 P.M.

Visitor Services: Rest rooms; visitors center.

Directions: Located in Arlington National Cemetery.

Charles City

6 **Site:** BERKELEY PLANTATION, 12602 Harrison Landing Rd., Charles City, VA 23030, 804-829-6018

Description: The Berkeley Plantation was used by Gen. George B. McClellan as headquarters during his Peninsula Campaign. President Lincoln conferred with him here, and "Taps" was composed here by Gen. Daniel Butterfield during the campaign.

Admission Fees: Adults: $8.50; Children (6–12): $4; Groups (10 or more): $4.50/person; Student groups: $2.50/person; Seniors/military/AAA members: 10 percent off the adult admission.

Open to Public: Daily: 8 A.M.–5 P.M.

Visitor Services: Guided tours; gift shop; museum; Coach House Tavern open daily for lunch, including Sun. brunch and dinner and by reservation on weekends (804-829-6003).

Regularly Scheduled Events: *First Sun. of Nov.:* First Thanksgiving festival.

Directions: From I-295: take Rte. 5. Located on Rte. 5, halfway between Richmond and Williamsburg.

Clover

7 | **Site:** STAUNTON RIVER BRIDGE BATTLEFIELD HISTORIC STATE PARK, Rte. 1, P.O. Box 183, Randolph, VA 23962-9801, 804-454-4312 or 804-786-1712

Description: On June 25, 1864, a ragtag band of Confederate soldiers, boys, and old men commanded by Capt. Benjamin L. Farinholt repelled a Union force sent to burn the Southern Railroad bridge over the Staunton River. Brig. Gen. James H. Wilson and Brig. Gen. August V. Kautz led the Union cavalry. Today, the remains of Farinholt's fortification stands on the high bluff overlooking the river and bridge site, on the south side of the river.

Admission Fees: Free.

Open to Public: *Fort Site:* Daily: Dawn to dusk. *Visitor Center:* Wed.–Sat.: 9 A.M.–4 P.M.; Sun.: 11 A.M.–4 P.M.

Visitor Services: Trails; tours in summer; museum; gift shop; information; visitors center; rest room; handicapped access to visitors center and part of trail; handicapped access planned for earthworks.

Regularly Scheduled Events: Call for events, dates, and times.

Directions: Take Rte. 360 to Rte. 92. One mile north of Clover, turn right onto Rte. 600. Proceed about 2.5 miles to entrance. Turn right and follow signs.

Danville

8 | **Site:** SUTHERLIN MANSION, Danville Museum of Fine Arts and History, 975 Main St., Danville, VA 24541, 804-793-5644

Description: For one week, April 3–10, 1865, Major William and Mrs. Sutherlin opened their home to Jefferson Davis and the Confederate government. The Confederate president delivered his final proclamation to the Confederacy on April 4. Danville has become known as the "Last Capital of the Confederacy."

Admission Fees: Free.

Open to Public: Tues.–Fri.: 10 A.M.–5 P.M.; Sat.–Sun.: 2 P.M.–5 P.M.

Visitor Services: Guided tours; gift shop; handicapped access.

Directions: Located on Rte. 29 Bus. (Main St.) in Danville.

Dayton

9 | **Site:** SHENANDOAH VALLEY FOLK ART & HERITAGE CENTER, 382 High St., Dayton, VA 22821, 540-879-2681

Description: The museum, among other Civil War exhibits relating to the Shenandoah Valley, features Stonewall Jackson's "Valley Campaign" as explained through the narrative program of a 12-foot electronic relief map where 300 lights follow the movements of the contending armies.

Admission Fees: Adults: $4; Children under 18: $1; Harrisonburg/Rockingham Historical Society members: $2.

Open to Public: Wed.–Sat: 10 A.M.–4 P.M.; Sun.: 1 P.M.–4 P.M.

Visitor Services: Handicapped access; museum; gift shop; rest rooms; picnic area.

Directions: From I-81: take exit 245 at Harrisonburg; go west on Port Republic Rd.; turn left on VA Rte. 42; turn right on Rte. 732; follow Rte. 732 as it turns sharply left; site is on the right at the corner of Bowman Rd. and High St.

Ewing

10 **Site:** CUMBERLAND GAP NATIONAL HISTORICAL PARK, U.S. 25E South, P.O. Box 1848, Middlesboro, KY 40965, 606-248-2817

Description: Cumberland Gap is the historic mountain pass on the Wilderness Road that opened the pathway for westward migration. During the Civil War, Cumberland Gap was first held by the South, then captured by Union troops. Each side held the gap twice.

Admission Fees: Free.

Open to Public: Mid-June–Labor Day: Daily: 8 A.M.–6 P.M.; Labor Day–mid-June: Daily: 8 A.M.–5 P.M.

Visitor Services: Gift shop; rest rooms; trails; museum; information; camping; handicapped access.

Directions: From I-81 at Bristol: follow U.S. 58 west to Cumberland Gap National Historical Park. Visitor Center is located 3 miles north on U.S. 25E.

Fairfax

11 **Site:** FAIRFAX MUSEUM AND VISITORS CENTER, 10209 Main Street, Fairfax, VA 22030, 703-385-8414

Description: Local history museum located in 1873 school building. Museum features exhibits and information on Fairfax during the Civil War. Walking tours of Historic Fairfax are available during certain

seasons and include the following Civil War–related sites:

Joshua Gunnell House (now a bed & breakfast, The Bailiwick Inn, open for

lodging, tea, and dinner; call 1-800-366-7666) Open on walking tour.
4023 Chain Bridge Road
Fairfax, VA 22030

**Confederate Memorial at
the Fairfax Cemetery**
10565 Main St.
Fairfax, VA 22030

Dr. William Gunnell House
Open on walking tour.
10520 Main St.
Fairfax, VA 22030

Fairfax County Courthouse
Open on walking tour.
4000 Chain Bridge Rd.
Fairfax, VA 22030

Admission Fees: *Museum:* Free. *Walking tours:* Adults: $2; Children: $1.

Open to Public: *Museum:* Daily: 9 A.M.–5 P.M.; *Walking tours:* Apr.–June and Sept.–Nov.: Sat. mornings at 10 A.M.

Visitor Services: Tours; museum; gift-shop; visitors center; rest rooms; handicapped access.

Directions: From I-66: exit onto Rte. 50 east. Follow until 50 becomes Main St. (Rte. 236). Proceed 4 miles, and museum is on the right.

Fort Monroe

12 Site: THE CASEMATE MUSEUM/FORT MONROE, P.O. Box 51341, Fort Monroe, VA 23651-0341, 804-727-3391

Description: This fort was never attacked by the Confederacy. Lee knew its strength; he helped build it. Fort Monroe denied the Confederacy access from the ocean to Norfolk and Richmond. Jefferson Davis was imprisoned here after being accused of plotting Lincoln's assassination.

Admission Fees: Free.

Open to Public: Daily: 10:30 A.M.–4:30 P.M.

Visitor Services: Rest rooms; handicapped access; gift shop.

Regularly Scheduled Events: Guided tours.

Directions: From I-64: take exit 268; follow signs to Fort Monroe.

Fredericksburg

13 Site: FREDERICKSBURG & SPOTSYLVANIA NATIONAL MILITARY PARK, 120 Chatham Ln., Fredericksburg, VA 22405, 540-371-0802

Description: Portions of major Civil War battlefields—Fredericksburg, Chancellorsville, the Wilderness, Spotsylvania Court

House, and several other smaller historic sites—comprise the park. The battles occurred during 1862, 1863, and 1864.

Admission Fees: Free.

Open to Public: Park and Visitors Center: Daily: 9 A.M.–5 P.M.; Extended hours in summer: 8:30 A.M.–6:30 P.M.

Visitor Services: Rest rooms; handicapped access; picnic area; trails.

Directions: From I-95: take exit 130A east on Rte. 3 to Fredericksburg battlefield.

Front Royal

14 **Site:** BELLE BOYD COTTAGE, 101 Chester St., Front Royal, VA 22630, 540-636-1446

Description: 1860 interpretation of a middle-class house, emphasizing the life of famed Confederate spy Belle Boyd. The information she gathered helped General Jackson win the Battle of Front Royal.

Admission Fees: Adults: $2; Children: $1.

Open to Public: Mon.–Fri.: 11 A.M.–4 P.M.; Sat. & Sun. by appointment.

Visitor Services: Guided tours; gift shop.

Regularly Scheduled Events: *Sat. nearest May 23:* Reenactment of the Battle of Front Royal; *Second weekend in Oct.:* Festival of Leaves.

Directions: From Washington, D.C.: take I-66 west; take exit 13 (Linden/Front Royal); then go 5 miles on Rte. 55 west to Rte. 522. Follow Rte. 522 (Commerce St.) into Front Royal; turn left onto Main St. and right onto Chester St.

15 **Site:** WARREN RIFLES CONFEDERATE MUSEUM, 95 Chester St., Front Royal, VA 22630, 540-636-6982

Description: Exhibits include memorabilia of Belle Boyd, Mosby's Rangers, Stonewall Jackson, Robert E. Lee, Jefferson Davis, and others, together with arms, uniforms, and historic documents.

Admission Fees: Adults: $2; Children under 12: Free.

Open to Public: Daily: 9 A.M.–4 P.M.

Visitor Services: None.

Directions: From I-66: take Front Royal exit; follow Main St. to Chester St.

Green Bay

16 **Site:** SAILOR'S CREEK BATTLEFIELD HISTORICAL STATE PARK, Rte. 2, P.O. Box 70, Green Bay, VA 23942, 804-392-3435

Description: Lee's ragged, hungry army fled Petersburg and Richmond, planning

to converge and meet a supply train at Amelia. The expected supplies did not arrive. Then disaster struck. Lee's column bogged down along Sailor's Creek near Rice, and Federals overtook and decimated the stalled Confederates. Total Confederate losses have been estimated at approximately 8,000—nearly a fourth of Lee's men.

Admission Fees: Free.

Open to Public: Daily: Dawn to dusk.

Visitor Services: Interpretive driving tour.

Directions: From Rte. 360: take Rte. 307; turn right onto Rte. 617, which goes through the park. From Rte. 460: take Rte. 307; turn left onto Rte. 617, which goes through the park.

Lexington

17 **Site:** LEE CHAPEL AT WASHINGTON AND LEE UNIVERSITY, Lexington, VA 24450, 540-463-3777

Description: Built in 1867 during Lee's term as president of Washington College, the Chapel contains his office, a museum with items belonging to Lee and his family, the Washington-Custis-Lee portrait collection, his tomb, and the famous recumbent statue of General Lee by Valentine. His horse Traveller is buried nearby.

Admission Fees: Free.

Open to Public: Apr.–Oct.: Mon.–Sat.: 9 A.M.–5 P.M.; Sun.: 2 P.M.–5 P.M.; After Oct.: Mon.–Sat.: 9 A.M.–4 P.M.

Visitor Services: None.

Regularly Scheduled Events: *Oct. 12 at noon:* Special service on the anniversary of General Lee's death.

Directions: From the intersection of I-81 & I-64: follow Rte. 11 south (Jefferson St.) 1 mile; campus is on the right.

18 **Site:** STONEWALL JACKSON'S GRAVE, Stonewall Jackson Memorial Cemetery, South Main St., Lexington, VA 22450, 540-463-2552

Description: Stonewall Jackson's grave is marked by Valentine's bronze statue of the general.

Admission Fees: Free.

Open to Public: Daily: Dawn to dusk.

Visitor Services: None.

Directions: From I-64: take exit 55 to Rte. 11 south, which becomes Jefferson St. Follow Jefferson St. until it ends; turn left onto South Main, where the cemetery is located.

19 **Site:** STONEWALL JACKSON HOUSE, 8 East Washington St., Lexington, VA 24450, 540-463-2552

Description: The only home famed General Thomas "Stonewall" Jackson ever owned, located in restored 1850 setting. Contains many of his personal possessions.

Admission Fees: Adults: $4; Children (6–12): $2; Adult group: $3.50/person; Youth group: $1.50/person.

Open to Public: Mon.–Sat.: 9 A.M.–5 P.M.; June, July, & August: open until 6 P.M.; Sun.: 1 P.M.–5 P.M.

Visitor Services: Rest rooms; handicapped access.

Regularly Scheduled Events: *Jan. 21:* Stonewall Jackson's birthday.

Directions: From I-81: take 188N or from I-64: take exit 55. Follow the Historic Lexington Visitor Center signs to Washington St. in downtown Lexington. The Jackson House is located one block west of the Visitors Center.

---

20 Site: VIRGINIA MILITARY INSTITUTE MUSEUM, Jackson Memorial Hall, Lexington, VA 24450, 540-464-7232

Description: Shelled and burned by the Union army after the Battle of New Market. In Jackson Memorial Hall is a mural of the famous cadet charge during that battle. Includes Stonewall Jackson's war horse, Little Sorrel, among other Civil War exhibits.

Admission Fees: Free.

Open to Public: Mon.–Sat.: 9 A.M.–5 P.M.; Sun.: 2 P.M.–5 P.M.

Visitor Services: Handicapped access; rest rooms; food; tours.

Directions: Located on the Virginia Military Institute Campus. From I-81: take Lexington exit (Rte. 11) 2 miles to VMI campus.

Lynchburg

21 Site: THE PEST HOUSE MEDICAL MUSEUM, Fourth and Taylor St., Lynchburg, VA 24504, 804-847-1811

Description: Audio commentary describes medical conditions at this medical office of Dr. John J. Terrell during the Civil War. Serves as monument to the memory of 365 soldiers who died of smallpox during the Civil War. Audio speaker located outside museum. For tour inside museum, call in advance.

Admission Fees: Free.

Open to Public: Daily: Dawn to dusk.

Visitor Services: Information; tours by appointment.

Directions: From I-81: exit at Rte. 130 east; turn right onto Rte. 29 south; cross John Lynch Memorial Bridge; Bus. Rte. 29 becomes Fifth St; follow Fifth St. to Taylor St.; turn right onto Taylor St. and look for gates.

Manassas

22 **Site:** THE MANASSAS MUSEUM, 9101 Prince William St., Manassas, VA 22110, 703-368-1873

Description: Interprets the history of the Northern Virginia Piedmont, emphasizing the Civil War. The museum grounds were the site of camps, fortifications, and Stonewall Jackson's raid.

Admission Fees: Adults: $2.50; Children: $1.50; Seniors: $1.50; Groups: $1.50/person; Tues: free.

Open to Public: Tues.–Sun.: 10 A.M.–5 P.M.; closed Mon. except federal holidays.

Visitor Services: Walking and driving tours; museum; gift shop; information; rest rooms; handicapped access.

Regularly Scheduled Events: *First weekend in Feb.:* Anniversary weekend; *June–Oct.:* Weekend programs/living history; *First Fri. in Dec.:* Holiday open house.

Directions: Take I-66 to exit 47, to VA 234 south. Proceed south about 3 miles; bear right, following 234; enter Old Town area; travel under the railroad overpass; turn left at the stoplight (Prince William St.). Proceed to the top of the hill; museum is on the right.

23 **Site:** MANASSAS NATIONAL BATTLEFIELD PARK, 6511 Sudley Rd., Manassas, VA 22110, 703-361-1339

Description: General Thomas J. "Stonewall" Jackson figured prominently in two Confederate victories here. Also known as "Bull Run," the First Battle of Manassas on July 21, 1861, ended any illusion of a short war. The Second Battle of Manassas, August 28–30, 1862, brought Southern forces to the height of their military power. The two battles are commemorated on this 5,000-acre battlefield park.

Admission Fees: Adults: $2; Children under 17: Free; Seniors may purchase a "Golden Age Pass," which is good for life: $10.

Open to Public: *Park:* Dawn to dusk. *Visitors Center:* Daily: 8:30 A.M.–5 P.M.

Visitor Services: Trails; picnic area; rest rooms; handicapped access.

Directions: The park is 26 miles southwest of Washington, D.C. The Visitors Center is on VA Rte. 234, .75 mile north of I-66 interchange (exit 47).

Middletown

24 **Site:** BELLE GROVE PLANTATION, 336 Belle Grove Rd., Middletown, VA 22645, 540-869-2028

Description: This 18th-century home, located on 100 acres, served as Sheridan's headquarters before and after the Battle of Cedar Creek in October 1864.

Admission Fees: Adults: $5; Children under 12: Free; Seniors: $4.50; Groups: $4.50/person.

Open to Public: Mon.–Sat.: 10 A.M.–4 P.M., last tour at 3:15 P.M.; Sun.: 1 P.M.–5 P.M., last tour at 4:15 P.M.

Visitor Services: Gift shop; quilt shop.

Directions: From I-66: take I-81 north to exit 302 (Rte. 627); go west on Rte. 627 to U.S. Rte. 11. Located 13 miles south of Winchester off Rte. 11; go 1 mile south of Middletown.

---

25 **Site:** CEDAR CREEK BATTLEFIELD VISITORS CENTER, P.O. Box 229, Middletown, VA 22645, 540-869-2064

Description: Cedar Creek Battlefield is the site of the only documented battle where both sides won and lost in the same day.

Admission Fees: Free.

Open to Public: Mon.–Sat.: 10 A.M.–4 P.M.; Sun.: 1 P.M.–5 P.M.

Visitor Services: Bookstore; visitors center.

Regularly Scheduled Events: *Oct.:* Cedar Creek living history and reenactment weekend.

Directions: From I-66: take I-81 north to exit 302 (Rte. 627); go west on Rte. 627 to U.S. Rte. 11; go 1 mile south to Cedar Creek.

New Market

26 **Site:** THE MUSEUM OF THE AMERICAN CAVALRY, 298 W. Old Crossroads, New Market, VA 22844, 540-740-3959

Description: The museum houses a collection of cavalry-related arms, armor, uniforms, and more, with special emphasis on the Civil War.

Admission Fees: Adults: $4.50; Children: $2.50, Children under 6: Free.

Open to Public: Apr.–Nov.: Daily: 9 A.M.–5 P.M.

Visitor Services: Gift shop; rest rooms; handicapped access.

Directions: From I-81: take exit 264; go west on Rte. 211; make an immediate right onto Collins Dr. (Rte. 305). Museum is on the left.

27 **Site:** NEW MARKET BATTLEFIELD HISTORICAL PARK & HALL OF VALOR CIVIL WAR MUSEUM, P.O. Box 1864, New Market, VA 22844, 540-740-3101

Description: At New Market in 1864, about 6,000 Federals under General Franz Sigel clashed with 4,500 Confederates led by General John Breckinridge. The Hall of Valor, focal point of the 280-acre battlefield park, presents a survey of the entire Civil War through its exhibits.

Admission Fees: Adults (age 16 & over): $5; Children: $2; Children under 5: Free; Adult group: $4/person for self-guided tour; Youth groups: $1/person.

Open to Public: Daily: 9 A.M.–5 P.M.

Visitor Services: Picnic areas; rest rooms; handicapped access.

Directions: From I-81: take exit 264 at New Market; turn onto Rte. 211 west and immediately turn right onto Rte. 305 (George Collins Pkwy.), and travel to the end.

28 **Site:** NEW MARKET BATTLEFIELD MILITARY MUSEUM, 9500 Collins Dr., P.O. Box 1131, New Market, VA 22844, 540-740-8065

Description: The Museum is located on Manor's Hill, where the fiercest fighting took place during the Battle of New Market. Of the 16 marble and granite markers, 15 are located on this part of the battlefield and mark the exact Federal and Confederate positions. Each side held a position on this property, first the Federal forces, and then the Confederate forces, as the Union army was forced to retreat north. The Confederate victory here on May 15, 1864, was the last Confederate victory in the Shenandoah Valley. John C. Breckinridge led 4,500 Confederate troops, and Franz Sigel led 6,000 Federal troops. About 70 percent of the museum exhibits are on the Civil War; other exhibits include items from the Revolutionary War to the present. The largest collection is from the Battle of New Market, and there is a 35-minute film on the Civil War.

Admission Fees: Adults: $6; Children (6–14): $2; Seniors: $5; Groups: call for rates.

Open to Public: Mar. 15–Dec. 1: Daily: 9 A.M.–5 P.M.

Visitor Services: Trails; museum; information; gift shop; rest rooms; handicapped access to museum and relic and gift shop.

Regularly Scheduled Events: *Monthly:* Living history weekends.

Directions: From I-81: take exit 264 at New Market. Turn west; turn right at next road (Collins Dr./Rte. 305). Travel .25 mile. Museum entrance is on left at top of the hill. Days Inn is located beside the museum.

Newport News

29 **Site:** DAM NO. 1, Newport News Park, 13560 Jefferson Ave., VA Rte. 143,
Newport News, VA 23603, 804-886-7912

Description: To halt McClellan's march up
the peninsula toward Richmond, General
Magruder built three dams to create im-
passable lakes on the Warwick River and
fortified the dams to prevent breach by the
Union.

Admission Fees: Free.

Open to Public: *Park:* Daily: Dawn to
dusk. *Interpretive Center:* Wed.–Sun.:
9 A.M.–7 P.M.

Visitor Services: Interpretive center.

Directions: From I-64 east: take exit 250B,
Fort Eustis Blvd. Turn left at junction of
Eustis Blvd. and Rte. 143 (Jefferson Ave.).
Park is on the right.

30 **Site:** WAR MEMORIAL MUSEUM OF VIRGINIA, 9285 Warwick Blvd.,
Newport News, VA 23607, 804-247-8523

Description: Offers a comprehensive
review of U.S. military history since 1775,
and within this context, the museum provides its visitors with a detailed survey of
the Civil War.

Admission Fees: Adults: $2; Children (6–
15): $1; Seniors: $1; Groups: $1/person;
Active military: $1.

Open to Public: Mon.–Sat.: 9 A.M.–5 P.M.;
Sun.: 1 P.M.–5 P.M.

Visitor Services: Picnic area; rest rooms;
handicapped access.

Directions: From I-64: take the Mercury
Blvd./James River Bridge exit (263A from
east/263B from west); follow south on
Mercury Blvd. and take Rt. 60/Ft. Eustis
exit on right. Turn left at first light, Horner
Blvd. Turn right to museum.

Petersburg

31 **Site:** BLANDFORD CHURCH AND CEMETERY, 319 South Crater Rd.,
Petersburg, VA 23803, 804-733-2396

Description: The church features 15
stained-glass windows, 13 of which were
donated by states in memory of 30,000 Confederate soldiers buried in the cemetery.

The church was used as a field hospital
during the war.

Admission Fees: Adults: $3; Seniors: $2.

Open to Public: Daily: 10 A.M.–5 P.M.; tours every half hour.

Visitor Services: Rest rooms; picnic area; book and gift shop; guided tours.

Regularly Scheduled Events: *June:* Confederate Memorial Day ceremony.

Directions: From I-95 north: take the Wythe St. exit to Crater Rd. and turn right at the church. From I-95 south: take Crater Rd. exit from the interstate.

Site: **CENTRE HILL MANSION**, Centre Hill Ct., Petersburg, VA 23801, 804-733-2401

Description: The mansion was built in 1823 by Robert Bolling and is a combination of federal, Greek Revival, and colonial architectural styles. The home was visited by two United States presidents, including Abraham Lincoln.

Admission Fees: Adults: $3; Children (7–12): $2; Seniors: $2; Active military: $2.

Open to Public: Daily: 10 A.M.–5 P.M.; tours every half hour.

Visitor Services: Rest rooms; gift shop.

Regularly Scheduled Events: *Jan.:* Ghost Watch Night.

Directions: From I-95 south: take the Petersburg/Washington St. exit; go one stoplight; turn right onto Justin; take first left onto Franklin St.; take immediate right to Centre Hill Ct.

Site: **CITY POINT UNIT, PETERSBURG NATIONAL BATTLEFIELD**, P.O. Box 549, Petersburg, VA 23804, 804-458-9504

Description: Between June 1864 and April 1865, City Point was transformed from a sleepy village of fewer than 300 inhabitants into a bustling supply center for the 100,000 Federal soldiers on the siege lines in front of Petersburg and Richmond.

Admission Fees: Free.

Open to Public: Daily: 8:30 A.M.–4:30 P.M.

Visitor Services: Visitors center; books; rest rooms.

Directions: From I-95: take Hopewell exit; follow Rte. 10 east into Hopewell. At second traffic light turn onto Main St., which becomes Appomattox St. Go 1 mile; turn left onto Cedar Ln., approximately two and a half blocks to parking lot.

---

34 **Site:** DRIVING TOUR OF THE ROUTE OF LEE'S RETREAT, P.O. Box 2107, Petersburg, VA 23804, 1-800-6-RETREAT

Description: The final days of the Civil War are interpreted on a 110-mile route of Lee's retreat from Petersburg to Appomattox through a 20-stop radio transmission tour.

The route remains virtually unchanged since the Civil War. Call to receive map of tour.

Admission Fees: Free.

Open to Public: Daily: Dawn to dusk.

Visitor Services: Rest rooms; information.

Directions: Start tour at intersection of U.S. Rte. 460 and State Rte. 708 at Sutherland in Dinwiddie County.

---

35   Site: FIVE FORKS UNIT, PETERSBURG NATIONAL BATTLEFIELD, P.O. Box 549, Petersburg, VA 23804, 804-458-9504

Description: On April 1, 1865, Union forces were able to capture this important crossroads that protected a nearby railroad supply line. The next evening, Petersburg was evacuated and Lee began his retreat that ended at Appomattox Court House.

Admission Fees: Free.

Open to Public: Daily: Daylight hours. Brochure available outside contact station.

Visitor Services: Information; rest room; handicapped access.

Directions: From I-85: take Dinwiddie exit and follow signs to Five Forks Unit, approximately 6–7 miles.

---

36   Site: PAMPLIN PARK CIVIL WAR SITE, 6523 Duncan Rd., Petersburg, VA 23803, 804-861-2408; 804-861-2820

Description: Interpretive Center contains exhibits, fiber-optic map, and interactive video displays on events leading to the April 2, 1865 battle resulting in the Union capture of Petersburg. Visit historic Tudor Hall plantation, an antebellum home and Confederate general's headquarters.

Admission Fees: Adults: $3; Children (7–11): $1.50; Groups of 10 or more: $2/ person; Children under 6: Free.

Open to Public: Daily: 9 A.M.–5 P.M.

Visitor Services: Rest rooms; handicapped access; 1.5 miles of interpretive trails; guided walks; living history.

Directions: From I-85: take exit 63A (U.S. 1 south) to Rt. 670 (Duncan Road); park entrance on left 1 mile.

---

37   Site: PETERSBURG NATIONAL BATTLEFIELD, State Rte. 36, Petersburg, VA 23804, 804-732-3531

Description: The Union army waged a 10-month campaign here in 1864–65 to seize Petersburg, the center of railroads supplying Richmond and the Confederate Army of Northern Virginia.

Admission Fees: Cars: $4.

Open to Public: *Battlefield:* Dawn to dusk. *Visitors Center:* Daily: Summer: 8 A.M.– 5:30 P.M.; Winter: 8 A.M.–5 P.M.

Visitor Services: Bookstore; picnic area; trails; rest rooms; handicapped access.

Directions: From I-95: take exit 52; take Wythe St (Rte. 36) east to park. The park is located 2.5 miles east of the center of Petersburg on State Rte. 36.

 Site: SIEGE MUSEUM/TRAPEZIUM HOUSE, 15 West Bank St., Petersburg, VA 23803, 800-368-3595 or 804-733-2400

Description: The human side of the 10-month siege of Petersburg is portrayed in exhibits and in a film narrated by Petersburg native, Joseph Cotton.

Admission Fees: Adults: $3; Children: $2; Seniors: $2; Groups: $2/person.

Open to Public: Daily: 10 A.M.–5 P.M.

Visitor Services: Rest rooms; handicapped access.

Regularly Scheduled Events: Special tours.

Directions: From I-95: take exit 52 (Washington St.). At third traffic light turn right onto Sycamore St. and go to Petersburg Visitors Center at the end of the street for directions.

Port Republic

 Site: PORT REPUBLIC BATTLEFIELD, Rockingham County, managed by Association for the Preservation of Civil War Sites (APCWS), II Public Sq., Ste. 200, Hagerstown, MD 21740, 301-665-1400

Description: The last and most fiercely contested battle of Jackson's 1862 Valley campaign was fought here on June 9, 1862. The APCWS owns nine acres of the "Coaling" part of the Federal position.

Admission Fees: Free.

Open to Public: Daily: Dawn to dusk.

Visitor Services: Information.

Directions: From I-81 at Harrisonburg: take Port Republic Rd. (Rte. 659) south through Port Republic to Rte. 340. Turn left and drive 1.5 miles to Rte. 708. Turn right and parking is on the right.

Richmond

40 **Site:** HOLLYWOOD CEMETERY, 412 South Cherry St., Richmond, VA 23220, 804-648-8501

Description: Most impressive and gorgeously landscaped cemetery. Contains graves of Confederate President Jefferson Davis, General J. E. B. Stuart, General Fitzhugh Lee, and other Confederate notables, as well as President James Monroe and President John Tyler. Magnificent holly trees give the cemetery its name.

Admission Fees: Free.

Open to Public: Daily: 8 A.M.–6 P.M.

Visitor Services: None.

Directions: From I-95: take exit 76B; proceed south on Belvedere St. and follow signs to Hollywood Cemetery.

---

41 Site: THE MUSEUM AND WHITE HOUSE OF THE CONFEDERACY,
1201 East Clay St., Richmond, VA 23219, 804-649-1861

Description: The museum houses the world's most comprehensive collection of Confederate artifacts, documents, and art. The White House is the restored executive mansion of Confederate President Jefferson Davis.

Admission Fees: Adults: $8; Children (6–college): $5; Seniors (55 and over): $7.

Open to Public: Mon.–Sat.: 10 A.M.–5 P.M.; Sun.: Noon–5 P.M.

Visitor Services: Handicapped access; rest rooms; gift shop.

Regularly Scheduled Events: *Mid-Aug.:* Down-Home Family Reunion; *Late Nov.:* Court End Christmas.

Directions: From I-95: take exit 74C (Broad St.) to 11th St.; turn right onto 11th; museum is two blocks down on Clay St.

---

42 Site: RICHMOND NATIONAL BATTLEFIELD PARK/CHIMBORAZO VISITORS
CENTER, 3215 East Broad St., Richmond, VA 23223, 804-226-1981

Description: Commemorates several battles to capture Richmond, which was the Confederate capital during the Civil War. From the beginning of the war, "On to Richmond" was the rallying cry of Union troops, and the city was their primary objective for four years. Extensive remains of Union and Confederate earthworks are preserved. Included battlefields are: Gaines' Mill and Malvern Hill.

Admission Fees: Free.

Open to Public: *Park:* Daily: Dawn to dusk. *Visitors Center:* Daily: 9 A.M.–5 P.M.

Visitor Services: Handicapped access; rest rooms; picnic area; self-guided tours.

Directions: From I-95: take East Broad St. exit. Begin tour at Chimborazo Visitors Center.

---

43 Site: THE VALENTINE MUSEUM & RIVERSIDE PARK, 1015 East Clay St.,
Richmond, VA 23219, 804-649-0711

Description: The studio contains the bust statues of Robert E. Lee, "Stonewall" Jackson, Albert Sidney Johnston, Jefferson Davis, G. E. Pickett, and other Civil War figures, as well as the plaster cast of "Recumbent Lee." Lunch is served year-round in the garden. Riverside Park is located at the site of the Tredegar Iron Works, where 50 percent of the Confederate cannons produced during the Civil War were forged. Call for events.

Admission Fees: *Museum:* Adults: $5; Children: $3; Seniors: $4. *Riverside Park:* $5.

Open to Public: *Museum:* Daily: 10 A.M.–5 P.M.; Sun.: Noon–5 P.M. *Riverside Park:* Mon., Thurs., Fri., & Sat.: 10 A.M. to sunset; Sun.: Noon–sunset.

Visitor Services: Food; rest rooms.

Directions: From I-95 north or south and I-64 east: take exit 10 (Broad St); turn right onto Broad St.; turn right onto 11th; turn right at Clay St.; turn left on 10th. The museum parking lot is on the right.

---

44 **Site:** THE VIRGINIA CAPITOL, Capitol Square, Richmond, VA 23219, 804-786-4344

Description: Designed by Thomas Jefferson, this officially became the capital of the Confederacy on May 21, 1861. A statue of Robert E. Lee and busts of Confederate heroes Stonewall Jackson, J. E. B. Stuart, Joseph E. Johnson, Fitzhugh Lee, among others, are located here.

Admission Fees: Free.

Open to Public: Daily: 9 A.M.–5 P.M.

Visitor Services: Guided tours.

Directions: From I-95: take Third St. exit (Coliseum); continue straight; turn left onto Franklin St.; turn left onto Ninth St.; Capitol Square is the first right.

---

45 **Site:** VIRGINIA HISTORICAL SOCIETY/CENTER FOR VIRGINIA HISTORY, The Battle Abbey, 428 N. Boulevard, Richmond, VA 23221, 804-358-4901

Description: The Museum of Virginia History offers seven galleries exhibiting rare Virginia treasures. Travel through Virginia history with the exhibit, "The Story of Virginia, an American Experience." Explore the development of Virginia from the Colonial period and the Civil War, through World War I and World War II and into the present. Tour the exhibit using handheld gallery guides that let you decide how much information you want about each object, and open drawers of "please touch" objects. Visit the Library of Virginia History for historical and genealogical research. See dramatic Civil War murals and a renowned collection of Confederate-made weapons. Original building, the Battle Abbey, is a memorial to the Confederate soldier. Allow one hour minimum.

Admission Fees: *Museum:* Adults: $4; Seniors: $3; Students and children: $2; Free for Historical Society members.

Open to Public: Mon.–Sat.: 10 A.M.–5 P.M.; Sun.: 1 P.M.–5 P.M.; Library closed Sun.

Visitor Services: Museum; gift shop; library; handicapped access; free parking; picnic area.

Regularly Scheduled Events: Call for information on lectures and special events held year-round.

Directions: From I-95: take exit 78; follow signs to Virginia Historical Society.

Strasburg

46 **Site:** FISHER'S HILL BATTLEFIELD CIVIL WAR SITE, managed by the Association for the Preservation of Civil War Sites (APCWS), II Public Sq., Suite 200, Hagerstown, MD 21740, 301-665-1400

Description: APCWS maintains 194 acres of the Fisher's Hill Battlefield where Gen. Jubal Early's Confederates were defeated on September 22, 1864.

Admission Fees: Free.

Open to Public: Daily: Dawn to dusk.

Visitor Services: Walking trail; information.

Directions: From I-81: take exit 298 to Rte. 11, through Strasburg; go right from VA Rte. 1 to State Rte. 601 and follow signs.

Stratford

47 **Site:** STRATFORD HALL PLANTATION, Stratford, VA 22558, 804-493-8038

Description: Built in the 1730s, this magnificent Potomac River plantation was the home of four illustrious generations of Lees. It was also the birthplace of Robert E. Lee.

Admission Fees: Adults: $7; Children: $3.

Open to Public: Daily: 9 A.M.–4 P.M.

Visitor Services: Tours; gift shop.

Directions: From Richmond: take 360 through Tappahannock to Warsaw; take Rte. 3 west to State Rte. 214 to Stratford Hall. From I-95 at Fredericksburg: take Rte. 3 east to State Rte. 214; go 1 mile.

Winchester

48 **Site:** CONFEDERATE AND NATIONAL CEMETERIES, Mt. Hebron, 305 East Boscawen St., Winchester, VA 22601, 540-662-4868 or 540-662-8535

Description: These two cemeteries contain the remains of 3,000 Confederate soldiers and 4,500 Union soldiers killed in nearby battles.

Admission Fees: Free.

Open to Public: *Summer:* Daily: 7:30 A.M.– 6 P.M.; *Winter:* Daily: 7:30 A.M.–5 P.M.

Visitor Services: None.

Directions: From I-81: take Rte. 7, which turns into Berryville Ave.; turn left on Pleasant Valley Rd.; proceed one block.

---

49 **Site:** STONEWALL JACKSON'S HEADQUARTERS MUSEUM, 415 North Braddock St., Winchester, VA 22601, 540-667-3242

Description: From this brick house Stonewall Jackson commanded his forces in defense of the strategic Shenandoah Valley.

Admission Fees: Adults: $3.50; Children (6–12): $1.75; Seniors: $3.

Open to Public: Apr. 1–Oct. 31: Daily: 10 A.M.–4 P.M.

Visitor Services: Gift shop; rest rooms.

Directions: From I-81: take exit 313; follow the signs.

Yorktown

50 **Site:** COLONIAL NATIONAL HISTORICAL PARK, P.O. Box 210, Yorktown, VA 23690, 804-898-3400

Description: Though established to commemorate the Colonial era, this park also possesses extensive vestiges of the Civil War related to the Siege of 1862 during the Peninsula Campaign.

Admission Fees: Free.

Open to Public: *Visitors Center:* Daily: Winter: 8:30 A.M.–5 P.M.; Summer: 8:30 A.M.–6 P.M.

Visitor Services: Information; visitors center; rest rooms.

Regularly Scheduled Events: *Memorial Day weekend:* Civil War weekend; *Spring:* Half-day Civil War tours by reservation only.

Directions: From I-64: take exit 199 and follow the signs to Colonial Pkwy.

WASHINGTON, D.C.

*I*n 1861, the capital of the United States remained incomplete. The Capitol's dome was unfinished, and sanitary conditions were horrible. There were deep political divisions. The Civil War transformed the capital that antebellum Americans called Washington City.

From the firing on Fort Sumter, South Carolina, the war became the central fact of the city's life. During the conflict's early days, fear reigned as Southern sympathizers in Maryland attempted to isolate the city. Order returned when the first Union volunteers poured into the District, but in July, the Union rout at First Bull Run produced near panic. During the following months, thousands of drilling soldiers and an elaborate defensive perimeter that included 68 forts, 22 batteries, and sprawling earthworks brought security to the city. Washington, D.C., like its Confederate counterpart, Richmond, Virginia, 100 miles to the south, became a nation's symbol, the one place that could not be surrendered to the enemy.

The war brought growth, activity, and problems. The city's population, fueled in part by freed slaves who poured in from the South, quadrupled from 41,000 in 1860 to 160,000 at its wartime peak. With the advent of Northerners, the city's distinctive antebellum Southern atmosphere changed. Besides the many soldiers, the city attracted lobbyists, speculators, inventors, and job seekers who came in droves, each looking for a share of the money to be made in the wartime economy.

The mood of the city's inhabitants reflected the fortunes of the Union army: euphoria after a victory, despair following a defeat. Government buildings, including the Capitol, the Treasury, and the Patent Office were used to house and supply the troops, and cattle grazed on the Mall. Numerous private residences, taken over by the Federal government, became hospitals teeming with wounded young men.

Workmen finally completed the Capitol's dome in time for Lincoln's second inaugural in March, 1865. On April 14, 1865, just five days after Lee's surrender at Appomattox, the president was assassinated at downtown Ford's Theater, delaying for a time the restoration of the American Union.

Washington, D.C.

1   **Site: FORD'S THEATER AND PETERSEN HOUSE NATIONAL HISTORIC SITE,**
         511 & 516 10th St., NW, Washington, D.C. 20004, 202-426-6924

Description: President Abraham Lincoln was shot while attending a play at Ford's   Theater on April 14, 1865. Following the shooting, he was moved to the Petersen

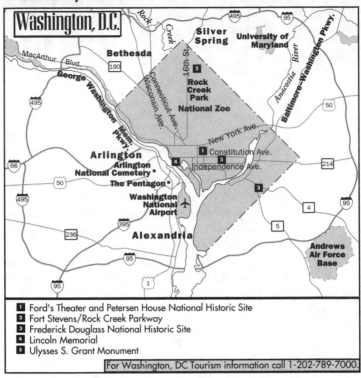

Washington, D.C.

MacArthur Blvd.
Bethesda
George Washington Mem. Pkwy.
Silver Spring
University of Maryland
Rock Creek Park
National Zoo
New York Ave.
Constitution Ave.
Independence Ave.
Arlington
Arlington National Cemetery
The Pentagon
Washington National Airport
Alexandria
Andrews Air Force Base

☐1 Ford's Theater and Petersen House National Historic Site
☐2 Fort Stevens/Rock Creek Parkway
☐3 Frederick Douglass National Historic Site
☐4 Lincoln Memorial
☐5 Ulysses S. Grant Monument

For Washington, DC Tourism information call 1-202-789-7000.

House, a neighboring boardinghouse, where he died nine hours later.

Admission Fees: Free.

Open to Public: Daily: 9 AM–5 PM.

Visitor Services: Handicapped access; museum; bookstore.

Directions: Located on 10th St., NW between E and F Streets.

---

2 **Site:** FORT STEVENS/ROCK CREEK PARKWAY, Piney Branch Rd., NW (13th St.), Washington, D.C.

Description: At the outset of the Civil War, a system of flanking forts and batteries was constructed around Washington. One such spot was Fort Massachusetts, built along the Seventh Street Pike, a thoroughfare leading to and from Washington. The fort was enlarged on two occasions. In 1863 its name was changed to Fort Stevens, in memory of Brigadier General Isaac Ingalls Stevens, who lost his life at Chantilly,

Virginia. On July 11, 1864, Fort Stevens was the site of the only battle within the District of Columbia.

Admission Fees: Free.

Open to Public: Daily: Dawn to dusk.

Visitor Services: None.

Directions: From I-495: exit at Georgia Ave. Go south into the District until Georgia Ave.

intersects with Military Rd. (on the right). Turn right onto Military Rd., then immedi- ately turn right again at 13th St./Piney Branch Rd. The fort is ahead.

Frederick Douglass (1818–95)

Frederick Douglass National Historic Site, Washington, D.C. (Photograph courtesy of The Civil War Trust.)

Frederick Douglass spent his early years in a home broken beyond most people's comprehension. His mother, a slave, was forced to leave him as an infant. He never knew the identity of his father. He lived in poverty, crowded into two rooms with grandparents and cousins. Beyond that, Frederick was a slave—listed on an inventory along with mules and bushels of wheat. His owner could sell him on a whim, because then in America slavery was legal. But all this adversity did not break the spirit of young Frederick, for he possessed an intellectual curiosity undeterred by his circumstances.

At age eight, he was sent to Baltimore as a house servant. He became fascinated by the "mystery of reading" and decided that education was "the pathway from slavery to freedom." Because it was illegal to educate slaves, Frederick learned how to read and write by trading bread for reading lessons and tracing over words in discarded spelling books until his handwriting was smooth and graceful. By age 13, he was reading articles about the "abolition of slavery" to other slaves. When he escaped to freedom at age 20, Douglass shared his hard-earned wisdom.

His lifetime triumphs were many: abolitionist, women's rights activist, author, owner-editor of an antislavery newspaper, fluent speaker of many languages, minister to Haiti, and most respected orator of the 19th century. In his closing years at Cedar Hill he was deemed the "Sage of Anacostia," an accolade that celebrated the intellectual spirit within him that never grew old.

3 **Site:** FREDERICK DOUGLASS NATIONAL HISTORIC SITE, 1411 W St., SE, Washington, D.C. 20020, 202-426-5961

Description: Frederick Douglass, the nation's leading black spokesman during the 19th century, lived at this home from 1877 to 1895. Douglass was U.S. minister to Haiti, 1889.

Admission Fees: Free.

Open to Public: Summer: Daily: 9 A.M.– 5 P.M.; Winter: Daily: 9 A.M.–4 P.M.

Visitor Services: Visitors center; museum.

Regularly Scheduled Events: *Feb. 14:* Wreath laying on Douglass's birthday.

Directions: From downtown: cross the 11th St. (Anacostia) Bridge to Martin Luther King (MLK) Ave.; turn left on W St. The home is on top of the hill at 14th and W Streets, SE. From I-295 north or south: take Pennsylvania Ave. east exit. Proceed east on Pennsylvania Ave. two blocks to Minnesota Ave. Turn right on to Minnesota to Good Hope Rd. Turn right on Good Hope Rd.; proceed one-half block; turn left on 14th St; turn left on W.

4 **Site:** LINCOLN MEMORIAL, 23rd St., NW, Washington, D.C. 20242, 202-485-9880

Description: This classical structure contains Daniel Chester French's monument sculpture of the 16th president of the United States. Lincoln's Gettysburg Address and Second Inaugural Address are carved on the marble walls.

Admission Fees: Free.

Open to Public: Daily: 8 A.M.–midnight.

Visitor Services: Handicapped access.

Directions: The memorial is located at the western end of the Mall, in downtown Washington between Constitution and Independence Avenues at 23rd St., NW.

5 **Site:** ULYSSES S. GRANT MONUMENT, U.S. Capitol Grounds West, Washington, D.C.

Description: The Grant Memorial is one of the most important sculptural groups in Washington. It consists of a central equestrian statue of Grant with two sculptured groups of military figures situated at either end of a large marble platform.

Admission Fees: Free.

Open to Public: Daily: 24 hours.

Visitor Services: None.

Directions: Located at Union Square at the east end of the Mall, directly below the west grounds of the Capitol.

WEST VIRGINIA

$\mathcal{T}$he slavery question, which between 1830 and 1860 tore at the fabric of the nation, left the Commonwealth of Virginia equally as divided. Perhaps the most incendiary of events connected with the slavery issue took place on what is now West Virginia soil, with the seizure of the federal arsenal at Harpers Ferry in 1859 by the fiery abolitionist, John Brown. His plan for arming the slaves of northern Virginia and inciting a general uprising, together with the secrecy with which his plan was carried out, threw the South into a panic.

In the wake of Fort Sumter and President Lincoln's call for volunteers, sentiment in the Virginia Convention shifted. Many delegates who had opposed secession now just as vigorously opposed the president's intention to use coercive federal powers against a state. When the questions of Virginia's position came to a vote, the majority cast their ballots to join the newly formed Confederate States of America. However, of the 47 delegates from western Virginia, 32, more than two-thirds, voted against leaving the Union.

The future of the newly proposed state depended on control of western Virginia by the Union. From the outset of the war, both the Union and Confederate governments endeavored to hold West Virginia because of its valuable salt resources, its productive farms, and the strategic section of the Baltimore and Ohio Railroad that traversed the eastern and northern sections of the state. Moreover, both sides were well aware of the psychological advantages in controlling West Virginia.

Most of the decisive fighting in West Virginia took place before the end of 1861. In the eastern Panhandle positions sometimes changed hands with bewildering rapidity. Military action there revolved around efforts to gain or retain control of valuable segments of the Baltimore and Ohio Railroad. In the campaigns in the Shenandoah Valley, West Virginia's distinguished Confederate General Thomas Jonathan "Stonewall" Jackson, played a vital part. Farther south, the Confederates took the initiative and pushed Union troops out of Fayetteville and Charleston. Other than some daring Confederate raids in central West Virginia, there were few important battles in the state after 1862. With the engagements at White Sulphur Springs, or Rocky Gap, and Droop Mountain in the autumn of 1863, the Confederates had been forced out of most of West Virginia.

During the early years of the Civil War, the statehood issue continued to be debated. The restored Government of Virginia eventually approved the separation, and Congress passed the West Virginia statehood bill. Although he had misgivings, President Lincoln issued a proclamation under which West Virginia entered the Union on June 20, 1863, as the 35th state.

by Jeffrey Harpold, West Virginia Division of Tourism

West Virginia

1 Camp Allegheny
2 Rich Mountain Battlefield Civil War Site
3 Bulltown Historic Area
4 West Virginia State Museum in the Cultural Center
5 Cheat Summit Fort
6 Grafton National Cemetery
7 Harpers Ferry National Historical Park
8 Droop Mountain Battlefield State Park
9 Lewisburg National Register Historic District/Visitor Center
10 Belle Boyd House/Civil War Museum of the Lower Shenandoah Valley
11 Philippi Covered Bridge
12 Philippi Historic District

13 Shepherdstown Historic District
14 Carnifex Ferry Battlefield State Park
15 Jackson's Mill Historic Area
16 West Virginia Independence Hall

For West Virginia Tourism information call 1-800-CALL-WVA.

Bartow

Site: CAMP ALLEGHENY, Mailing address: 200 Sycamore St., Elkins, WV 26241, 304-636-1800

Description: Established by Confederate forces in the summer of 1861 to control the Staunton-Parkersburg Turnpike, this camp, at 4,400 feet above sea level was one of the highest of the Civil War. Although Confederate General Edward Johnson's troops won the battle against Union forces under the command of General R. H. Milroy, the loss of men because of the harsh winter climate and the logistical nightmare of keeping the camp supplied contributed to the decision to abandon it in April 1862.

Admission Fees: Free.

Open to Public: Daily: Dawn to dusk.

Visitor Services: None.

Directions: From I-81 at Staunton: take U.S. 250 west to just beyond the Virginia/West Virginia line; turn left at County Rd. 3; take a right at the T; go 2 more miles. NOTE: Road is sometimes closed due to snow; call 304-636-1800 for road information.

Beverly

2 **Site:** RICH MOUNTAIN BATTLEFIELD CIVIL WAR SITE, P.O. Box 227, Beverly, WV 26253, 304-637-RICH (7424); 800-422-3304

Description: Rich Mountain Battlefield Civil War Site includes the battle site, Confederate Camp Garnett, and connecting section of the old Staunton-Parkersburg Turnpike. On July 11, 1861, Union troops under General George B. McClellan routed Confederates holding the pass over Rich Mountain. This victory led to General McClellan's appointment to command the Army of the Potomac. It also gave the Union control of northwestern Virginia, allowing the formation of the state of West Virginia two years later.

Admission Fees: Free.

Open to Public: Daily: Dawn to dusk.

Visitor Services: Trails. NOTE: Visitor information, a display, and a gift shop are located in Beverly.

Regularly Scheduled Events: *July 1997 and semiannually:* Reenactment/living history.

Directions: From I-79: take exit 99 at Weston; take U.S. Rte. 33 east to Elkins, then U.S. Rte. 219/250 south to Beverly; turn west in Beverly onto Rich Mountain Rd.; follow road 5 miles up the mountain to battlefield. Camp Garnett is 1.5 miles farther. NOTE: Road is sometimes closed due to snow. Call ahead and check local weather information.

Burnsville

3 **Site:** BULLTOWN HISTORIC AREA, c/o Burnsville Lake, Corps of Engineers, HC 10, P.O. Box 24, Burnsville, WV 26395, 304-452-8170 (number for visitors center, May–Sept.)

Description: The Battle of Bulltown occurred at the site of fortifications on a knoll overlooking a key covered bridge that once crossed the Little Kanawha River along the Weston-Gauley Turnpike. The highway was the artery for transportation in Central West Virginia connecting the northern and southern portions of the state. Had Confederate Commander "Mudwall" Jackson's (Stonewall's cousin) assault on Bulltown been successful, he would have cut communications between troops in northern West Virginia and the Kanawha Valley, creating an opportunity to march on

Wheeling, the center of Union support in West Virginia.

At the site are fortifications dug to protect the fort, the burial site of seven unknown Confederate soldiers, intact sections of the Turnpike, and the Cunningham House. The Cunningham House housed supporters of the Confederacy at the time of the Civil War. Today it serves as the center for Historic Bulltown Village, which includes farm buildings, two relocated log homes, and the log St. Michael's Church, that date from before the Civil War.

Admission Fees: Free.

Open to Public: *Interpretive center:* May–Sept.: 10 A.M.–6 P.M.

Visitor Services: Camping; trails; interpretive center; information; rest rooms; handicapped access (some trails are paved; unpaved trails may require someone to assist those in wheelchairs); seasonal tours of battlefield and historic village, or by appointment.

Directions: From I-79: exit at Flatwoods, WV or Roanoke, WV and follow signs for Bulltown, Burnsville Lake (approximately 14 miles from Flatwoods and 20 miles from the Roanoke exit on U.S. 19 and State Rte. 4).

Charleston

4 **Site:** WEST VIRGINIA STATE MUSEUM IN THE CULTURAL CENTER, 1900 Kanawha Blvd., East, Charleston, WV 25305-0300, 304-558-0220

Description: The West Virginia State Museum in the Cultural Center has exhibits about the Civil War in West Virginia featuring artifacts, graphics, and maps.

Admission Fees: Free.

Open to Public: Mon.–Fri.: 9 A.M.–5 P.M.; Sat.–Sun.: 1 P.M.–5 P.M.

Visitor Services: Museum; gift shop; information; rest rooms; handicapped access.

Directions: Adjacent to I-64 & I-77 in the Capitol Complex. Exit on Greenbriar St.; proceed south toward the river and the Capitol; turn left at the first light (Washington St.) into the parking lot. The museum is in the Cultural Center.

Durbin

5 **Site:** CHEAT SUMMIT FORT, Mailing address: 200 Sycamore St., Elkins, WV 26241, 304-636-1800

Description: General George B. McClellan ordered this pit and parapet fort to be built in 1861 to secure the Staunton-Parkersburg Turnpike and protect the Baltimore and Ohio Railroad. The Confederate failure to take the fort in September, 1861 was central in the failure of Robert E. Lee's western Virginia campaign.

Admission Fees: Free.

Open to Public: Daily: Dawn to dusk.

Visitor Services: Trails.

Regularly Scheduled Events: *Apr. or early May:* Semiannual living history and reenactment.

Directions: From I-79 near Weston, WV: take U.S. 33 east to Elkins, then U.S. 250 south to just before Cheat Bridge; turn right at the sign and right again at the T. Go about 1 mile to the top. NOTE: Road is sometimes closed due to snow; call 304-636-1800 for road information.

Grafton

6 **Site:** GRAFTON NATIONAL CEMETERY, 431 Walnut St., Grafton, WV 26354, 304-265-2044

Description: Grafton was established in 1867 by Congressional legislation to offer a final resting place for the men who died during the Civil War. Burials were removed from other cemeteries to make Grafton the final resting place for 2,133 soldiers, including 664 unknown soldiers. Grafton is notably the site of the grave of the first casualty of land engagement of the Civil War, Private T. Bailey Brown.

Admission Fees: Free.

Open to Public: Daily: Dawn to dusk.

Visitor Services: Information; rest rooms.

Regularly Scheduled Events: *May:* Memorial Day parade and service—continuous since 1879; *Nov.:* Veterans Day service.

Directions: From I-79: take Rte. 250 for approximately 10 miles; then take Rte. 50 into Grafton.

Harpers Ferry

7 **Site:** HARPERS FERRY NATIONAL HISTORICAL PARK, P.O. Box 65, Harpers Ferry, WV 25425, 304-535-6223

Description: Site of abolitionist John Brown's 1859 raid on the First Federal Arsenal. Harpers Ferry changed hands eight times during the war. It became the base of operations for Union invasions into the Shenandoah Valley. Stonewall Jackson achieved his most brilliant victory here in September 1862, when he captured 12,500 Union soldiers.

Admission Fees: Bicycles, motorcycles, and walk-ins: $3; Cars: $5.

Open to Public: Daily: 8 A.M.–5 P.M.

Visitor Services: Trails; museum; gift shop; information; rest rooms; handicapped access.

Regularly Scheduled Events: *Second full weekend in Sept.:* Civil War living history

View of Harper's Ferry National Historical Park from Maryland Heights. (Photograph courtesy of Harper's Ferry National Historical Park.)

weekend; *Second full weekend in Oct.:* Election Day, 1860; *Dec.:* Illumination.

Directions: From Washington: take I-270 north to I-70 to west Rte. 340. From Gettysburg: take MD Rte. 15 south to west Rte. 340. From Shenandoah Valley: take I-81 north to WV 51 east. From Baltimore: take I-70 west to Rte. 340 west.

Hillsboro

8 **Site:** DROOP MOUNTAIN BATTLEFIELD STATE PARK, HC 64, P.O. Box 189, Hillsboro, WV 24946, 304-653-4254

Description: Droop Mountain Battlefield is the site of one of West Virginia's largest and last important Civil War battles. The battle was fought on Nov. 6, 1863, between the Union army of Gen. William Averell and the Confederate army of Gen. John Echols. Echols's army was pushed south into Virginia and never regained control of southeastern West Virginia.

Admission Fees: Free.

Open to Public: Daily: 6 A.M.–10 P.M.

Visitor Services: Trails; museum; information; rest rooms.

Directions: Take I-64 to Lewisburg, WV; travel north on U.S. Rte. 219 for 27 miles.

Lewisburg

9 **Site:** LEWISBURG NATIONAL REGISTER HISTORIC DISTRICT/VISITOR CENTER, 105 Church St., Lewisburg, WV 24901, 304-645-1000, 800-833-2068

Description: Lewisburg was the site of a Civil War battle on May 23, 1862, when Union forces attempted to sever railroad communications between Virginia and Tennessee. There is a Confederate cemetery in town; a library used as a hospital with Confederate graffiti on the walls; a church with a cannonball hole; another church that served as a Confederate morgue; and a monument to the Confederate dead.

Admission Fees: $3 for the North House.

Open to Public: *Visitors Center:* Mon.–Sat.: 9 A.M.–5 P.M.; Sun.: 1 P.M.–5 P.M. *Museum:* Mon.–Sat.: 10 A.M.–4 P.M.

Visitor Services: Lodging; gas; food; museum; gift shop; information; rest rooms.

Directions: From I-64: take exit 169; travel south on U.S. 219 for 1.5 miles; turn right on U.S. 60 (Washington St.); proceed two blocks; turn left onto Church St.

Martinsburg

 Site: BELLE BOYD HOUSE/CIVIL WAR MUSEUM OF THE LOWER SHENANDOAH VALLEY, 126 East Race St., Martinsburg, WV 25401, 304-267-4713

Description: Belle Boyd, West Virginia's best-known Civil War spy, lived in this house. Belle endorsed the Confederate cause, even shooting a Yankee soldier. She supplied information to Stonewall Jackson about enemy activities and was imprisoned twice. Also on-site is the Civil War Museum of the Lower Shenandoah Valley and the Berkeley County Museum. The archive division offers facilities to research the local Berkeley, Jefferson, and Morgan areas.

Admission Fees: Free.

Open to Public: Wed.–Sat.: 10 A.M.–4 P.M.

Visitor Services: Gift shop; information; rest rooms; handicapped access.

Regularly Scheduled Events: *Third weekend in May:* Belle Boyd's Birthday; *Three weekends following Thanksgiving:* Christmas open house.

Directions: The Belle Boyd House is located in Martinsburg, WV at 126 E. Race St. Martinsburg is immediately east of I-81 and is reached via West Virginia exits 12, 13, and 16; U.S. Rte. 11 and State Routes 9 and 45 run through Martinsburg on Queen St. Queen St. is Martinsburg's main street and divides the cross streets. From Queen St. proceed east on Race St., one block to the Belle Boyd House at 126.

Philippi

11 **Site:** PHILIPPI COVERED BRIDGE, 124 North Main St., Philippi, WV 26416, 304-457-1225

Description: The bridge witnessed the first land battle of the Civil War on June 3, 1861. During this battle, Union troops took command of the bridge and used it as a barracks.

Admission Fees: Free.

Open to Public: Daily: Dawn to dusk.

Visitor Services: Lodging; gas; camping; trails; gift shop; information; rest rooms; handicapped access.

Directions: From I-79: take exit 115; follow Rte. 20 south to Rte. 57 east; take U.S. Rte. 119 north to Philippi (22 miles from exit 115).

12 **Site:** PHILIPPI HISTORIC DISTRICT, 124 North Main St., Philippi, WV 26416, 304-457-1225

Description: The City of Philippi was the site of the first land battle of the Civil War

on June 3, 1861. It was also the site of the first amputation of the Civil War on

James Hanger. Philippi is home to many historic sites, as well as a historical museum containing Civil War–era artifacts.

Admission Fees: Free.

Open to Public: Daily.

Visitor Services: Lodging; gas; camping; trails; food; museum; gift shop; information, rest rooms; handicapped access.

Regularly Scheduled Events: *First weekend of June:* Blue and Gray Reunion (including reenactment of the Battle of Philippi).

Directions: From I-79: take exit 115; follow Rte. 20 south to Rte. 57 east; take U.S. Rte. 119 north to Philippi (22 miles from exit 115).

Shepherdstown

13 Site: SHEPHERDSTOWN HISTORIC DISTRICT, Shepherd College, Shepherdstown, WV 25443, 304-876-5399

Description: In the wake of the battle of Antietam, the town became one vast Confederate hospital with public and private buildings in town serving as military hospitals for the wounded. On September 20, 1862, the last significant battle of the Maryland campaign occurred at Boteler's Ford, about a mile down the Potomac River from Shepherdstown.

Admission Fees: Free.

Open to Public: Daily: Dawn to dusk.

Visitor Services: Lodging; gas; food; gift shops; information.

Directions: From I-81 south: take exit 16E; take Rte. 9 east to Rte. 45 east, 8 miles to Shepherdstown. From I-81 north: take exit 12; take Rte. 45 east to Rte. 9 east, 7 miles to Kerneysville; left on Rte. 480 (at Kerneysville); 4 miles to Shepherdstown.

Summersville

14 Site: CARNIFEX FERRY BATTLEFIELD STATE PARK, Rte. 2, P.O. Box 435, Summersville, WV 26651, 304-872-0825

Description: Site of a Civil War battle on September 10, 1861. This Union victory halted any further attempt to take the Kanawha Valley.

Admission Fees: Free.

Open to Public: *Park:* Daily: Dawn to dusk; *Museum:* Memorial Day weekend–Labor Day weekend: Sat., Sun., holidays.

Visitor Services: Trails; museum; information; rest rooms; picnic facilities.

Regularly Scheduled Events: *Second weekend in Sept.:* Battle reenactment during Civil War Weekend.

Directions: Located off Rte. 129 approximately 5 miles west of U.S. Rte. 19 near Summersville; U.S. Rte. 19 is a north-south connection between I-77 & I-79.

Weston

15 **Site:** JACKSON'S MILL HISTORIC AREA, P.O. Box 670, Weston, WV 26452, 304-269-5100

Description: The Jackson's Mill Museum is the midpoint of a historic area representing the life of General Thomas "Stonewall" Jackson. Greatly influenced by his Uncle Cummins who raised him after the death of his parents, young Tom developed much of his character by building and working in this mill.

Admission Fees: Adults: $3; Children: $2; Groups (25 or more): $2/person.

Open to Public: Tues.–Sun.: 10 A.M.–5 P.M.; Nov.–Apr.: closed.

Visitor Services: Trails; museum; gift shop; information; rest rooms; handicapped access.

Regularly Scheduled Events: *Labor Day Weekend:* Stonewall Jackson Arts & Crafts Jubilee.

Directions: From I-79: take exit 99 and turn west on U.S. Rte. 33 toward Weston. Go approximately 4 miles to the third stoplight; turn right on U.S. Rte. 19 north. Go approximately 5 miles to Jackson's Mill Rd. on the left; turn left on Jackson's Mill Rd. and go approximately 2.5 miles to Jackson's Mill on the right.

Wheeling

16 **Site:** WEST VIRGINIA INDEPENDENCE HALL, 1528 Market St., Wheeling, WV 26003, 304-238-1300

Description: The site of statehood debates during the Civil War years of 1861–63, which led to the new state of West Virginia, the only state to have acquired its sovereignty by proclamation of a U.S. president.

Admission Fees: Guided tours: $2/person (reservation required).

Open to Public: Daily: 10 A.M.–4 P.M.; Closed on state holidays and Sun. in Jan.–Feb.

Visitor Services: Museum; rest rooms; handicapped access.

Directions: Located between I-70 and I-470 in downtown Wheeling. From I-70: proceed south on Main St. to 16th St.; turn left and go one block to Market St. The building is across Market St. on the left; proceed through the light and turn left into the parking lot behind the building

Index

GET THE DIRT ON THE CIVIL WAR.

Nearly 130 years after the last shot was fired, the final battle of the Civil War is just beginning. Today, dozens of historic battlefields are endangered and completely unprotected by federal, state or local laws. Join in our plot to save them. For ever $25 you send, we'll preserve one acre of historic and threatened battlefield in your name, a loved one's or ancestor's and send you an honorary deed of ownership. Call or mail the coupon. And help keep America's history from becoming just a memory.

THE CIVIL WAR TRUST™

Enriching Our Future By Preserving Our Past.

1-800-CW-TRUST

HERE'S THE SCOOP.

I wish to have ____ acre(s) of endangered battlefield preserved in the following name(s):

_____   _____

I am enclosing $25 for each acre. Please mail ____ honorary deed(s) of ownership to:

Name _____

Address _____

City _____

State _____

Zip _____

Phone _____

Payment enclosed:

Check Money Order VISA MasterCard AmericanExpress

Card # _____

Exp. Date _____

Signature: _____

Contributions are tax deductible to the extent allowed by law.

Mail to: The Civil War Trust, 1225 Eye St., NW, Suite 401, Washington, DC 20005. Or call 1-800-CW-TRUST.

AFTER CHASING THE
BATTLES OF YESTERYEAR,

CONTINUE YOUR VISIT TO THE PAST
AT CRACKER BARREL
OLD COUNTRY STORE.

Cracker Barrel Old Country Store™ is proud to partner with The Civil War Trust in the national campaign to preserve the historical, environmental and cultural heritage of our American battlefield lands.

As part of our commitment, Cracker Barrel is pleased to be an official sponsor of The Civil War Discovery Trail™ which links more than 400 sites in 24 states. The trail inspires and teaches the story of the Civil War and its haunting impact on America.

While visiting the stops along the trail, we would be honored if you would drop by any of our 260 restaurants and country stores in 28 states.

Visit with us and step back in time when the pace was a little slower and we will try our best to make your meal special.

At Cracker Barrel Old Country Store, breakfast, lunch and dinner are prepared according to time-proven recipes, with a traditional country fondness for good food and honest value.

READY TO BE TREATED LIKE SOMEONE SPECIAL?

Alamo's Membership Program offers you:
- Discounted rates in the U.S.A. and Europe
- No charge for additional drivers
- Frequent Flyer benefits with Alaska, American, British Airways, Delta, Hawaiian, Midwest Express® Northwest, Southwest, TWA, United, and USAir

Alamo features fine General Motors cars like this Buick Skylark.

JUST ASK ALAMO.℠

For reservations, call your Professional Travel Agent, access us at http://www.goalamo.com or call Alamo Rent A Car. Be sure to request **I.D. #**_____**430629**_____ and **Rate Code BY**.

1-800-354-2322

1011-2-196